K2259

D0627154

Faulkner's Apocrypha

A Fable, Snopes, and the Spirit of Human Rebellion

Faulkner's Apocrypha

A Fable, Snopes, and the Spirit of Human Rebellion

Joseph R. Urgo

University Press of Mississippi
Jackson and London

Manufactured in the United States of America

92 91 90 89   4 3 2 1

The paper in this book meets the guidelines for permanence
and durability of the Committee on Production Guidelines for
Book Longevity of the Council on Library Resources.

All William Faulkner texts cited are the most recent Vintage/
Random House paperback editions.

Library of Congress Cataloging-in-Publication Data

Urgo, Joseph R.
  Faulkner's Apocrypha : a fable, snopes, and the spirit of
human rebellion / by Joseph R. Urgo.
      p.   cm.
  Bibliography: p.
  ISBN 0-87805-404-9 (alk. paper)
  1. Faulkner, William, 1897–1962—Political and social
views.
  2. Faulkner, William, 1897–1962—Characters—Snopes family.
  3. Faulkner, William, 1897–1962. Fable. 4. Radicalism in
literature. I. Title.
  PS3511.A86Z9795 1989
  813'.52—dc20   89-34381
                                           CIP

British Library Cataloguing in Publication data is available.

This book was made for Lesley

Contents

Acknowledgments

Thank you, George Creeger, for listening and responding to these ideas when they began a long time ago, and thank you, George Monteiro, for your support, encouragement, and guidance. Thanks go also to those people who read or offered advice, including Robert Scholes, Barton L. St. Armand, Richard Meckel, Michael Kreyling, Cecelia Tichi, and the anonymous readers along the way. Thank you Seetha Srinivasan at the University Press of Mississippi for the many gestures of faith in this project. Thank you to the Mellon Foundation for funding my position at Vanderbilt University, where this book was completed. And thanks to Joseph and Rose Urgo, my parents, who when they sent their son off to college probably thought it was only temporary. And ultimately, thank you, Lesley, for everything there is.

Faulkner's Apocrypha

A Fable, Snopes, and the Spirit of Human Rebellion

1. The Apocryphal Vision

WILLIAM FAULKNER'S fictional production is a sustained assault on common sense ideas about reality and on what passes by ordinary for truth, authority, and perception. He called his life's work his "apocrypha," but no one until now has taken him seriously in his use of this descriptive term. William Faulkner was not very comfortable in life, and his fiction is seldom comfortable with the world it depicts. The man would often totally obliterate himself from the world through the consumption of amazing quantities of liquor; he would then sober up and produce amazing quantities of words. His words have always intoxicated his readers, confusing and stupifying some, enlightening and enthralling others. Here was a man who lived and produced many of these kinds of contradictions, contradictions that need to be characterized and understood, but not ironed out or deceptively and patly explained. His books often contain contradictory points of view, for he seemed to relish complexities. His fictional heroes, for example, are seldom without horrendous character flaws. Many of his strongest characters commit suicide, are ineffectual, never quite say what they need to express or do what they intend. Despite the confusions and intoxications, the canonized Faulkner, the product of fifty years of scholarly attention, is often presented as a sagacious old man with strong humanist moral fiber who believed in God and did not mean to drink so much.

This book takes a different track. It takes seriously the contention that what Faulkner was creating was an apocrypha, a self-consciously "other" interpretation of reality. The apocrypha challenges sacred notions about who or what Jesus Christ was, political notions about how power is wielded, and historical notions about how the present has been created as real. To do justice to Faulkner's major apocryphal productions, however, a number of preliminaries are necessary. First, the idea of an apocrypha must be explained on theoretical grounds. It also needs to be demonstrated critically in terms of Faulkner's fiction and his biography. Once the idea is fully presented, Faulkner's two greatest literary works, those projects on which he expended the most time and effort, and for which he was the most proud, can be placed where they belong. *A Fable* and the *Snopes* trilogy form the apex of Faulkner's career but are usually considered minor works, or at least they are deemed less powerful than the work he did previous to their completion. Faulkner judged *A Fable* to be his greatest work and thought enough of *Snopes* to spend thirty-four years on it. It is odd that the writer who so many readers consider so "right" about life and literature should think him so wrong on this particular issue. When the *Snopes* trilogy and *A Fable* are placed at the center of Faulkner's apocrypha and not on the fringes of his literary output, his entire production demands a new critical perspective.

This study contends, finally, that Faulkner is a far more politically challenging and politically radical writer than has yet been explicated in any systematic fashion. The radicalism of his apocrypha has been muted partially because of the personal image he cultivated in the 1950s, a nonconfrontational, cordial, and rather self-indulgent style of Nobel Laureate. His radicalism has been further muted by a specific reluctance on the part of critics to address issues raised in his most ambitious projects as well as by a more general failure to appreciate the implications of his apocrypha. Faulkner's apocrypha includes much more than the county he called Yoknapatawpha, which is only a synecdoche for the writer's larger production of alternatives of self and place and time. The apocrypha in its entirety, as I explain, stands as a political and ideological alternative to what Faulkner considered to be the totalitarianism of modern society.

I

On December 10, 1950, William Faulkner received the 1949 Nobel Prize for Literature. His speech of acceptance is now famous, and

Faulkner critics have generally regarded it as marking a turning point in his career.[1] The gloom and doom of the pre-Laureate Faulkner would be supplanted, as the career formula goes, by the post-Laureate Faulkner and a sense of redemption. According to the story, the post-Laureate Faulkner suffered a decline in creative power and artistic intensity, the result of which is that "Faulkner redeemed" was never quite as powerful or convincing as the "fallen" Faulkner. I believe that both of these assertions, for a variety of reasons which this book will make clear, are wholly misleading.

There are shifts in Faulkner's career, shifts in emphasis and artistic aim, as in the career of any writer. Yet the shifts Faulkner began to make at the time of the Nobel Prize were not in the direction that critics either expected or preferred. At a time when many readers were going back to *The Sound and the Fury, Absalom, Absalom!,* and *Light in August,* Faulkner was moving away from Yoknapatawpha with *A Fable.* When Faulkner did return to that apocryphal county, writing a "sequel" to *Sanctuary* and finishing the *Snopes* trilogy, his vision of the cosmos was radically different from what most readers were anticipating. As a result, Faulkner's novels in the 1950s were received with disappointment, and despite his receiving the Nobel Prize and world recognition, Faulkner continued to be misread and misunderstood. In the 1930s, Faulkner was writing fiction that would eventually win him the acclaim he craved and felt his work deserved—regardless of the fact that his books were not selling. In the 1950s, readers began to recognize the greatness of that early fiction but were ignoring and often denigrating what the "great" writer was doing at the time. Readers in the 1950s wanted Faulkner to write *Absalom!* again so they could no doubt be present at the creation, but Faulkner had already written that. In a career pattern that would have him continually altering his fictional purposes and goals,[2] Faulkner found himself once again alone with his vision. Unlike in the 1930s and early 1940s, when Faulkner was making his way from obscurity to recognition, in the 1950s he was engaged in a different kind of struggle. To a large extent he was struggling against the confines of his own literary reputation. In 1953, Faulkner told confidante Joan Williams that if she meant to be a serious writer of fiction, she could expect "scorn and horror and misunderstanding" throughout her life. He was actually describing his own career experience.[3]

Malcolm Cowley is primarily responsible for delivering Faulkner from obscurity in the 1940s, a rescue mission which was, perhaps, among the more timely in the history of American literature. Cowley has been credited with anticipating and leading a wave of interest in Faulkner that has yet to crest.[4] In *The Faulkner-Cowley File,* Cowley refers to his correction of Faulkner's critical neglect as something "every critic dreams of . . . [to] come upon an author whose reputation is less than his achievement and in fact is scandalously out of proportion with it, so that other voices will be added to the critic's voice, in a swelling chorus, as soon as he has made the discovery." As a result of Cowley's efforts, there indeed arose a chorus of critical voices singing praises for William Faulkner—but they were, as can be expected, almost to a voice singing Cowley's tune. Due to the breadth and coherence of Cowley's reading of Faulkner, emblematically packaged in *The Portable Faulkner,* the chorus produced an author who would come to be understood as a Southern mythmaker, the clearest voice in the Southern literary renaissance, a gentle, pipe-smoking conservative and a brooding, self-educated, moralist anomaly in American letters who was sadly neglected in his own country and badly treated by those people in Hollywood who took advantage of his need for money.

The point of *The Portable Faulkner,* of course, was to correct the neglect and the need for the money, to revere properly the genius and to lead readers back to the early works he produced. In his introduction to *The Portable Faulkner,* Cowley claims that Faulkner had accomplished two things in his fiction, two things which would form the nucleus of Cowley's view of Faulkner. First, Faulkner created "a Mississippi county that was like a mythical kingdom," and second, he made the "story of Yoknapatawpha County stand as a parable or legend of all the Deep South."[5] At the same time that Cowley found the lost kingdom—in 1944, the books in which Faulkner "had created a mythical county in northern Mississippi," says Cowley, "were effectively out of print"—he also found what he would come to see a tired and diminished king. "It had better be said that his later books, in general, had not the freshness and power of the early ones," Cowley asserts at the end of *The Faulkner-Cowley File.* "That is the common fate of imaginative writers . . . some original force goes out of them. The books they write after the age of fifty most often lose in genius what they may possibly gain in talent."[6]

The resurrection of Faulkner by Cowley, then, was accompanied by the chilling assessment that there survived in the flesh of the genius a kind of ghost, a Quentin who had not jumped but had just kept on brooding—and writing. It seemed that way because to Cowley, "None of his later books was on a level with *The Sound and the Fury* or *Go Down, Moses*,"[7] the traditional gates of Faulkner's golden period of phenomenal achievement. There is no reason to assume that critics, including Malcolm Cowley, who in the 1940s and 1950s had just begun to come to terms with what Faulkner had been doing for two decades, were prepared for what he would do next. In other words, whatever the critical value of Cowley's view of Faulkner's pre-Laureate "mythical county," there is no reason to believe it said anything pertinent about Faulkner's career after the publication of *The Portable Faulkner*. The assumption is especially wrong-headed if we see, as this study proposes, that what Faulkner was doing in the 1950s was largely in *response* to Cowley's interpretation of him—an interpretation which Faulkner may have initially welcomed for its service to his career but which he finally rejected as a definitive, or even accurate assessment of his purposes as a writer of fiction.

Cowley's *Portable Faulkner* is, in many ways, an astonishing, almost incredible work of critical intervention. Alternatives to Cowley's pastoral subdivisions easily come to mind, and we can imagine "The Last Wilderness" and "The Old People" replaced with far more textually organic categorizations. A different "portable" edition might open with "Murder and Mutilation" (featuring Percy Grimm on Joe Christmas as well as Lee Goodwin's lynching from *Sanctuary* and Vardaman's drilling holes into Addie's corpse) and continue with these subdivisions: "Rape and Misogyny," "Racial Horror Stories," "Sibling Violence and Fratricide," "Drunkenness and Disorderly Conduct," and "Long-winded Young Men from Mississippi." Formalistic categories might also be included, such as "Made-up Words in Context," "Inexplicable Prose," and "Significant Departures from Common Knowledge." These sorts of things come to mind when Faulkner's name is invoked, not "The Peasants" and "The Old People." The new collection might be called "The *Profane* Faulkner," something far too damning and heretical to be toted around like a pocket Bible. Cheryl Lester, in her study of *The Portable Faulkner*, perceptively sees that "lost in the transfer" of Faulkner to Cowley is "the unruly writing Faulkner left behind." *The Portable Faulkner* amounts to "a violent imposition of order on something wild" in "an attempt to establish the legitimacy of Faulkner's writings."[8] This, of course, is precisely the point. Cowley chose Faulkner (as he had previously selected Hemingway) for canonization, which marshals good angels, not rebellious Lucifers embittered with what the Creator has accomplished. Cowley certainly had his hands full when he went about domesticating and making Faulkner palatable. We could borrow Faulkner's words from the preface to the Modern Library edition of *Sanctuary* and say, in a similar spirit, that Cowley did "a fair job" of it.

There are, of course, historical justifications for the "job" Malcolm Cowley did on Faulkner in 1946. The late 1940s, "The Age of Suspicion"[9] in America, was an era of profound national reassessment. It was also an imperial time in America, before the giant demonstrated its helplessness, and on many levels the nation attempted to fulfill its newly crowned role as world power. Cowley's specific act in producing *The Portable Faulkner* was itself an imperial gesture (a lost *kingdom*, after all), but it also followed a more general move toward a national, postwar cultural recuperation. In the 1930s, Malcolm Cowley may have been concerned with the writer's role in the revolution; in the late 1940s, he was equally concerned with the writer's role in the empire. In 1946, Cowley was himself awakened from what he has since called "a daydream of revolutionary brotherhood"[10] to characterize his activities of the previous decade, when he was a Communist Party fellow traveller awaiting the twilight of capitalism in the United States. The inspiration provided by the American Left to many writers in the early 1930s must have seemed remote to Cowley a decade later.

Did Faulkner's ability, in Cowley's imagination, to produce an artistic literary program out of a backwater region somewhere in Mississippi have any psychic connection to the career Malcolm Cowley was trying to forge out of the radical decade and the Second World War? Cowley had just "done" Hemingway when he approached Faulkner with the ambition to commodify him in the Viking Books series of "portable" authors. He would recuperate Faulkner's career and make the author legitimate—while doing the same for himself and contributing to the nation's recuperation. The revolutionist's dream of the 1930s was over, but new dreams would come of Deep South legends, American myths, and "The Undying Past," to quote another *Portable* subdivision.

Malcolm Cowley was not acting alone. "Cowley's involvement with Faulkner," according to Lawrence Schwartz, "represented a personal renunciation of Marxist culture and radical politics but also was reflective of the broader intellectual realignment" throughout the American literary elite. Schwartz explains the postwar cultural matrix out of which Faulkner's reputation was produced in America. A cultural consensus made up of the New Critics on the political right, the New York intellectuals on the political left, and backed by the financial support of the Rockefeller Foundation, worked in concert to promulgate "very specific cultural values" in the postwar period. Aesthetic formalism emerged as the single literary program to enable left, right, and corporate interest to overcome, or set aside, political concerns in the name of American cultural hegemony. "The intelligentsia understood that the defense of culture was part of a larger economic and political struggle with the Soviet Union," Schwartz contends, "in which the United States represented Western values and traditions." William Faulkner—or at least the William Faulkner created by Malcolm Cowley, Robert Penn Warren, Irving Howe, and others—served the "comprehensive effort in cultural planning" that characterized this era. Faulkner became one of the primary showpieces of American cultural achievement.[11]

Faulkner was "perfectly suited to represent the new conservative liberalism and humanitarianism of American democracy" after the Second World War, as Schwartz explains. "And analogously, Cowley's rediscovery of Faulkner's 'greatness' was perfectly suited to the prevailing formalist aesthetics of the postwar period which claimed, in part, that literature in its fully realized form was universal and apolitical." Faulkner's individualist themes, his technically challenging prose, and his mix of rural-agrarian, modernist, and romantic traditions served the ideological (or what was shrewdly claimed to be non-ideological) program of a closed community of literary intellectuals in which "dissent was suppressed and oppositional literary criticism was displaced."[12] Along with American factories retooled to produce consumer goods, automobiles, washing machines, and refrigerators, Faulkner was revived and reorganized by literary critics to serve the interests of the cultural Cold War abroad and cultural hegemony at home. He was, in Schwartz's terms, the "great new American novelist" who would "represent the dominance of humanist values."[13] The author was projected, by New Critics and other literary, cultural, and corporate interests, as a universal emblem of personal freedom under capitalism, a mythmaker who spun tales of American local strength, woodsy origins, and characteristic endurance, a "chronicler of the plight of man in the modern world." He became the representative man of literary modernism. As Schwartz makes clear, it is imperative to see "the re-interpretation of Faulkner" by the American literary intelligentsia in "the context of postwar cultural readjustment." An elitist aesthetic, called New Criticism, a repudiation of 1930s-style "socially conscious" fiction, an explicit anti-Communism, and funding by the Rockefeller Foundation for graduate programs in English and for literary journals in the humanities all "came together in the 1940s to set a cultural agenda, and they used and promoted Faulkner for their own ends."[14]

There would be no audience in 1946 for the *profane* Faulkner outlined above. That Faulkner, the one associated with the "cult of cruelty" in the 1930s, was suppressed. Cowley sanitized and recuperated William Faulkner for a middle class, postwar culture in which such cleanliness and healing were becoming national virtues. The nation, the culture, and Malcolm Cowley were cleaning house. Nationally, the tidying up would soon become cutthroat, and Faulkner's vision of a violent, fascistic culture would again be demonstrated in the careers of Joe McCarthy and other "red-blooded Americans" of the era. Sexual politics were no less subject to sanitation. The Kinsey report, published in 1948, would scandalously announce that masturbation, promiscuity, adultery, bestiality, and other "deviant" sexual practices were quite common in America— but as common as in Faulkner's fiction? This report, of course, was taken as a sign of America's moral dissolution and as a falling apart of the nation's moral fiber. In addition, Communism threatened the United States with the loss of its right to an imperial ascendency. An acceptable cultural image was sought and debated nationally in the immediate postwar period, and the ideological divisions formed in that era would continue to characterize cultural politics in subsequent decades. Into this context Malcolm Cowley brought his version of the gentleman farmer from Mississippi, the moralist, the mythmaker, whose literary accomplishments were passing by a culture in dire need of guidance and, as Faulkner would later say himself, props.

Faulkner, on the other hand, believed in his talents and genius long before many others did, including Malcolm Cowley. This confidence—or arrogance—helped him get through the long and often frustrating journey from obscurity to international acclaim. Simply put, he did all he could to achieve the recognition eventually given him. He told the editor of *The Saturday Evening Post* in 1927, for example, "Hark in your ear: I am a coming man, so take warning."[15] David Minter describes Faulkner's slowly emerging self-confidence in the 1920s and his tendency to believe "that he was a genius who would one day be famous," which was finally solidified by Sherwood

Anderson's encouragement.[16] Yet if Faulkner craved recognition, he did not necessarily welcome fame with its celebrity connotations and resultant loss of privacy. In 1931, following the wide-ranging critical reception to *Sanctuary,* Faulkner wrote to his wife Estelle about "luncheons in my honor," "evening parties," and "people who want to see what I look like." He is, however, somewhat wary that all the attention might affect his ability to create. "I'm glad I'm level-headed, not very vain. But I dont think it has gone to my head," he added. "Anyway, I am writing. Working on the novel, and on a short story."[17] What Faulkner wanted from recognition was not so much fame as fortune, the financial security to allow him to continue writing free of monetary anxiety. For all the attention showered upon him after the publication of *Sanctuary,* it was hardly the beginning of the end of Faulkner's financial problems. The publisher of *Sanctuary,* Harrison Smith, went bankrupt following the book's publication, and Faulkner received little, if any, profits from its sale.

Financial security did not come to Faulkner until 1948, according to Joseph Blotner, when Random House sold the movie rights to *Intruder in the Dust* to MGM for $50,000.[18] The sale marked the end of Faulkner's money problems and the beginning of his fame. In many ways, what he experienced fleetingly in the early 1930s returned to him permanently in the last fifteen years of his life, and he would find it increasingly difficult to escape luncheons filled with "people who want to see what I look like." Blotner explains that "the same paradoxical situation" was happening to Faulkner "over again; when he had wanted recognition it had largely been denied, and now when it came he wanted none of it that was directed at him personally."[19] Faulkner always wanted to maintain a distinction between the works, which deserved the awards, and the man, who deserved the privacy. In the years following the Nobel Prize, Faulkner would come to accept the impossibility of the distinction and attempt to fulfill the role of Laureate. Yet in the 1940s, when Faulkner and others, most notably Malcolm Cowley, attempted to revive and create interest in his work, Faulkner himself did all he could to protect his privacy and maintain control over his reputation. He would lose the effort, however, as critics who had more to say about the works than did the author would create a literary figure whose hailed accomplishments would eventually stagger the man responsible for them. In 1953, Faulkner wrote Joan Williams that he had finally managed to "have some perspective on all I have done. I mean, the work apart from me, the work which I did, apart from what I am. . . . And now I realize for the first time what an amazing gift I had."[20]

Ten years before this letter to Joan Williams, Faulkner was anything but amazed with himself or his work. In the years immediately following the publication of *Go Down, Moses* (1942), he experienced periods of severe depression and self-doubt, feelings compounded by his unwitting and irresponsible commitment to a seven-year contract with Warner Brothers in Hollywood.[21] As a result of the contract, Faulkner worked for Jack Warner at a starting salary of $100 per week in a deal that gave Warner complete control over when Faulkner worked as well as rights to what he wrote for seven years. This contract, more than anything else, may explain the "dry spell" in Faulkner's writing from 1942 through 1948.[22] By 1945, Faulkner felt completely trapped in Hollywood. He wrote to Harold Ober in August:

> I feel bad, depressed, dreadful sense of wasting time, I imagine most of the symptoms of some kind of blow-up or collapse. . . . Feeling as I do, I am actually afraid to stay here much longer. For some time I have expected, at an early age, to reach that period (in the early fifties) which most artists seem to reach where they admit at last that there is no solution to life and that it is not, and perhaps never was, worth the living. . . . My books have never sold, are out of print; the labor (the creation of my apocryphal county) of my life . . . will never make a living for me. . . .[23]

In the midst of Faulkner's despair in the summer of 1945 came an indication that things might change. The reference to "the creation of my apocryphal county" is clearly a sign of his reaction to Malcolm Cowley, as is the information that the Faulkner list was out of print at the time. In August 1945, Cowley wrote to Faulkner with good news: Viking had agreed to publish a *Portable Faulkner,* a sign that interest in Faulkner was on the rise.

Cowley first wrote to Faulkner in February 1944. In May, Faulkner answered the letter from Hollywood, from "the salt mines" as he put it. He agreed to discuss the Viking project with Cowley. "I have worked too hard . . . to leave no better mark on this our pointless chronicle than I seem to be about to leave."[24] The correspondence between Faulkner and Cowley in compiling *The Portable Faulkner* presents an interesting struggle between author and critic, where the stakes are the writer's very definition. Although Faulkner would express an enthusiasm for the final product that led to a renewed self-confidence ("By God, I didn't know myself what I had tried to do, and how much I had succeeded"),[25] the process of collaboration with Cowley was often frustrating and disappointing. It was Faulkner's first extended experience with a critic whose ideas about "Faulkner" were as strong—and at times more informed— than those of the author. Although Faulkner always remained favorable to intelligent analysis of his works, this was the first time that an interpretation of what he was doing artistically would directly influence a collaborative production aimed at renewing his reputation. Cowley told him in 1944 that "in publishing circles your name is mud. They are all convinced that your books won't ever sell, and it's a pity, isn't it?" Cowley had just completed a *Portable Hemingway* and must have represented, to Faulkner, a potential deliverance from obscurity to the recognition he knew he deserved. "So," Cowley told him, "a good piece on your work has to be written."[26] So, Faulkner agreed. "The result should be a better sale for your new books," Cowley encouraged, "and a bayonet prick in the ass of Random House to reprint the others."[27]

Faulkner always maintained that *The Portable Faulkner* was "not a new work by Faulkner. It's a new work by Cowley all right through."[28] Responsible for this distinction is a definite disagreement between the two men over the essence of what Faulkner's work represented. Their first divergence occurred in the course of their exchange concerning *Absalom, Absalom!* Cowley's biographical inferences from the text led Faulkner to insist that although "I was writing the story" it was Quentin, not Faulkner, who "was brooding over a situation."[29] Cowley was an aggressive editor and critic, however, and even implied on one occasion that he would like to have "managed" Faulkner. *Absalom, Absalom!*, Cowley suggested, "would be better if cut by about a third."[30] In regards to *The Portable Faulkner*, the author generally agreed to Cowley's editorial corrections and changes. As the editorial details continued to occupy his time, and as Cowley presented more alterations for his approval, Faulkner seems to have detached himself from the project. At one point, he agreed to Cowley's switching around a clause in a sentence from the "Appendix: Compson," written for *The Portable Faulkner*. When the appendix was included in *The Sound and the Fury*, however, the sentence appeared in its original form.[31]

A far more important divergence between the two men arose over the word to be used to describe Faulkner's total Yoknapatawpha production. In August 1945, Faulkner wrote, "By all means let us make a Golden Book of my apocryphal county," and in

December suggested that the front jacket should read, "A chronological picture of Faulkner's apocryphal Mississippi county. . . ." Yet
when Cowley wrote to his Viking editor, he phrased the line this
way: "The Saga of Yoknapatawpha County, 1820–1945, being the
first chronological picture of Faulkner's mythical county in Mississippi. . . ."[32] The difference is significant. Cowley was contributing to a tradition in Faulkner criticism of interpreting the work as
"saga" and as "myth"—not as apocrypha. As myth, Faulkner's work
remained safely outside the "real" world, the historical world, and
thus could be mined for its moral content while leaving its political
implications muted. When Faulkner demanded the word "apocryphal," he insisted upon his relevance and his challenge to "official,"
historical reality. After reading Cowley's introduction to *The Portable Faulkner,* the author responded to the Deep South "legend" and
"myth" thesis with characteristic restraint, but not without getting
his point across. "I dont see too much Southern legend in it," he
commented.[33]

The distinction between Cowley's "mythical" and Faulkner's
"apocryphal" cannot be overstated. A myth helps to interpret reality
by transforming what is mysterious or "other" in life into intelligible
patterns and forms. Myths explain how things came to be; they tell
us how we got here, and why things are the way they are. Frank
Kermode has identified the conservative program that underlies
mythmaking. "Myth operates within the diagrams of ritual, which
presupposes total and adequate explanations of things as they are
and were." According to Kermode, myths amount to "a sequence of
radically unchangeable gestures. . . . Myths are the agents of stability."[34] Aprocrypha, on the other hand, exists as a *challenge* to the
real by offering alternatives to what is commonly accepted as authoritative, official, or genuine. The impulse behind composing an
apocrypha is not to explain, harmonize, or put into order. An
apocrypha aims to upset and to create a sense of *competing* accounts,
not a single version, of the real. Myth reinforces an authoritative
reality by answering questions about the world; apocrypha subverts
the real and raises questions about the way we understand it. The
issue between Cowley and Faulkner, then, was far from semantic, for
it concerned Faulkner's political definition as a writer of fiction and
as the creator of a fictional county. In Cowley's view, Faulkner's
"mythical" world of Yoknapatawpha "explained" something—the
South, its history, its people. To Faulkner, his "apocryphal" vision

offered an alternative view to something which, without the apocrypha, would be taken for granted as real.

Readers and critics of Faulkner have never taken seriously his insistence upon the term "apocrypha" to describe his literary production. The term generally refers to biblical writings excluded from the established, canonical Bible for various reasons, most often having to do with issues of authority and content. Willis Barnstone, in his introduction to *The Other Bible*, a collection of Old and New Testament apocrypha, points to "fierce political and religious rivalry between sects, between factions, between Jew, Christian, and Gnostic," which influenced the collation of what has come to be accepted and known as the Bible. "The exclusion of many texts was often as arbitrary and dubious as was the inclusion of such magnificent and dangerous books as Ecclesiastes and Song of Songs." The impulse among early Church authorities to establish a fixed canon of *Biblical* writings was, according to Barnstone, something of a contradiction.

> The word bible, from *biblia,* Greek for "small books," signifies broadly a collection of books by which a person or people can live. The ancient Bible was sacred, for its composition was held to be inspired by God. . . . So the act of inspired composition, whether of a Blake or a Whitman or a biblical patriarch, whether of the West or the East, appears to be a universal human endeavor, not restricted to one people or religion. After the closing of the Old Testament and during the first centuries of the Common Era, inspired authors continued to write inspired scripture. They were written by Jews, Christians, Gnostics, and Pagans. Many of these texts were of amazing beauty and religious importance and competed with books within the canon. The Jewish texts are in large part called pseudepigraphica, which includes the Dead Sea Scrolls; the Christian texts are called Christian Apocrypha. . . .

Barnstone concludes that the Bible as we have inherited it is a distortion of its own professed divine representations. He says, "categorically that the Bible, with the absence of sacred texts from the intertestamental period, with its acceptance of a small and repetitious canon for the New Testament, with the exclusion of all later Christian Apocrypha, and the total rejection of Gnostic scriptures, has given us a highly censored and distorted version of ancient religious literature."[35]

By closing the Bible to subsequent amendment and addition, early Christian authorities subverted and attenuated its symbolism as a repository of divinely inspired composition. All subsequent claims to inspired writing would be, by definition, of dubious authenticity, or apocryphal. Statements such as that made by Faulkner to Cowley in 1948—"I listen to the voices . . . and when I put down what the voices say, it's right. Sometimes I don't like what they say, but I don't change it"[36]—can only be met with skepticism, or some other appropriate secular or psychological response. After all, how should we react to Faulkner's insistence that he heard and responded to "voices" when he composed fiction? His demands for complete silence in his home, his discomfort with music, especially recorded music, his ban on radio and television at Rowan Oak for many years: all this is evidence that Faulkner may have been listening to "something." We can cite the Romantic's muse or the psychologist's schizophrenia (or even Faulkner's own word, "demons"), but we cannot espouse divine inspiration in the twentieth century with any degree of credibility.

Nonetheless, a difference exists between claiming to be the maker of myths (which we can accept today, and which is probably why Cowley picked the term) and being the vehicle of apocryphal composition. The divergence on one level lies in that, as stated above, the mythmaker explains reality or makes the real intelligible and known, while the writer of apocrypha amends reality or makes the real more problematic. More important, the writer of apocrypha denies that anything divinely inspired can be claimed as "canonical," that is, not subject to subsequent reversal or redefinition. Divine inspiration, in the apocryphal tradition, may occur at any time to overturn previously established understandings of the divine. (This is why the idea of an "apocryphal tradition" is actually impossible.) To the maker of apocrypha, not even God's Truth is truth for all eternity. Multiple viewpoints and rejected truths and conclusions are central aspects of biblical apocrypha.

Barnstone explains "the great diversity of ancient thought" in *The Other Bible:*

> Each view, it seems, is contradicted by a second and a third. The reader has several perspectives to aid in interpretations and judgments. . . . We may find three conflicting views of a single event. Thus after Jesus Christ is crucified the Jews think him another man and go on seeking the messiah, the Christians proclaim the crucified Jesus both man and God, and the Gnostics take the Docetic view that Jesus was only a simulacrum on the cross, for God is always God. In fact, in the Gnostic works, *The Second Treatise of the Great Seth* and the *Apocalypse of Peter,* Jesus the

Savior stands above the cross, laughing at the ignorance of his would-be executioners who think that men can kill God.[37]

Successive contradiction and multiple perspectives are central motifs in the apocryphal bible, and it was largely because of these inconsistencies that the writings were originally considered ingenuine. In the apocryphal *Felicity and Perpetua,* martyrdom is presented successively as an erotic and spiritually significant event and then as wasteful cowardice. In other books the Fall is put forth in competing versions, including the gnostic one, which claims that Adam and Eve were innocent of wrongdoing and that the Creator itself was the first sinner. These contradictions and discrepancies, however, were considered signs of forgery, inauthenticity, and bogus divinity on the part of Church authorities who assumed that truth was, by definition, characterized by consistency, singularity, and definitive, authoritative statement.

Faulkner made a political statement to Malcolm Cowley in his insistence on the word apocrypha, which ought not be ignored in assessing his writing. To consider an apocrypha as a legitimate source of knowledge and truth is to make a statement about the political nature of knowledge and truth. Elaine Pagels has explained, for example, how certain orthodox views of Christ's resurrection served to reinforce the incipient institutional structure of the early Church. The idea "that all authority derives from certain apostles' experience of the resurrected Christ, an experience now closed forever—bears enormous implications for the political structure of the community." First, according to Pagels, "it restricts the circle of leadership to a small group of persons . . . of uncontestable authority. Second, it suggests that only the apostles had the right to ordain future leaders as their successors." Dissenting views concerning the resurrection, such as the gnostic position that a *literal* resurrection is "the faith of fools," were suppressed by orthodoxy. In fact, gnostic ideas about the resurrection may help to clarify Faulkner's ambitions in writing *A Fable.*

According to gnostic tradition, recorded in apocryphal writings, the resurrection "was not a unique event in the past: instead, it symbolized how Christ's presence could be experienced in the present." Pagels adds that "what interested these gnostics far more than past events attributed to the 'historical Jesus' was the possibility of encountering the risen Christ in the present."[38] Orthodox Christianity has been no more able to incorporate gnostic views into its canon than have Faulkner scholars been able to integrate *A Fable* into theirs. In the gnostic case, this anarchic, anti-institutional, and unstructurable challenge to orthodox hegemony has resulted in gnostic texts being labelled apocryphal and gnostic beliefs being categorized as heretical.

When Cowley began the canonization of Faulkner, the author insisted on his apocrypha. What did he mean? Was he ridiculing Cowley's position as apostle? As kingmaker? Or was he trying, in the only way he knew, to communicate what he saw as the essential nature of his production to a man who had, as Cowley did in the 1940s, the power to impart that essence internationally? The institutional history of orthodox Christianity and the suppression of certain texts as apocrypha demonstrate the political nature of truth. What is considered truthful, genuine, or authentic implies a specific form or institution (or *myth*) to perpetuate and to preserve that truth. Why was Faulkner being chosen for canonization? Which texts would Cowley choose for his "bible"? How would these be arranged? What would be the orthodox view of the fiction itself? All these questions arise at the point of canonization.

When Faulkner insisted on labelling his works "apocrypha," he called into question Cowley's entire enterprise, and Cowley, for his own interests, did well to ignore him. It was heresy. Faulkner was out of print and headed for obscurity. Like an early Church founder contemplating the future of Christianity, Cowley knew that Faulkner had two choices: institutional legitimacy (orthodoxy) or oblivion. The development of the institution took precedence over ideas or views about the material that might harm the institution. In the context of cultural Cold War, a very specific kind of Faulkner would have to be developed in order to achieve canonical status. The politics of Faulkner's "development" were precisely those of any conscious effort at universal, institutional foundation. "In simplest terms," according to Pagels, "Ideas which bear implications contrary to that development came to be labelled as 'heresy'; ideas which implicitly support it become 'orthodox.'"[39]

Cowley's ideas about Faulkner coincide, in much the same way, with his program of canonization. The nation needed a moralist of laureate proportions, a mythmaker to tell it of its origins, to explain its history and to assure it of its stability—and its longevity. Faulkner's "apocrypha" would complicate forever Cowley's package and his program of recuperation, and so it was suppressed. Yet the evidence survives (in the Dead Sea, at Nag Hammadi), and apocryphal texts always seem to resurface despite orthodox gestures at hegemony. It seems clear today why Cowley said what he did about Faulkner in 1946, and why he packaged him the way he did to make him *Portable*. Now, however, the hidden or "secret text" needs to be read for its heretical, apocryphal essence.

Readers familiar with Faulkner's works should recognize the apocryphal nature of not just his "Yoknapatawpha County" but of his entire aesthetics. A defining principle of the apocryphal, or "other" bible is that there exists, legitimately and purposefully, multiple versions, glosses, or interpretations of any single event, as opposed to the canonical assumption of a single, authoritative account. Hence, the Bible contains a single story of the Fall, with Eve tempting and Adam succumbing. All other versions of the Fall are excluded for being of dubious authority.

In my personal copy of the King James Version of the Bible, an appendix called "Bible Study Helps" (a curiously orthodox pun in itself) contains a section entitled "Harmony of the Gospels," which lists 186 examples of parallel incidents, teachings, and miracles that "harmonize" the four Gospels.[40] The obvious implication is that the *consistency* of the Gospels is further evidence of their divine inspiration. St. Augustine provides an exemplary display of canonical logic when he explains that "writings as fall outside the canon," or apocrypha, have no spiritual value. "In a word, it is because they might be spurious that they are not to be trusted; and this is pre-eminently the case with works that contain declarations that run counter to the faith as contained in canonical writings, for then we can be absolutely sure that the attribution is spurious."[41] Here, then, is an unbridgeable gulf between the apocrypha and the canon. In the tradition of the apocrypha, contradiction, inconsistency, and multiple perspective are signs of the richness of divinely inspired human thought, of the changing and revolving (not evolving) nature of God's words. In the tradition of the canonical Bible, on the other hand, contradiction is a sign of fallibility and spuriousness, an obvious misrepresentation of God's *word*. In concise terms, the canon expunges discrepencies in an attempt to freeze the one true faith into a knowable pattern. The apocrypha, recognizing perhaps that "life is motion," depends upon the existence of these same discrepencies to certify its very vitality.

"Apocryphal" county[42] describes with precision Faulkner's aims as a fiction writer, while "mythical" county falls wide of the mark. When Faulkner told Jean Stein in 1955 that he had discovered, after writing *Sartoris*, "that my own little postage stamp of native soil was worth writing about," he spoke candidly, but apparently not quite clearly enough. The "postage stamp" was not worth writing about as an act of explication or even explanation, but as an act of imaginative rebellion *against* the native soil. It was his place and his time, usually understood as limitational or categorical qualities, which Faulkner wrote against. As he explained to Stein, his "discovery" about his native soil was that "by sublimating the actual into the apocryphal," he could allow himself what no man firmly rooted to his time and place is given: "complete liberty." The apocrypha does not accept time and place—native soil—as definitive, but as *postage stamp*. As such the native soil is merely the medium, a symbol of the carrier, through which the letter, or the story, is posted. By liberating himself from the authority of the stamp, only using it as his medium of expression, Faulkner in the apocrypha "opened up a gold mine" and "created a cosmos of my own"[43] in another series of perspectives on the native soil.

A good example of the workings of Faulkner's apocryphal habit of thinking is found in his experience writing "The De Gaulle Story" for Warner Brothers in the early 1940s. He was given this project in 1942 and responded to the assignment with enthusiasm.[44] Faulkner's idea of what a "De Gaulle story" might be, however, proved at odds with the conceptions of representatives of the Free French/Fighting French, who were consulting on the project. For one thing, Faulkner's version of De Gaulle's story barely included the general in the plot and action. Second, Faulkner had little patience with the exact details of the French culture and politics that served as a background and setting for his story. The report on Faulkner's story treatment compiled by Free French representative Adrien Tixier includes a long section called "Observations on Inexact Details." Tixier points out the impossibility of the main characters, Jean and Georges, being on military furlough in May 1940. (Although without their furlough, Faulkner's story, which takes place largely in Jean and Georges' home town, would be impossible.) He also corrects such items as, "In a cafe in France one does not play dominoes or cards but billiards." Primarily, Tixier believed that, in the words of producer Robert Buckner, "we have not enough of De Gaulle in our story."[45] Faulkner's story treatment keeps De Gaulle for the most part outside the action as a source of inspiration for occupied France, while his "story" concerns those common people for whom De Gaulle, even in his absence, *was* that source of inspiration.

Faulkner wrote a two-page memorandum in which he defended his story treatment and suggested ways to gain "complete liberty" from the Free French consultants to the project. His memorandum on "The De Gaulle Story," dated February 19, 1942, opens boldly. "Let's dispense with General De Gaulle as a living character in the story." Faulkner explains: "If we use him as a living character, we must accept the supervision of his representatives, and at least satisfy them, even if we can't please them. . . . These supervisors, being Free French, will insist upon an absolute adherence to time and fact, no matter how trivial the incident nor imaginary the characters acting it, and regardless of the sacrifice of dramatic values or construction or the poetic implications or overtones."

This is the voice of the apocryphal writer, wary of the "supervision" of the representatives of canonical "time and fact" who have an interest in the story proceeding in a certain, authoritative way. The De Gaulle *story,* to Faulkner, is not about one man. In fact, De Gaulle himself "is nothing more than a figurehead of his time," according to Faulkner's memorandum. Rather, the story of De Gaulle lies in "the sum of his acts, . . . the sum of the little people whom he slew or raised, enslaved or made free." Faulkner concludes, "Let's tell what he has done by means [of] its poetic implications, in terms of some little human people, with their human relationships which an audience can understand, whose lives and destinies were affected, not by him but by the same beliefs that made him De Gaulle."[46]

In applying himself to "The De Gaulle Story," Faulkner began by "sublimating the actual into the apocryphal." He denied first of all that the story, in his words, had to be "about De Gaulle in the heroic sense." Seeking to liberate himself from "the people who knew [De Gaulle] in the flesh and who insist on fact," Faulkner treated the French leader as a postage stamp, a simple validation on the letter or story he wanted to tell about "destinies" and "beliefs" which were, in his view, central to the fate of occupied France. His apocryphal vision ran counter to the historical facticity of Adrien Tixier, who, quite understandably, wanted to produce effective propaganda in a wartime situation. The maker of an apocrypha was not interested in De Gaulle the figurehead (and would deny that an "actual" De Gaulle could be definitively represented). Instead, he was enthusiastic about the kind of story the figurehead inspired. Faulkner's story of De Gaulle is about resistence, commitment, and divided loyalties—qualities that would, of course, outlive any single historical leader or political circumstance and continue to characterize the historical image of an occupied France. His story is not about the particular actions of a man to whose historical stature few may aspire. On the contrary, it deals with "little people," whose lives are always affected by such commanding figures, and whose lives "create in the hearts" of the audience "a feeling of warmth and affection and pride" toward their predicament. To accomplish this, facts and historical consistency had to be treated loosely and held secondary to the film's main thematic concerns.

His memorandum argues the dismissal of twin authorities: that of De Gaulle as historical personage, and that of his representatives over the creation of "The De Gaulle Story." Faulkner's story of De Gaulle would be just that: *Faulkner's* story of De Gaulle, just as Matthew's Christ is Matthew's Christ, and (the apocryphal) Thomas' Christ is Thomas' Christ, and as will be explained later, Faulkner's Christ is Faulkner's Christ in *A Fable*. The fact that Faulkner centers his story on "the little people" indicates his own opinion of what is historically significant, a view neither true nor false but apocryphal, or among many possible views. De Gaulle must be eliminated from the story treatment because as a living political force, Faulkner says, he is without dramatic value ("He becomes colorful and dramatic only after he has been dead for years"). He would only be disruptive to the story line. Tixier must be eliminated from the collaboration because his interest is not in getting a story from William Faulkner but in cementing certain facts with political positions for the record, in essence, to attach a particular, singular interpretation to De Gaulle's story that will have a particular, singular effect on history. Both of these authorities run counter to the aims of the apocryphal vision.

In his lifetime Faulkner transformed his childhood inclination to tell lies ("It got so that when Billy told you something, you never knew if it was the truth or just something he'd made up")[47] into an adult theory of the relationship between facts and truth. "I don't have much patience with facts," he said in Virginia in 1957, "and any writer is a congenital liar to begin with or he wouldn't take up writing. And so I couldn't tell the truth even about history. That's why I'll never write a biography. I couldn't tell the truth about Faulkner, I'm sure."[48] When he was less candid, Faulkner could offer elaborate defenses for disregarding facts. Indeed, a familiar Faulkner "formula" runs something like "fact and truth have very little to do with each other,"[49] or what he told Jean Stein in 1955: "If a writer concentrates on what he does need to be interested in, which is the truth of the human heart, he won't have much time left for anything else, such as ideas and facts like the shapes of noses or blood relationships, since in my opinion ideas and facts have very little connection with truth."[50] What Faulkner meant in his lifelong criticism of "facts" and defense of "truth" was to argue a kind of poetic license or ontological freedom—the right to reconstruct reality and to use whatever aspect of the environment is necessary to tell a story.

It is not simple mimesis which concerns Faulkner so much as the process of mimesis: how reality is transformed into represented reality, how the mind transforms sensation and knowledge into belief and value. Claude-Edmonde Magny has observed that the present "can never be known" in Faulkner's works. "One never sees it: one does not see what is in the process of happening at the moment it is happening; one sees only the past."[51] In other words, one "knows" only what is known or remembered. "Consciousness, therefore, is mostly memory," according to Jean-Jacques Pouillon. "But not the kind of memory which attaches the present to a past known as past and no longer existing. For memory is so much a part of what actually exists that it does not know itself as memory, does not know itself as anything but the sense of reality."[52] Many critics have concluded from this sense of memory's primacy that for Faulkner, only the past is real. "According to Faulkner," R. W. B. Lewis states, "events become real not when they occur but only when they are looked back on in memory."[53]

This may be true, but it is the *activity* of looking and remaking which interested Faulkner, not the resurrection or the making into legend of the past, whether it be the Sutpen saga or the McCaslin wilderness-genesis "myth." As Hubert McAlexander, Jr., has said, Faulkner believed "that history for any one man becomes essentially what he perceives it to be," and that the act of perception, the "constantly turning historical fact in the light in order to reveal as many meanings as possible" occupies not only Faulkner but also many of his characters as well.[54] At its base level, then, Faulkner's apocrypha resists the idea of a single body of "authentic" representations of reality. It is as simple as that, although its implications are profound. Reality, according to the apocryphal writer, cannot be pinned down once and for all by any system or theory. There are no authorities in the field.

Faulkner's avowed mimetic purpose was not to transfer historical or contemporary reality onto a representational field but to demonstrate (or to imagine) how the human mind makes that transference in the natural course of its operation, and then show with equal force how that transference might result in a different form, next time. "My ambition," he admitted to Malcolm Cowley, "is to put everything into one sentence—not only the present but the whole past on which it depends and which keeps overtaking the present, second by second." He told Cowley that in his long sentences he attempted to "convey a sense of simultaneity" to the reader,[55] attempting, I would suggest, to present the mind on an eternal quest to understand, comprehend, and assimilate its present and its past simultaneously. At the same time, however, the mind is *creating* the very object it seeks to comprehend.

Michael Millgate has noted that Faulkner displays a "persistent effort to hold in suspension a single moment of experience, action, or decision and to explore the full complexity of that moment by considering, in particular, its total context of past, present and future and its emergence as the often paradoxical product of many contrasted forces and pressures."[56] Faulkner examines and turns over and over the single moment, the single event, the single act of comprehension in an effort to reveal the full implications and workings of the mind's creation. Through the device of the frozen moment, Faulkner compels himself to work at an understanding of a "fact," which he would call a "truth," while it is being explored from every possible temporal, spatial, and epistemological angle by the various characters and, vicariously, by the reader. In this sense, Faulknerian mimesis not only "challenges reality's right to be as it is"[57] but also tests the individual's right to understand reality in *any* fixed way. From Faulknerian mimesis emerges an endorsement of the continually created meaning, the eternally overturned fact. This is the logic of the apocryphal vision.

Until now, the implications of Faulkner's apocrypha have been obscured by what has been an intensive critical examination of Faulkner's narrative logic. His epistemological concerns have been the focus of a major branch of Faulkner criticism, an area that seems to be growing in recent years and has yielded important insights into the effects of the author's language and style. Arthur Kinney suggests that "Faulkner does not rely, finally, on any single narrative consciousness, but on the reader's own *constitutive consciousness,* his ability to select what terms he will accept, his means of combining them, and, just as importantly, what he will reject."[58] Faulkner thus makes the reader's ability to piece together meaning "the focal point of the fiction, where all the stories become congruent and coalesce," and thus, "the author disappears."[59]

Early critics such as Magny pointed to Faulkner's success "in bringing that notoriously lazy being, the reader of novels, under this hard and truly Socratic discipline."[60] Warren Beck has described Faulkner's invitation "to experience discovery not just as information but as process, subject to revision and enlargement, and never resting in absolutes or in finalities."[61] With more urgency, Joseph Gold depicts the Faulknerian world as one "so designed that meaning must be found or made by man" as an effort to sustain life.[62] Robert Penn Warren explains that the struggle "to achieve meaning" and "the awareness that meaning, if achieved, will always rest in perilous balance" is what accounts for Faulkner's sense "that the great ungirding and overarching meaning of life is in the act of trying to create meaning through struggle."[63] Hence, the epistemological tradition in Faulkner criticism takes various forms, all pointing to the observation that with Faulkner the creation of meaning amounts to an independent drama within the fiction. John T. Irwin sees "the almost meaningful—the sense of the meaningful as the always deferred" as Faulkner's "sense of the tragic absurd" in epistemology.[64] Walter Slatoff's view of this phenomenon is that Faulkner's refusal to be pinned to a particular meaning amounts to a failure to choose and that his frequent use of oxymorons to hold meaning in suspension is a kind of sustained epistemological avoidance.[65]

To argue that Faulkner raises epistemology to a dramatic level or that the creation of meaning is a kind of motif running through his work can easily be mistaken for the suggestion that Faulkner's is a purely aesthetic approach to literature. Slatoff's assertion that Faulkner suspends resolution and meaning certainly points to such a conclusion, and it is thus wholly possible to regard Faulkner's fiction as being without ideological significance. To claim, however, that Faulkner lacks ideological content is only to suggest that it has not been recognized and explicated, for no fictional representation of social reality can be devoid of the one system of meaning that makes social reality intelligible. As Edward W. Said has pointed out, all "literary activities" are ideological, unless we consider the humanities as "essentially ornamental" and without social significance.[66] What needs to be outlined, then, is the theoretical ground upon which

Faulkner's apocrypha, with its epistemological strategy, can be understood not only as a literary method but also as an ideological stance.

II

We live in a world of authorities, of canonical understandings and teachings about phenomena, a world divided between fiction and nonfiction, reality and fantasy, the authentic and the "apocryphal." Our Bible does not include series of contradictory versions of single events, nor do our teachers generally tolerate multiple perspectives and competing visions as the *basis* of a practical, working epistemology. What we accept in theory, or in literary theory at least, we find nearly impossible to accept in daily practice. Indeed, it is difficult to envision a discipline based upon a belief in slippery fact and contradictory truth. Our very terminology, or "discipline," precludes the possibility. Faulkner's apocryphal vision cannot be taken seriously, that is, taken outside the literary academy, without profoundly disrupting our received (and transmitted) notions of how truth operates and what "authority" means in representations of reality. The world as we know it does not tolerate, much less value, inconsistency (despite Emerson's definition of "the hobgoblin of little minds"), multiplicity of meaning, and divided perspective. It instead values and rewards consistent argument, final and definitive conclusion, and singular, unvarying vision.

The town of Oxford, Faulkner's home in Mississippi, provides ironic demonstration of this problem. We know that Faulkner sought to sublimate the actual Oxford into the apocryphal Jefferson, thus liberating himself from the twin authorities of the "real" town and its representatives. The "exact reversal of what Faulkner performed," however, is occurring in Oxford, according to geographer Charles Aiken, "a prime example of how the fictional becomes the real," or in my formulation, a prime example of how an apocrypha, in a world of authorities, gets canonized. "One factor in Oxford's movement to preserve buildings is recognition of their relationship to Jefferson" as well as the fact that thousands of tourists now come to Oxford, Mississippi, to see where Lucas Beauchamp was jailed, or where Jason Compson worked in the hardware store, or to find Holsten House.[67] Faulkner wanted to capture life's motion on paper, and perhaps he did. He also succeeded, in direct contradistinction to his aims as a writer, in fossilizing Oxford, Mississippi. Seeking and employing the principles of revolving vision and competing truth, Faulkner ironically managed to freeze in place and "canonize" Oxford, preserving as a tourist center the very place he sought to sublimate.

Faulkner was well aware of the resistence to his apocryphal program. His last novel, subtitled "A Reminiscence," is a long reflection inspired by the apocryphal temperament. Directly opposed to this frame of mind is the canonical: the principle behind the fixed, eternal Bible, the singular, authoritative vision. Barnstone refers to numerous "other bibles" in modern times, including William Blake's "rebellious scripture, influenced by the canonical Bible as well as such texts as [the apocryphal] *Book of Enoch*. . . . Other poets—Walt Whitman, Charles Baudelaire, Jorge Guillen— gave themselves to one book, to recording their personal religion, sacred or profane, in a bible for their times."[68] To achieve the creation of an "other bible," the artist, in Faulkner's conception, must be "ruthless" if necessary. He must stop at nothing to answer the divine voice within him (or the demonic one, as Faulkner would say, as he quite obviously could not claim divine inspiration). This point was most clearly presented to Jean Stein. "An artist is a creature driven by demons. He doesn't know why they choose him and he's usually too busy to wonder why. He is completely amoral in that he will rob, borrow, beg or steal from anybody and everybody to get the work done. . . . Everything goes by the board: honor, pride, decency, security, happiness, all, to get the book written. If a writer has to rob his mother, he will not hesitate. . . ."[69]

The Reivers (1962), as its title indicates, is about stealing: stealing guns, stealing cars, stealing horses, *stealing experience and meaning* from those who control these icons of power and authority. In his first novel, *Soldier's Pay,* Faulkner wrote, "Only the ageing need conventions and laws to aggregate to themselves some of the beauty of this world. Without laws the young would rieve us of it as corsairs of old combed the blue seas."[70] In his last novel, Faulkner made clear the absolute need of the young to reive (as he preferred to spell the word in 1962) from the old authority over their inherited world. Like Blake, Whitman, Baudelaire, Guillen—and Faulkner—the young must reive experience and authorship, and write their own "other bible." Dedicated to his grandchildren, this final novel is wholly conclusive, a fitting "book of revelations" to Faulkner's apocrypha. For what "Grandfather says" in the novel is to beware of making him into the kind of icon which prohibits, or even inhibits, future creation. In his "Reminiscence," Faulkner as grandfather explains how and why he stole, and how important the act was in forming his character. Faulkner's "actual" stealing, of course, is sublimated into the apocryphal, into the tall tale that makes *The Reivers* a plot. As reiver, the author is inviting his grandchildren, his apocryphal grandchildren, to follow his example.

The novel opens with a disavowal of the narrator's own credibility. "I'm sure you have often noticed how ignorant people beyond thirty or forty are. I dont mean forgetful. That's specious and easy" (5). Here the narrative immediately demands critical intervention, or "reader participation" as Faulknerians often say. *The Reivers* achieves a balanced presentation of wisdom and knowledge (about itself as well as about the world it depicts) as being equally dependent upon the experience and guidance of elders, and upon the resources and imaginative powers inherent only in the young. Yet the young are not given their chance until the elders die away. In fact, until their authority is negated in death, the old stand in the way of young people's creative life experience. For example, Lucius Priest knows that "when mother got the message that Grandfather Lessup was dead," he was well on his way to the act of disobedience that would mark his "fall," as he terms it (50). The rebellion in this case is the stealing of his other grandfather's automobile—a symbol, in 1905, of the future, of Lucius' own inheritance, his own era. Lucius' living grandfather, aptly nicknamed "Boss," bought the automobile only as a status symbol, because the president of the other bank, Sartoris, owned one, and Boss would not let his competitor show him up. To Lucius, on the other hand, the automobile is no reactionary symbol but instead embodies and holds promise to the future, to his maturity, to his inheritance of freedom, authority, and power.

Boss Priest would like to keep the automobile locked safely out of the hands of the young (Lucius), the irresponsible (Boon Hogganbeck), and the dispossessed (Ned). In *The Reivers,* this is what the representatives and holders of authority do with symbols of power and with their control over the future: keep them locked away, unexamined, and out of the reach of potential and eventual usurpers. There are plenty of examples in the novel of what happens when this social order is violated. When Boon steals John Powell's gun in the opening scene of the novel, his inability to "handle" the symbol of power results in damaged property and injury to an innocent bystander. Lucius' grandfather settles this incident in a particularly paternalistic manner, paying damages out of his own pocket and acting as lawyer, judge, and jury. The meaning of the social order is clear. Power and responsibility must be controlled and guarded closely against usurpation by the young, the innocent, or the (allegedly anyway) inept.

Nonetheless, for Lucius to accomplish his "fall," or his loss of innocence (actually "Grandfather" calls it the onset of his appetite), he must disobey the "law" of his elders and become a "reiver." Significantly, he does not consider it stealing, because to the young, what the elders call stealth is simply the *taking* of what is owed them. It is seizing the world promised them by their birth but withheld from them by their jealous living forebears. And so, Lucius maintains his innocence even as his appetites increase, "We were worse than amateurs: innocents, complete innocents at stealing automobiles even though neither of us would have called it stealing since we intended to return it unharmed; and even, if people, the world (Jefferson anyway) had just let us alone, unmissed" (62). To Lucius, it is not the automobile that is being stolen—for it will be returned—but the *experience* provided by the automobile, which will not be turned. As a symbol, the automobile is truly a *vehicle* for something greater than itself. It is Lucius' "postage stamp," the means by which he will reive from his native circumstance "some of the beauty of the world."

Faulkner's code of stolen experience, actually a reification of the apocryphal vision, is masked behind what appears to be a harmless and trivial tall tale, a kind of reversal of his more familiar novelistic tendency to obscure faith and "the uplifting of the heart" beneath violent and even "horrific" plot lines and story themes. Critics have worked hard to find the light glimmering behind the stories of Temple Drake's sexual ordeal in *Sanctuary* and Joe Christmas' gruesome, wasted life and death in *Light in August*. They search for statements of faith and hope in the dissolution of the Compson family in *The Sound and the Fury* and the Sutpen family in *Absalom, Absalom!* The critical assumption in Faulkner studies has always been that there is more to Faulkner than meets the eye, more than incident of plot. In fact, Faulkner criticism depends upon this supposition for its own existence.

Critical analysis of *The Reivers,* on the other hand, has generally taken the novel at its word, echoing, for example, the "gentlemanly code" that Faulkner articulates through Boss Priest at the end of the book and a code that Lucius seems to endorse. The code says that "a gentleman can live through anything. He faces everything. A gentleman faces the responsibility of his actions and bears the burden of their consequences, even when he did not himself instigate them but only acquiesced to them, didn't say No though he knew he should" (302). Joseph Gold characterizes Faulkner's "world view," especially evident in *The Reivers,* as "neither an optimism nor a pessimism, but a humanism, a comprehensive acceptance of the human condition as a meaningful phenomenon."[71] William Rossky has called the novel "Faulkner's summing up— . . . his final, most complete acceptance of time, of the human condition."[72] Judith Bryant Wittenberg sees *The Reivers* as more than a summation or a triumph of what she identifies as Faulknerian principles. "By the end of *The Reivers,* Lucius has become a triumphant figure," according to Wittenberg, "and the gentlemenly 'code' has proved vital and operable in a way never before possible in a Faulkner novel." She compares Lucius to earlier Faulkner protagonists, such as Bayard Sartoris of *The Unvanquished,* who come close but do not emerge with "the more positive morality" achieved by Lucius Priest.[73] In all, there appears to be critical consensus that *The Reivers* sums up and actually celebrates certain Faulknerian values about the past and morality. "Faulkner's fiction," concludes Panthea Reid Broughton, "establishes that man escapes history only by coming to terms with it and accepting all its implications. . . . Only by accepting the past, living with it," as Boss argues, "does one gain control over experience."[74] Within the plot of *The Reivers,* according to the consensus, Lucius learns just this lesson.

It is odd that a novel about stealing—from petty to grand larceny—should generate so much criticism about "acceptance." The observations made about the gentlemanly code are accurate, of course, but only as explications of what lies at the surface of what is usually called a "light" Faulkner novel. First of all, we need to recall that "Grandfather," the aged Lucius who narrates the tale, is well beyond "thirty or forty or so" and is, by his own admission, "ignorant." *His* interpretation of what he learned from this exercise in felonious adventurism is therefore highly suspect. The deceptively comfortable ending of male generational bonding and adolescent initiation ought to be seen through eyes trained, by nearly twenty of Faulkner's previous novels, to be suspicious of the obvious or of the narrator's own avowed interpretation. No one believes Jason when he calls Caddy (or Quentin) a bitch. No one believes Sutpen when he says he made only one mistake in his design. Faulkner's readers are used to distrusting his narrators. Why believe the Grandfather?

The Reivers may be Faulkner's final reminder not to be so trusting of the authority of the Word. The need to delve beyond the surface or the plainly stated is an aspect of Faulkner's entire apocrypha, not simply a critical approach to his last novel. The actual term apocrypha comes from the Greek words *apo* ("away") and *kryptein* ("to hide, conceal"). *Apokryptein* thus means "to hide away," and the noun *apokryphos* means "hidden, concealed, obscure."[75] Biblical scholar W. O. E. Oesterley explains that the term apocrypha was first used to describe "books containing hidden teaching not to be disclosed to ordinary people." A distinction between two categories of holy books is found in II Esdras xiv:44–47 and Oesterly quotes the passage. "The first [twenty–four holy books] that thou has written publish openly, and let the worthy and the unworthy read it; but keep the seventy last, that thou mayest deliver them to such as be wise among the people; for in them is the spring of understanding, the fountain of wisdom, and the stream of knowledge." According to Oesterley, the first category of books became the Old Testament while "the seventy last" became the Jewish apocrypha, at least according to apocryphal legend.[76]

Faulkner held, for example, a similar view concerning his two "categories" of fiction: short stories and novels. He tended to write simpler, straightforward narratives for mass-consumption and profit in such magazines as *Colliers* and *The Saturday Evening Post,* but he would revise and add complexity to the same material if he needed to include it in a novel. The various versions of "The Bear," a chapter in *Go Down, Moses,* provides exemplary demonstration of this categorization.[77] It may be that Faulkner's very stature as a literary master in the twentieth century is owed to his belief that "literature" is for the initiated and for posterity, while mass-market fiction is something done for money. Certainly the high yield Faulkner's novels provide to critical scrutiny has acted, at least in part, to undergird his reputation as a master of the art. The critical history of *Sanctuary,* for instance, offers evidence of the rehabilitation of that novel from "cheap idea" to "a fair job" to masterpiece—all the product of a steady critical engagement in that novel's complexity to which Faulkner consciously added in order to make it "a fair job."[78]

With *The Reivers,* however, critics have been far from rigorous and engaged. If the dark surface of *Sanctuary* could obscure "hidden" rays of beauty and affirmation, why is it that the light, bright surface of *The Reivers* cannot conceal something more serious, more deadly? After all, when Boon shoots John Powell's gun in wild abandon, he causes serious injury to a young black woman, whose cries for justice ("screaming and bleeding like a stuck pig" [15]) are considered irrelevant to "father's" patriarchal authority and to Grandfather's story. Lucius' father and Judge Stevens handle the matter extralegally. "If [it] is not legal," the Judge asserts, "it ought to be" (16), and of course, no one can argue with him. The world of *The Reivers* is one in which lying, stealing, and unnecessary convolutions of "fact" are in the natural order of things, so much so that they all contribute to the "light" storyline. The plot of the novel is actually uncalled for. "All that striving and struggling and finagling to run a horse race with a horse which was not ours, to recover an automobile we never had any business with in the first place, when all we had to do to get the automobile back was to send one of the first family colored boys to fetch it" (229). Although *The Reivers'* plot is unnecessary and none of it had to happen, not much of what does happen is of great consequence. As a tale of initiation and lost innocence, the novel does not amount to much either. As apocrypha, however, the inconsequential novel belies its own seeming triviality.

In *The Reivers,* the willingness to reive is paired with the need to say no to authority when its demands run counter to desires or ambitions within one's own conscience. Lucius says no to Boss' locked garage; Everbe says no to her life as a prostitute; and even Boon, at one point, is transformed by knowledge of his own capacity to refuse. Reflecting on Everbe's decision, Boon realizes his own rather sorry position in the Priest's extended family. "But now she's done quit," he says. "For private reasons. She cant no more. She ain't got no more private rights to quit without my say-so too than I got to quit without Boss' and Mr Maury's say-so too—." Here, Boon glimpses into his own predicament. "He stopped," Faulkner continues, "furious and baffled, raging and helpless; and more: terrified" (197). His terror is in response to a vision of something that Boon seems unable, at this point, to accept, despite his being engaged at the time in the motions of its accomplishment. He too is a reiver, and by the end of the novel he has stolen his own place away from the juvenile relationship he previously had with the Priests, is paying his own way, and is raising his own child with Everbe.

The Reivers: A Reminiscence, then, depicts the powerless, the juvenile, and the ambitious achieving control, maturity, and authority by way of stealth and refusal. The novel endorses the will to take what is needed to accomplish a movement, peacefully or by force, away from the ignorance of age and establishment. The stakes involved are life and death, money and power, and the transition of authority is far from ritualistic or even orderly. Instead, it is rather compelled and reived. If this marks an "acceptance" on Faulkner's part, it is more a reassertion of what his fiction has always maintained and accepted. Struggle and loss, ambition and violence, are the hinges upon which more than one of Faulkner's characters have swung. Even Lucius Priest at one point sounds like Faulkner's quintessential adolescent, Quentin Compson, in his confrontation with human debasement. "I was ashamed," Lucius says of learning that Everbe is a whore, "and hated myself for listening, having to hear about it, learn about it, know about it; hating that such not only was, but must be, had to be if living was to continue and mankind be a part of it" (174). Quentin, of course, came to the same conclusion, but that conclusion had another effect on his actions.

Lucius' surviving grandfather tells him what an old person must in the context of *The Reivers*, to "Live with it" and to accept his responsibilities as an adult in a fallen world. This advice is particularly "ignorant" given the role Lucius has played in the reformation of Everbe and the maturation of Boon. It points again to the novel's insistence upon the blindness of age. Nonetheless, Boss Priest is the authority here, and his words reduce Lucius to tears. His entire journey will be misread by his grandfather and turned into an occasion for the delivery of some stock homilies about being a gentleman before it is dismissed. Meanwhile, the "reivers" have indeed triumphed. Ned reveals in the final pages of the novel how much money he has made on the horserace (at Boss' expense) and how important it is that he and Lucius lie to Boss about the wagering so he will never know what he has lost and to whom. It is youthful stealth and the subterfuge of the underclass (and race), not a "gentlemanly code" or an acceptance of the human condition, that wins the race in *The Reivers*.

III

The tragedy facing so many of Faulkner's early characters "is that their interior world has been co-opted by an external world they never made and apparently no one can ever unmake," observes Myra Jehlen.[79] The typical Faulknerian tragic hero—Quentin Compson, Isaac McCaslin, any of the Bundren children, the Reporter—finds himself in a world in which definition, meaning, problem, and solution have all come before and all the structures and contracts for the social order have long been agreed upon before he or she was born. Even the way in which a person must "think" has been established, with logic, rationality, and ratiocination demanded of the human mind from its first initiations into human intellectualism. Faulkner identified with this predicament and made it into his own apocryphal impetus. In Virginia, Faulkner said it was his intention "to take man's dilemma, the old familiar things in which there is nothing new and can't be anything new, and by the light of my own experience and imagination and a great deal of hard work, to make something which was a little different, and wasn't here yesterday."[80] This sentiment accounts for Faulkner's numerous and highly quotable lines about creating a cosmos of his own, about inventing "much more interesting people than God ever did,"[81] or about improving on God's creation "who, dramatic though He be, has no sense, no feeling for, theatre."[82] If "the sorry, shabby world" does not "quite please you," he told students at Virginia, "you create one of your own."[83] The world Lucius Priest makes for Lucius Priest Hogganbeck, for example, is "a little different, and wasn't there yesterday" because of Lucius' will to appropriate—or reive—something new by the light of his own experience and *against* his elders.

The compulsion, and later in life the insistence, that meaning be continually reformulated has an American tradition dating back at least as far as Thomas Jefferson's suggestion that each successive generation make its own revolution. Although the world seems to be fixed and society seems to predate the individual, in the Faulknerian ideal the individual nonetheless has an obligation to attempt to communicate his or her personal divergence or private rebellion. In 1950, Faulkner told Dayton Kohler that "if you just keep on trying to say a thing long enough and hard enough, it will emerge; someone will hear it."[84] For this reason, Faulkner always insisted on the free exchange of ideas, including ideas about his own work. When confronted with a Freudian analysis of his writing which seemed a bit overblown, Faulkner deferred to what he said might be the beginning of a credible approach. "I'm convinced, though, that that sort of criticism whether it is nonsensical or not is valid because it is a symptom of change, of motion, which is life, and also it's proof that literature—art—is a living quality in our social condition."[85] In this sense, then, Faulkner seems to stand for what Frank Kermode has called "the radiant obscurity of narratives" against any notion of a single truth or a single meaning.[86] The evidence bears this out despite Faulkner's formulaic insistence that there exists one Truth, though perhaps Faulkner had a more pragmatic, process-oriented view of truth than has been yet identified. "Why insist that knowing is a static relation out of time when it practically seems so much a function of our active life?" asked William James in *Pragmatism*. "When the whole universe seems only to be making itself valid and to still be incomplete (else why its ceaseless changing?) why, of all things, should knowing be exempt?"[87]

Faulkner's pragmatistic view of truth is exemplified clearest in his use of history. To him, history is not so much the record of the past but the dramatic play of the motif of meaning in human life. A book such as *Absalom, Absalom!* demonstrates clearly that for Faulkner the past is the record of what people said and of the stories they told, not the activities that led to the tales and the telling. History, for Faulkner, is the record of men's and women's perceptions, not the things or events themselves. The implication, of course, is that to question or challenge perception or ways of perceiving the present is to suggest possibilities for change in history. How the phenomena of life are understood and interpreted is the "how" of history, and why certain phenomena are comprehended and included in the historical record—or in the historical consciousness of a people—is the "why" of progress, chaos, or doom in history.

If there is such a thing as a Faulknerian ethic, it is the human obligation to communicate, to speak out. Because we live in what Joseph Mazzeo calls an "age of exegesis"[88] and because, as Faulkner was fond of saying, "change must alter, must happen, and change is going to alter what was,"[89] the modern human mind is obligated to communicate continually interim reports on what it knows. As such, Faulkner is truly a critic's writer, encouraging divergent views and rewarding the revisionist mind. When James Divine read "Carcassone" in 1937, he asked Faulkner what it meant. Faulkner answered, "It means anything you want it to mean."[90] It is the reader's responsibility to find meaning, and if reading is a representation of thinking, it is the mind's function to interpret and make meaning in the world. "Man," Faulkner told Loic Bouvard in 1952, "is free and he is responsible, terribly responsible. His tragedy is the impossibility—or at least the tremendous difficulty—of communication. But human beings keep on trying endlessly to express themselves and to make contact with other human beings." When the artist creates, Faulkner continued, he attempts "man's most supreme expression." Due to the difficulties involved, "The artist must create his own language. This is not his right but his duty."[91] Yet he does not have to create his own language, or his own philosophy, if he is at home with the one given to him. It is the creation of new language and new structure, and the suggestion of alternative ways of perceiving reality that form the literary basis of Faulkner's apocrypha.

If communication is successful, then the object of communication—the reader—achieves understanding. Faulkner's idea of communication, however, was never polemical in the sense of his having a particular program or platform to expound. "I believe that speech is mankind's curse," the author wrote in 1959. "All evil and grief in this world stems from the fact that man talks. I mean, in the sense of one man talking to a captive audience."[92] To communicate is to invite the reader to understand, and Faulkner knew well that a person understands best what he desires or what he thinks of independently. Change occurs when comprehension is achieved, and comprehension occurs only when a person is willing to accept change in the way he is thinking. In Sartre's formulation, "To understand is to change, to go beyond oneself."[93] To take the apocrypha is to accept the unaccepted, to go beyond the parameters of the authentic or the official version of reality. Faulkner's implication beyond exegesis and textual analysis is that no prefabricated or canonical or "official" meaning can be accepted as definitive and that the source of truth in the world lies not in objective reality but in subjective purposefulness. What is true, in other words, is what is desired. This view contradicts Boss Priest's definition of intelligence in *The Reivers* as "the ability to cope with the environment" (121) in favor of young Lucius' demonstration of it as the ability to amend or alter the environment by sheer assertion or subversion, even chicanery if necessary. The way in which the individual is taught to think and to structure his thoughts, in Faulkner's ethic, must be questioned, turned over, and challenged. If Faulkner's creation of an apocrypha stands for anything, it advocates a vigorous and free interplay of ideas and criticism among human beings where nothing, not even the forum, is permanent. In the end, Faulkner's aesthetic strategy amounts to a political stance: society is composed of thousands of voices, and every voice has not just the right but the duty to attempt to be heard. If one person is ignored or denied a platform, then the opportunity must be *taken,* by stealth and by rebellion against authoritative attempts at suppression. The Faulkner aesthetic encourages and requires readers to come to conclusions and understandings about his texts and, by implication, about their world.

The understanding of Faulkner as a mythmaker and creator of a saga of the South resulted in the muting of the political implications of his work. As his early fiction was reassessed in the 1950s, it came to be understood as distinctly apolitical. Faulkner was seen as a sort of regional traditionalist, a singular example of American private initiative and individualism. In the 1950s, Faulkner would write against this assessment of his work. In his personal or public role as Laureate, however, Faulkner would fulfill the assessment of himself as an American moralist—and as a national prop. His various public formulations about human values and individualism in the 1950s (which will be examined in greater detail in Chapter 4) influenced critical readings of his work in unfortunate ways.

For Faulkner, the ideology of individualism amounted, in practical consequence, to an avoidance of political confrontation in his personal life. It was his way of appearing politically and socially conscious without having to defend the actual implications of his fiction. It allowed for survival, not political praxis. The same, of course, was true for Malcolm Cowley and the entire corporately funded cultural and literary consensus that produced Faulkner in the postwar era. "Individualism" (like "human values") was not something, by label alone, that would get anyone into any trouble (or cost anyone his funding) in the 1950s. Nevertheless, what Faulkner was *writing* in that decade was diametrically opposed, in an ideological sense, to what he was *saying*. And if anything has been proven reliable about Faulkner studies, it is that it is safer to trust his texts than to trust his talk. After all, as Faulkner said in 1957 (if this can be trusted), he "couldn't tell the truth about Faulkner" if he tried.

There is no question that Faulkner's reputation was "saved" by Malcolm Cowley's intervention in his career. Whether interest in Faulkner would have grown so quickly in the late 1940s without Cowley is, of course, unknowable, but Cowley is certainly a crucial player in the first wave of American critics to recognize (and to insist upon) Faulkner as a major literary figure. This recognition, however, was not without its price. Due to Cowley's peculiar understanding of the author, Faulkner criticism was limited for years to the "chronological picture of Yoknapatawpha County." Carvel Collins has reported that Faulkner had given "a great amount of pleasurable attention to preparing a detailed plan for a complete collected edition of his fiction if one were ever to be published." Yet Faulkner had no intention of ordering the collection chronologically, and his thoughts on his total output, according to Collins, had little in common with "the criticism which began years ago drumming the belief that one of the important features of Faulkner's work is the chronology of his fictional county."[94]

When *The Portable Faulkner* was completed, Faulkner was pleased with the job. He told Cowley that "even if I had beat you to the idea, mine wouldn't have been this good." At the end of the same letter, he added that he was "working at what seems now to be my magnum o," the manuscript of what would become *A Fable*.[95] It is quite possible that although Faulkner was grateful for Cowley's attention to his career, he was also anxious to prove wrong Cowley's thesis about his regional saga. *A Fable,* his "magnum o," would have nothing at all to do with Yoknapatawpha County and would use Southern materials only in a tall tale with allegorical relevance to the main events of the novel. *A Fable* is primarily concerned with rebellion and its place in the definition of the human spirit. What Faulkner was primarily resisting in his dealings with the critic was Cowley's materialistic characterization of him as some kind of Southern mythmaker and his description of Faulkner as an old-fashioned moralist. Perhaps writing the appendix to *The Sound and the Fury* (at Cowley's request) for *The Portable Faulkner* reminded the author of the immense satisfaction he got from writing that book and led him back to similar political and social concerns in *Requiem for a Nun* and *A Fable,* concerns which, after his experience with Cowley, he felt he had to make explicit.

What Faulkner defines in the fiction he would turn to following the Cowley affair are the political implications of his aprocryphal, not mythical, vision. As if to prove Cowley wrong, Faulkner begins to demonstrate in the 1950s that the literary impulse to create apocrypha translates, ideologically, into a program of political and social rebellion. He makes his first move in this direction in the "Appendix: Compson," which he wrote for *The Portable Faulkner*. According to Faulkner, he included in the appendix what he "should have done . . . when I wrote the book. The whole thing would have fallen into pattern like a jigsaw puzzle when the magician's wand touched it." The appendix actually places *The Sound and the Fury* in two patterns simultaneously, Cowley's and Faulkner's, and is surely the stroke of a "magician" writer of apocrypha for its double purpose.

First, the appendix introduces to the novel a Cowleyan mythos by bringing *The Sound and the Fury* to Yoknapatawpha. Dispossessed American Indians, trading posts, and long genealogies filled with colorful detail are surely the stuff out of which mythical counties are made. Yet there is nothing in the stories of Ik- kemotubbe, Andrew Jackson, Quentin MacLachan, Charles Stuart, or Jason Lycurgus that contributes anything substantial to the mean- ing of *The Sound and the Fury,* although the stories do add detail to the mythos of *The Portable Faulkner.* It is the appendix's second purpose, though, which truly does supplement the novel's effect on readers. In the material about Caddy Compson, Faulkner clarifies her place in the "pattern" of his political apocrypha, which he would subsequently develop in response to Cowley. Here, in Caddy's story, is found the true drama of "Appendix: Compson," a pattern which the magician accomplishes while his audience, including Malcolm Cowley, is looking elsewhere.

The ideological implications of Caddy's story—the missing nar- rative in the text of *The Sound and the Fury*—are made clear by placing her, in the appendix, in the company of the Nazi Staff General. The only Compson child with the will and the spirit to break away from the Compson "curse" has been prohibited from regenerating her family because of social strictures and conventions owing to her gender. Out of the repressive and authoritarian nature of her girlhood in America, including the influence of her unloving, insistent parents and her demanding, inhibiting brothers, emerges a woman far colder and far more "authoritarian" than any of the authority figures in her own life. The Compsons are "cursed," the "appendix" explains, because they sacrifice their own spirit, as em- bodied by the loving child Caddy, to such ideologically obsolete notions as the sanctity of womanhood and gentility.

Through Caddy, Faulkner begins to explore the place of re- bellion—rebellion based on love and on the regeneration of the human spirit—in the life and vitality of the community. In reflecting on his "heart's darling," Caddy Compson, Faulkner may also have sensed parallels between her predicament and his own struggle with Malcolm Cowley. The apocryphal writer, in the hands of the literary canon-maker, is prohibited from presenting his apocrypha as a legiti- mate body of work because the canonizer insists on an orthodox *order* to his fiction. Cowley will transform, with his own magician's wand, the disorderly, contradictory, anarchic apocryphal writer into a figure far more authoritarian than any apocrypha would tolerate. Caddy was driven away by the hegemonic impulses of her family, driven finally to a Nazi officer to make her point. Faulkner was forced from Yoknapatawpha by another kind of hegemonic program representing another kind of clan. He turned to the trenches of World War I France to make his point about authoritarian impulses to suppress apocrypha.

He had, of course, defined Caddy's political role in the Compson family in the original text of *The Sound and the Fury*. As a child, Caddy experiences intense repression and often threatens to "run away" (21), or claims she does not care about herself or her future (22). When her parents decide to change her brother's name to Benjamin after they learn he is mentally retarded, Caddy expresses a hatred for *"everything"* as she cries in Maury/Benjy's lap. In defiance of her parents she continues to call the boy Maury on occasion. Caddy's rebellion, however, is not tied to any specific event in her childhood but is a product of her own vision of a dismal, oppressive future. She is, quite simply, precluded by the political dynamics of her family from possessing a life of her own while she is in the Compson household. As they have renamed the idiot child to avoid unintended reference to a living member of the clan, the Compsons just as brutally attempt to mold, repress, and predetermine Caddy so she, too, reflects their sense of her proper place in the family.

Quentin, for one, would rather his sister be dead than pregnant and "unvirgin." When Quentin claims he cannot "believe it doesn't matter" that Caddy has had sexual relations with men, it is because he associates Caddy with "the dirty little sluts" of Cambridge (96). Rather than change his opinion of the town girls, and his view of his own status in relation to them, he condemns Caddy. Mrs. Compson, of course, would prefer her daughter marry the repulsive, dishonest Herbert Head than have Caddy live in violation of social forms. Both Quentin and his mother turn Caddy's normal desire to give and receive affection into something perverse and wicked because her activities challenge the structures of authority and propriety to which they vainly cling. Growing up under these circumstances, Caddy never fantasized about being "a queen or a fairy," Quentin recalls. "She was always a king or a giant or a general" (215). Blocked in her every effort to break free of the loveless, Compson "curse," when all she wanted was the same freedom enjoyed by her brothers ("she couldn't bear for any of you to do anything she couldn't," Mrs. Compson says [326]), Caddy chooses the only option available to her: flight. Her daughter, Quentin, is an attenuation of Caddy. She possesses all her mother's sense of repression, but none of her spirit or, to put it in Compson terms, none of Caddy's class.

Of all the biographical snippits in the appendix, Caddy's is by far the longest (it takes up one-third of the length of the appendix) and the most complete. It is the only one that contains a present-tense drama, that being the librarian's discovery of Caddy's photograph in the "slick magazine." (The librarian's "discovery" of Caddy is another possible reference to Faulkner's own discovery by Cowley.) When Caddy is introduced in "Appendix: Compson," the word "love" is used seven times, as if to emphasize the centrality of that emotion to her fate. Caddy "loved her brother despite him" and the fact that Quentin's values and expectations result not only in his hatred for her but also in her banishment from the family. She finds refuge in such places as Hollywood, California, (clearly associated with rejection in Faulkner's mind) and occupied Paris, an international symbol of resistence and captivity.

It is, perhaps, a sister in misery and resistance who "discovers" Caddy, a "mouse-sized and -coloredwoman who had never married, who had passed through the city schools in the same class with Candace Compson." This small town librarian, whom Faulkner depicts as a kind of slave to public, hypocritical morality, takes Caddy's photograph clipped from the magazine and performs what is to her truly an act of courage and defiance. She approaches Jason Compson, "trembling and aghast at her own temerity," and asserts, "It's Caddy! . . . We must save her!" Jason laughs cruelly at Caddy's fate and then denies her to the librarian. The librarian meets a similar dead end in Memphis, where even *The Sound and the Fury*'s great icon, Dilsey, cannot see a way to save Caddy *"because she knows Caddy doesn't want to be saved hasn't anything anymore worth being saved."* The librarian, keeper of the culture's literary works, returns home to where life is lived for her "too with all its incomprehensible passion."

One thing Faulkner adds as far as a book *(The Sound and the Fury?)* is concerned is that at the end of the day "you could close the covers on it and even the weightless hand of a child could put it back among its unfeatured kindred on the quiet eternal shelves and turn the key upon it for the whole and dreamless night." Closing its covers and putting the book away is what the magician claimed he was doing to *The Sound and the Fury* in the appendix. In fact, however, "Appendix: Compson" acts to reopen the covers of the book in a rare act of authorial audacity. If Cowley could re-write Faulkner and make him "Portable," so could Faulkner append a novel he had penned seventeen years before. In doing so, however, he would comment upon Cowley's authoritative, orthodox program of discovery and canonization. In any case, it is in the temperament of the apocryphal writer to consider no story ever finished or perspective final—and no perspective illegitimate, including, paradoxically, Malcolm Cowley's.

When Random House began plans to reprint *The Sound and the Fury* in 1946, Faulkner described the appendix as "the key to the whole book" and (perversely, to many critics and to Random House) insisted on placing the key *"first,"* before the original text, to allow the four sections to "fall into clarity and place."[96] Read this way, "Appendix: Compson" introduces the apocrypha first and only superficially as legend before getting to its real task of representing in the apocrypha a pattern of human defiance and rebellion. The "key to the whole book" lies in Caddy's rebellion born of love, in the librarian's kindred temerity, and in the resistence that arises organically from "incomprehensible passion." It is the librarian who refuses to "close the covers" of the book on Caddy by insisting on an attempt to save her. Faulkner's appendix makes clear, however, that the covers *are* closed. For Quentin, Caddy's daughter, who is abducted from her strong and defiant mother to be raised in the same authoritarian cruelty that banished Caddy, there would be "no chromium Mercedes; whatever snapshot would have contained no general staff." In driving out Caddy, the Compsons dispel all hope for the regeneration of the family, which depends not upon the maintenance and canonization of authority but upon resistance to it. Yet Caddy is written out of the text, and its survivors, from the evil Jason to the inimitable Dilsey, will no longer recognize her or see in her either threat or salvation.

In *A Fable,* Faulkner would thoroughly explore this "pattern" of rebellion, and later, in *Snopes,* he would apply it to his apocryphal county. When he places Caddy in the back seat of that German Mercedes, he imagines precisely the implications of the trammelled, cornered spirit and vividly portrays the perversion of life where rebellion is suppressed. The human spirit, as Faulkner would come to define it in his apocrypha, is inherently rebellious, or else it is doomed.

---

1. For example, Joseph L. Blotner calls it "a stirringly rhetorical statement, but how had William Faulkner arrived at this position of seeming faith and affirmation after the great novels which appeared to say the very opposite? . . . How could he say that man would prevail, he whose works seemed to some principally a chronicle of failure, anguish, and despair?" In *Faulkner: A Biography* (New York: Random House, 1974), p. 1366, hereafter cited as *Faulkner: A Biography.* Joseph Gold, *William*

Faulkner: A Study in Humanism, From Metaphor to Discourse (Norman: University of Oklahoma Press, 1966), p. 171, sees the post-Laureate Faulkner as "like a preacher, high up in the pulpit, wanting desperately to go down and mingle with the crowd, but knowing that they are looking up and waiting for the sermon which he must give." Andre Bleikasten describes the public Faulkner as largely the creation of the author in response to the Nobel Prize award, where Faulkner "addressed his audience from a standpoint that he had not chosen, and that he took up only from a sense of duty. What he said from that position did not spring from his deeper writing impulse, but was his response to a pressing social demand." See "For/Against an Ideological Reading of Faulkner's Novels," in Michel Gresset and Patrick Samway, S.J., eds., *Faulkner and Idealism: Perspectives from Paris* (Jackson: University Press of Mississippi, 1983), p. 33.

2. A valuable analysis of textual succession in Faulkner's career is Gary Lee Stonum, *Faulkner's Career: An Internal Literary History* (Ithaca: Cornell University Press, 1979). Stonum argues that each completed text both solved artistic problems raised by its predecessor and created new artistic problems for its successor novel to address.

3. Quoted in Blotner, *Faulkner: A Biography,* one-volume edition (New York: Random House, 1984), p. 561.

4. Cowley was preceded by two important articles published in 1939: George Marion O'Donnell, "Faulkner's Mythology," *Kenyon Review* (Summer 1939), pp. 285–99, and Conrad Aiken, "William Faulkner: The Novel as Form," *Atlantic Monthly* (November 1939), pp. 650–54.

5. Malcolm Cowley, ed., *The Portable Faulkner* (New York: Viking Press, 1946; rev. ed., 1967), p. vii. In 1967, Cowley added his endorsement to the original introduction and defended *The Portable Faulkner* as "the straightest path into Faulkner's imaginary kingdom" (xxxiii).

6. Malcolm Cowley, ed., *The Faulkner-Cowley File: Letters and Memories, 1944–1962* (New York: Viking Press, 1966), pp. 3, 5, 171, hereafter cited as *The Faulkner-Cowley File.*

7. *Ibid.,* p. 172.

8. Cheryl Lester, "To Market, To Market: *The Portable Faulkner,*" *Criticism* 29:3 (Summer 1987), pp. 388–89, 375.

9. William Manchester, *The Glory and the Dream: A Narrative History of America, 1932–1972* (Boston: Little, Brown & Co., 1974), p. 473.

10. Malcolm Cowley, *The Dream of the Golden Mountains: Remembering the 1930s* (New York: Viking Press, 1980), p. xii.

11. Lawrence H. Schwartz, *Creating Faulkner's Reputation: The Politics of Modern Literary Criticism* (Knoxville: University of Tennessee Press, 1988), pp. 100; 139–40. See Schwartz's chap. 5 for extensive details on the role played by the Rockefeller Foundation in situating literary criticism within the cultural Cold War. "The Foundation had created excellent connections to the leading critics through which initiatives were carried out. . . . [At the Rockefeller Foundation all] were agreed that preservation of cultural values required support for those individuals whose commitment was both to modern literature and 'high' culture" (137). In practical terms, this meant the distribution of grants, endowments, and other financial support to "approved" individuals, journals, and institutions.

12. *Ibid.,* pp. 202–203.

13. *Ibid.,* p. 210.

14. *Ibid.,* p. 4.

15. James B. Meriwether, "Faulkner's Correspondence with *The Saturday Evening Post,*" *Mississippi Quarterly* XXX (Summer 1977), p. 465.

16. David Minter, *William Faulkner: His Life and Work* (Baltimore: Johns Hopkins University Press, 1980) p. 51.

17. Joseph L. Blotner, ed., *Selected Letters of William Faulkner* (New York: Random House, 1977), p. 53, hereafter cited as *Selected Letters.*

18. *Faulkner: A Biography,* p. 1257.
19. *Ibid.,* p. 1270.
20. *Selected Letters,* p. 348.
21. *Ibid.,* p. 162. Faulkner's understanding was that the contract would be torn up and a new one more favorable to him would be drawn up "if I show that I am doing all right on this job." Apparently, Faulkner was misled or taken advantage of by story department head James Geller and director Robert Buckner of Warner Brothers. Faulkner claimed in August 1942 that "I was not aware that the deal included more than this one particular job, and on the strength of Geller's statement that, if I worked well, the contract would be voided by the studio, I decided to sign it. Afterward I talked to Buckner, who assured me that the contract would be voided." In August 1943, Faulkner still held to this verbal understanding over the letter of the contract. "I have a promise from the studio that, when I have written a successful picture, they will destroy the contract" (177). His patience may have begun to run out in May 1945 when he told his agent Harold Ober, that Geller "has promised about a dozen times that I am to get" a new contract (192).
22. In November 1945, Faulkner told Robert K. Haas of Random House that he was not writing anything until the Warner Brothers claim was made clear (*ibid,* 210). Minter suggests that Faulkner entered this dry spell with reluctance and "struggled against it repeatedly"; however, the experience "marked him permanently" (193).
23. *Ibid.,* p. 199.
24. *The Faulkner-Cowley File,* pp. 6–7.
25. *Ibid.,* pp. 90–91.
26. *Ibid.,* pp. 9–11.
27. *Ibid.,* p. 22.
28. *Ibid.,* p. 66, for example.
29. *Ibid.,* p. 15.
30. *Ibid.,* pp. 15; 29–30. Cowley later repudiated the opinion about cutting *Absalom, Absalom!*
31. *Ibid.,* p. 61.
32. *Ibid.,* pp. 25, 65, 69.
33. *Ibid.,* p. 78.
34. Frank Kermode, *The Sense of Ending* (New York: Oxford University Press, 1967), p. 39.
35. Willis Barnstone, ed., *The Other Bible* (New York: Harper and Row, 1984), pp. xvii, xviii–ix.
36. *The Faulkner-Cowley File,* p. 114.
37. Barnstone, *The Other Bible,* p. xvii.
38. Elaine Pagels, *The Gnostic Gospels* (New York: Vintage Books, 1981), pp. 11–12; 13.
39. *Ibid.,* p. xxxix.
40. *The Holy Bible: King James Version* (New York: New American Library, 1974), pp. 44–50.
41. St. Augustine, *City of God* (Garden City, NJ: Doubleday, 1958), p. 406 (book XVIII, Chap. 38).
42. Faulkner owned a fourteen-volume collection of Biblical materials, *The Holy Bible Containing the Old and New Testaments and the Apocrypha* (Boston: R. H. Hinkley Co., n.d.), and signed each volume "William Faulkner / Rowan Oak 1932." According to Joseph Blotner, his autograph was the only reliable sign of esteem for books in his library, and he signed merely 255 of his 1,200 volumes. Joseph L. Blotner, comp., *William Faulkner's Library: A Catalogue* (Charlottesville: University Press of Virginia, 1964), pp. 85, 7.
43. James B. Meriwether and Michael Millgate, eds., *Lion in the Garden: Interviews with William Faulkner, 1926–1962* (New York: Random House, 1968), p. 255, hereafter cited as *Lion in the Garden.*

44. Louis Daniel Brodsky and Robert W. Hamblin, eds., *Faulkner: A Comprehensive Guide to the Brodsky Collection, Volume III: The De Gaulle Story*, by William Faulkner (Jackson: University Press of Mississippi, 1984), p. xi.

45. *Ibid.*, pp. 354–55, 361.

46. *Ibid.*, pp. 395–98.

47. Sally Murray, quoted in *Faulkner: A Biography*, p. 128.

48. *Ibid.*, p. 6, from an unpublished portion of the classroom conferences at the University of Virginia in 1957.

49. James W. Webb and A. Wigfall Green, eds., *William Faulkner of Oxford* (Baton Rouge: Louisiana State University Press, 1965), p. 134. Speaking in 1947, Faulkner continued: "Truth is the sum of things that make man bid for immortality, that make him generous in spite of himself, or brave when it is to his advantage to be cowardly—that something that makes him better than his environment and his instincts." Hereafter cited as *William Faulkner of Oxford*.

50. *Lion in the Garden*, p. 252.

51. Claude-Edmonde Magny, *The Age of the American Novel: The Film Aesthetic of Fiction Between the Two Wars*, translated by Eleanor Hochman (New York: Frederick Ungar Publishing Co., 1972), p. 186.

52. Jean-Jacques Poullin, "Time and Destiny in Faulkner," in Robert Penn Warren, ed., *Faulkner: A Collection of Critical Essays* (Englewood Cliffs, NJ: Prentice Hall, Inc., 1966), p. 80.

53. R. W. B. Lewis, "William Faulkner: The Hero in the New World," in *ibid.*, p. 214.

54. Hubert McAlexander, Jr., "General Van Dorn and Faulkner's Use of History," *Journal of Mississippi History* 39:4 November 1977), p. 360.

55. *The Faulkner-Cowley File*, p. 112.

56. Michael Millgate, *The Achievement of William Faulkner* (New York: Random House, 1966), p. 214.

57. Erich Auerbach, *Mimesis: The Representation of Reality in Western Literature*, trans. by Willard R. Trask (Princeton, NJ: Princeton University Press, 1953), p. 401.

58. Arthur F. Kinney, *Faulkner's Narrative Poetics: Style as Vision* (Amherst: University of Massachusetts Press, 1978), p. 9. Kinney explains: "Faulkner's meanings come not simply in the narrative consciousness of one or more characters . . . but in our *constitutive consciousness* as readers, the integrated sum of our awareness of the work and the perceptions of all the characters whose thoughts are explicitly or implicitly provided for us: the epistemological emphasis in Faulkner's narrative poetics is finally on the reader" (101).

59. *Ibid.*, p. 243.

60. Magny, *The Age of the American Novel*, p. 208.

61. Warren Beck, *Man in Motion: Faulkner's Trilogy* (Madison: University of Wisconsin Press, 1961), p. 16.

62. Gold, *A Study in Humanism*, p. 38.

63. Robert Penn Warren, "Introduction: Faulkner: Past and Present," in Warren, ed., *Faulkner: A Collection of Critical Essays*, pp. 14–15.

64. John T. Irwin, *Doubling and Incest/Repetition and Revenge: A Speculative Reading of Faulkner* (Baltimore: Johns Hopkins University Press, 1975), p. 9.

65. Walter J. Slatoff, *Quest for Failure: A Study of William Faulkner* (Ithaca, NY: Cornell University Press, 1960), *passim.*

66. Edward W. Said, "Opponents, Audiences, Constituencies, and Community," in W. J. T. Mitchell, ed., *The Politics of Interpretation* (Chicago: University of Chicago Press, 1983), p. 26.

67. Charles Aiken, Faulkner's Yoknapatawpha County: Geographical Fact into Fiction," *Geographical Review* 67:1 (January 1977), p. 20.

68. Barnstone, *The Other Bible*, p. xvii.

69. *Lion in the Garden*, p. 239.

70. William Faulkner, *Soldier's Pay* (New York: Liveright, 1926; rpr. 1954), p. 58.

71. Gold, *A Study in Humanism*, p. 175.

72. William Rossky, "Faulkner's Tempest," *William Faulkner: Four Decades of Criticism*, edited by Linda W. Wagner (East Lansing: Michigan State University Press, 1973), pp. 358, 361.

73. Judith Bryant Wittenberg, *Faulkner: The Transfiguration of Biography* (Lincoln: University of Nebraska Press, 1979), p. 245.

74. Panthea Reid Broughton, *William Faulkner: The Abstract and the Actual* (Baton Rouge: Louisiana State University Press, 1974), p. 46

75. *Webster's New Universal Unabridged Dictionary*, second edition, 1983.

76. W. O. E. Oesterley, *An Introduction to the Books of the Apocrypha* (London: SPCK, 1935), p. 4.

77. See also the discussion of the composition of the *Snopes* trilogy in this volume.

78. See Faulkner's spirited and coy preface to the 1932 edition of *Sanctuary* for an account of his own efforts to "rehabilitate" the novel and his opinion of it as "a fair job."

79. Myra Jehlen, *Class and Character in Faulkner's South* (New York: Columbia University Press, 1976), p. 1.

80. Frederick L. Gwynn and Joseph L. Blotner, *Faulkner in the University: Class Conferences at the University of Virginia, 1957–1958* (New York: Vintage Books, 1965), p. 258, hereafter cited as *Faulkner in the University*.

81. As quoted by Emily Whitehurst Stone in Albert Isaac Bezzerides, *William Faulkner: A Life on Paper* (Jackson: University Press of Mississippi, 1980), p. 59.

82. Max Putzel, "Faulkner's Trial Preface to *Sartoris*: An Eclectic Text," in *Papers of the Bibliographic Society of America* 74 (1980), p. 375.

83. *Faulkner in the University*, p. 59.

84. *Selected Letters*, p. 296.

85. *Faulkner in the University*, p. 65.

86. Frank Kermode, *The Genesis of Secrecy: On the Interpretation of Narrative* (Cambridge, MA: Harvard University Press, 1979), p. 47.

87. William James, *Pragmatism: A New Name for Some Old Ways of Thinking* (Cambridge, MA: Harvard University Press, 1975), p. 235.

88. Joseph Anthony Mazzeo, *Varieties of Interpretation* (Notre Dame, IN: University of Notre Dame Press, 1978), p. 1. We take our cue, according to Mazzeo, from the study of nature, which "requires interpretation because its operations are hidden. What we see is not, in some sense, what is 'really' going on" (2).

89. *Faulkner in the University*, p. 277.

90. Quoted in *Faulkner: A Biography*, p. 976.

91. *Lion in the Garden*, pp. 70-71.

92. *Selected Letters*, p. 424, from a letter to Muna Lee of the State Department.

93. Jean Paul Sartre, *Search for a Method*, trans. and with introduction by Hazel E. Barnes (New York: Alfred A. Knopf, 1963), p. 18.

94. Carvel Collins, "Introduction" to William Faulkner, *Helen: A Courtship and Mississippi Poems* (New Orleans and Oxford, MS: Tulane University/Yoknapatawpha Press, 1981), p. 36.

95. *The Faulkner-Cowley File*, pp. 90–91.

96. *Selected Letters*, pp. 220–21. In subsequent editions of the text and on the advice of Faulkner scholars, Random House has ignored this request. The most recent edition of *The Sound and the Fury* (New York: Vintage Books, 1987), dispenses with the Appendix entirely, reverting to the "first edition and Faulkner's original manuscript" from 1929. ("Publisher's Note"). Therefore, citations to *The Sound and the Fury* in this study are taken from the 1954 Vintage books edition, which includes the Appendix: Compson.

> The voice of the amplifier, apocryphal, source-
> less, inhuman, ubiquitous and beyond weariness
> or fatigue, went on.
>
> —*Pylon*

2. The Apocryphal Voice
The Production of Self and Place and Time

I

FAULKNER'S "apocrypha" accounts for significantly more than his subject matter. His "apocryphal county" signifies not only Jefferson, Mississippi, but his whole literary production. It signals the ideological content of his novels, including those set outside Yoknapatawpha, in form and structure as well as in subject matter. The radical juxtapositioning of material and the habitual reworking of material not only from short story to novel but also between novels all suggest an apocryphal production indicative of the literary consciousness of one who sometimes seems, like Lucas Beauchamp of *Go Down, Moses,* to have *fathered himself.* Of course, this is hardly the case. Faulkner's literary generation and the production of Faulkner himself was accomplished by conscious, brazen stealth, a willingness to reive from his surroundings and his associations what he needed to create his art.

The "discovery" of the "postage stamp" that became Jefferson and Yoknapatawpha is clearly indebted to the example of Sherwood Anderson's *Winesburg, Ohio,* as well perhaps to the idea that an established truth is something grotesque. More specifically, Blotner's biographies indicate a number of occasions when Faulkner would appropriate a short story, an idea, at times even an entire unfinished manuscript, from his wife. Estelle had ambitions of her own to write, which went unfulfilled; but how much of her own sense of failure, her suicide attempts, and her alcoholism can be attributed to the fact that much of what she did attempt to write was so readily absorbed by her phenomenally prolific, "ruthless" husband? Blotner's biographies do not address this issue, and neither do those of Minter or Oates, so Estelle remains a kind of ghost figure aside the great writer. All of Faulkner's biographers have commented on his hesitancy to pursue a divorce despite the dramatic differences between him and Estelle, and his own extramarital affairs. Perhaps the man was indebted to this woman in ways which the biographers have not fathomed, a bond at least partially borne of secrecy and untold exchanges. As reiver, Faulkner knew that appearances could be produced, used, and protected. In *The Reivers,* Lucius recalls Grandfather's peculiar contention "that your outside is just what you live in . . . and has little connection with who you are and even less with what you do" (304).

Faulkner was a twentieth-century maker of apocrypha: writing against place and against time to produce place and time, denying the universal or perpetual authority of any single, established truth or experience or point of view, and creating instead a world of slippery accountability, radical dissonance, and multiple, revolving possibilities of telling and knowing. This apocryphalism manifested itself in Faulkner's personality as well. The apocrypha was no literary mask or opportunistic strategy but sprang from deep within the man himself, the product of a particular temperament and personality. My language here is misleading. There was no "Faulkner" in the sense of a singular, consistent character and personality; there were, in fact, many Faulkners, multiple Faulkners. The man had a kind of "revolving" personality. One reason why every biography of Faulkner has fallen flat, that is, failed to evoke a sense of the man outside of what he said and did, is because his biographers have assumed the existence of a unified (canonical? orthodox?) individual. In fact, "Faulkner" was an apocryphal production, and the same aesthetics that define the art also characterized the man. In other words, Faulkner did not stop at the creation of multiple possibilities of telling and knowing; he also created multiple possibilities, in his own lifetime, for being.

The cornerstone in what can be called Faulkner's apocryphal

biography is his sense of life's plasticity. "Constant change" and "motion" are signal words in Faulkner criticism, words he repeated himself in those curious classroom conferences and interviews of the 1950s, words that critics never tire of quoting and perpetuating. Faulkner used the idea of perpetual change to characterize the shift in his career from reclusive Mississippi writer to public American spokesman, and perhaps also to mark his reluctance to be the *authority* implied in that shift. "Well, sir," he informed his questioner at the University of Virginia, "you are constantly changing, your skin, your fingernails, are constantly changing. The only alternative, you know, is death, and let's hope that we won't have to keep on doing tomorrow what we are doing today. There won't be much fun in it."[1] These words have an especially curious ring coming from a man who had been saying since grade school, "I want to be a writer,"[2] a man for whom the vocation of the written word symbolized his best edge against the certainty of impermanence and change.

Joseph Blotner argues in *Faulkner: A Biography* that Faulkner's lifelong goal was to make a living as a writer—and only as a writer—despite his dabbling in farming and his insistence that he was, at heart, a man of the soil.[3] There is a tension, then, in the temperament of this man who saw around him constant change and impermanence and yet felt within him a single, driving ambition to write. His writing, of course, reflects that conflict, but the strain seldom interfered with the act of writing. Faulkner's friend Louis Cochran put it bluntly in 1931: "It should not be forgotten in studying the personality of this writer that he is, in common parlance, a man with one idea. Since his earliest childhood he had known he was to be a writer, or nothing else at all."[4] Looking back over his career in his semi-autobiographical essay "Mississippi," Faulkner recalled himself becoming "a professional fiction writer: who had wanted to remain a tramp and the possessionless vagabond of his young manhood but time and success and the hardening of his arteries had beaten him. . . ."[5] What changed more than anything else in Faulkner's career, however, was the account he gave of himself to people who asked.

Despite his singular ambition to be a writer, Faulkner was a man of many faces and various personal styles. Gilbert Rhyle has argued that to know a mind, the biographer must "know about your capacities, interests, likes, dislikes, methods and convictions by observing how you conduct your overt doings, of which by far the most important are your sayings and writings."[6] Faulkner had an adapta-

ble style, and his "sayings" are as closely tied to form and context as
are his writings. He had a stock set of responses that he applied to
predictable questions regarding artistic aims and literary purposes, as
clearly seen in such productions as *Faulkner in the University* and
Faulkner at Nagano. His friend Stephen Longstreet had a good sense
of what he called "the Faulkner act."

> Bill was never himself in any interview I witnessed, and all I've read in
> print. It was an act, the stealth of a shy, proud man. He didn't like to talk
> and [when I knew him in California] he didn't very much. Later when
> the Nobel Prize made him a part of the modern American scene, I
> noticed he still used the drama of the conflict in the human heart, and
> the whiskey, tobacco and paper line. He added the fact that he was
> uneducated. It was an untrue picture of himself, a juggling of the
> sequence of events, for he was well aware of his worth at most times,
> cold and chilly with strangers and with little respect for those material
> things most people held important. Any insufficiency he kept hidden
> inside.[7]

Longstreet said that Faulkner continually relied upon two lines
about "the conflict in the human heart" and about "the whiskey,
tobacco and paper" whenever he was cornered into saying something quotable to an interviewer. Faulkner told his audience at the
University of Virginia as much when he claimed to have a "split
personality." The author, he claimed, "is one thing when he is a
writer and he is something else when he is a denizen of the world."[8]
Longstreet was amused at the image Faulkner constructed for himself in the last decade of his life. "As he grew older and fame came to
him he became, some said, a snob." It was all an "act," Longstreet
explains. "The moustache grew longer in a British guardsman's
model, a bowler hat had appeared, and he wandered around with a
tightly furled umbrella. The only people to whom he freely offered
signed copies of his work were dull hunt club horsemen and fox
hunters. I sensed the self-examination and purification was over;
these were Bill's last self-indulgent years."[9]

James G. Watson has studied the various personae Faulkner
created in his letter writing, for example, and finds that Faulkner
presented distinct, discrete selves to his different correspondents. He
would write and revise in successive letters, describing his experiences with significant alterations, additions, and deletions. Watson
concludes that Faulkner's letters "are self-consciously inventive in
themselves, aware of their own imaginative language and artistic
effects."[10] Faulkner presented himself to the world in the same way

he presented his fiction. There were different styles for different audiences, and the complex relationship between subject (fiction as well as self) and circumstance revolved over time. Self and place and time, in Faulkner's mind, were continually revolving, continually produced.

Faulkner's character and genius have been mysteries to his biographers; the final word on "what he was like" has yet to emerge. Joseph L. Blotner has allowed that even after spending "a good part of my professional life thinking about his genius . . . I am not sure it *is* possible finally to say" where the source of Faulkner's genius lies.[11] David Minter portrays Faulkner as a "divided self," moving "to and fro between two worlds," alternating his allegience to his "imagination" and to the physical world of Oxford, Mississippi.[12]

> At times Faulkner as a writer made Faulkner as denizen his effective sign—as in his dramatizations of the dandy and the bohemian. But the firmer his sense of his literary self became, the more his roles changed. Most of his later dramatizations—of the pilot, farmer, or huntclubber— were expressions of his shy social self. Later he habitually described himself as not a literary man but a writer, and as not only a writer but a farmer. . . . Yet, though he brought little of the intensity or the talent to life that he brought to writing, and though none of his activities, including farming, became remunerative, they remained an essential part of the divided life he lived.

As a result of this "doubleness," Minter concludes, Faulkner "would never be wholly satisfied living in the world he imagined" nor would he "really belong to the world around him or to the creatures of it."[13] Although there is sufficient biographical evidence to support Minter's idea of the divided self,[14] I think it does little to illuminate a human being to draw the Cash Bundren conclusion that "this world is not his world; this life not his life" (*As I Lay Dying* [250]). Faulkner was more than simply *divided,* and by Minter's own evidence he was divided into more pieces than *two.*

Nonetheless, a neatly divided Faulkner—life versus art, imagination versus real world—is emblematic of the attempt to fit him into an orthodox, literary mold. Against the chorus of critics who would like to canonize William Faulkner[15] speak a number of people who knew the man and who object to the canonization. Howard Hawks, the only man who spoke up for Faulkner professionally in Hollywood and with whom Faulkner had a serious and productive working relationship, was astounded at what the literary community was doing to the reputation of his friend. "[N]ow I get the damnedest letters from these people in Oxford, Mississippi, who want to carry on as if Faulkner were a saint. And I won't be a part of that." Hawks continues, "Hell, he liked to get drunk, and he believed fidelity was an overrated virtue, like some of the rest of us. He wasn't a saint. And he'd be goddamned angry if he found out people were preparing him for sainthood, or whatever it is called."[16] More remarkable than Hawks' personal impression is A. I. Bezzerides' experience as scriptwriter for the public television production of *William Faulkner: A Life on Paper*. In his preface to the printed version of the documentary, Bezzerides all but repudiates the final product.

> All his friends, his relatives, his acquaintances, his admirers, and especially the professors, who teach Faulkner in 1-A and 1-B in the universities, and who deleted everything they thought to be offensive, because they respected Faulkner's image more than they did the all too fallible man, distorted reality not so much by controlling what was said as by controlling what was not said. [They claimed to be adhering to Faulkner's desire for privacy]. . . . I knew Faulkner well enough to know that if his privacy was to be violated, he would want it to be told as it was, warts and all. Faulkner would have balked at being corrupted into a legend, out of misguided deference to some concocted image, at cost to the man.[17]

If a single image of Faulkner emerges from the testimony of those who actually knew the man, it is that there were numerous images he felt free to turn on and off at will or in response to varying circumstances.[18] To Robert Coughlin he acted "like a farmer who had studied Plato and looks like a river gambler. In the way he looks there is something old-fashioned, even archaic."[19] To Saxe Commins, one of Faulkner's Random House editors, he acted like some personification of "Little Lord Fauntleroy," and there was an inexplicable incongruity between the very proper gentleman who would visit the Commins' home and the artist who created the books. Sometimes, however, "Fauntleroy" slipped: "Now and then Bill lapsed into colloquial expressions which didn't in any way fit his Little Lord Fauntleroy image," recalls Dorothy Commins, as when he said of his mother, "she ain't paintin' so good."[20] Maurice Coindreau, writing at Faulkner's death, expressed an awareness that Faulkner "did not show himself to everyone in the same light. There were several Faulkners."[21] Even Stephen Oates, whose popular biography of Faulkner published in 1987 intends to "elicit from the coldness of fact the warmth of a life being lived," falls short of accomplishing this goal. Oates is correct in his assertion that no biography has yet presented a sense of a "life being lived," but aside from recounting Faulkner's love affairs more candidly, presenting his difficult marriage in greater detail, and chronicling his alcoholic binges with less gentility than past biographers, Oates' Faulkner still, in my opinion, remains cold and flat. His many references to Faulkner's hypnotic eyes and personal intensity do not enliven the figure he presents, because Oates has not taken seriously the absence of a unified self in Faulkner's character, that is, he has not considered him apocryphally.[22]

Faulkner's life itself was an apocryphal production, a multi-faced, revolving structure of stories and images and poses existing simultaneously. He presented himself and performed the duties and activities of all these "people," including the farmer, the hunter, the mule breeder, the pilot, the horseman, the patriarch of an extended family, the romantic lover of young women, the "congenital liar," the Nobel Laureate, the American good-will ambassador, the national public spokesman, the Southern apologist, the classroom teacher, the poet, the screenwriter—and, of course, the great writer of literature and the sot. All these "people" were not roles, or guises or masks hiding the real Faulkner and protecting the true man. Each and all these people *were* the real Faulkner. This is the hinge on which all Faulkner biographies have failed to turn. Faulkner did make up stories about himself, fancying himself a veteran of World War I combat over France (which he recanted in later years) and claiming to have a steel plate in his head and to have fathered illegitimate children. These tall tales are all by-products of the "congenital liar" Faulkner and are not the same as the very real and many selves Faulkner did experience in his lifetime. His biographers have confused the issue and have assumed that there must exist beneath the multiple perspectives on Faulkner a singular, authoritative figure of the man. This simply is not the case. Apocryphal in spirit as well as in artistic performance, in life as well as in literature, Faulkner was all he produced himself to be. When he said in Virginia that he could never "tell the truth about Faulkner," perhaps he meant that there was no single truth to tell.

The plasticity of Faulkner's personality—his ability to juggle personality emphases and to move among various lives—is mirrored by his acceptance of competing ideas about the meaning of his work. As his life could comfortably mean a number of contradictory things to him, so could his fiction, since to him definitiveness had no meaning or value. Robert Linscott writes that he once advanced to the author a theory to explain "Faulkner." "He grinned and agreed, as he agreed to any theory about his writings you happened to advance, not caring in the least what ideas were attributed to him."[23]

Among the few things Faulkner always liked were horses, silence, whiskey, and the results of hard work and intense concentration. Due to the last on that list, any idea which reflected that Faulkner's interlocutor had read his work carefully and thought about its implications would most likely meet with agreement. Ideas were never as important to Faulkner as were their production; just as his "personality" was never as important to him as was his freedom to produce himself as he chose. If we understand the apocryphal production correctly, inspired creation outweighs any existing achievement, and epistemological freedom will always be held as more vital than the already-created or the canonized. Elaine Pagels explains that early gnostics, authors of numerous apocryphal texts, "considered original creative invention to be the mark of anyone who becomes spiritually alive." All were expected to revise and transform what they were taught. "Whoever merely repeated his teacher's words was considered immature."[24] To fully engage the apocrypha, then, means not to order and arrange it into some orthodox pattern but to *participate* in it by re-creating, in its spirit, something which it seems to have failed to articulate adequately. Production, not collection or recapitulation, is at the core of an apocrypha.

"We are here to work. It is either sweat or die," Faulkner told an interviewer in 1931. "Where is there a law requiring we should be happy. A man can be happy doing a tough job well or failing in a tough job. But contentment and happiness come only to vegetables when they sit still, never to man himself because he is the victim of his own thinking and his own sweat."[25] Faulkner repeated variations on the theme of hard work—and of the importance of silence to get thoughtful work done—all his life.[26]

He found the only outlets or relief from his lifelong devotion to his calling in horses, farming, and whiskey. The debilitating effects of intoxication no doubt offered relief to "the victim of his own thinking" and from the intense drive to continue working. The image of Faulkner as a kind of "alcoholic refugee, self-pursued" was advanced by his earliest biographer, Robert Coughlin.[27] Explanations and rationales for Faulkner's legendary drinking binges are numerous. Maurice Coindreau saw the whiskey bottle as the "Alice's mirror" of Faulkner's imagination, "for he drank less to destroy himself than to create," or perhaps to rehearse the logic of creativity by a kind of ritual process.[28] Robert Linscott characterized Faulkner as a cyclical alcoholic for whom periodic pressures would result in the "chemistry of craving" and he "would go overboard."[29] Faulkner's drunken sabbaticals were not productive, and he did not show any interest in "literature" when he was drinking. Hodding Carter recalls that when Faulkner "went on a prolonged binge he could be sickeningly vulgar and blindly stupid. He was not a day to day alcoholic but his heavy drinking was a periodic compulsion and when whiskey was in him no one was happy, including himself."[30]

Most all of Faulkner's biographers have attempted to explain his drinking, but none has ventured to assert its absolute centrality to his work and to his artistic production. Literary critics have said even less about the place of whiskey in the apocrypha. Thomas P. Gilmore, in a study of alcoholism and drinking in modernist literature, cites the "complete neglect" of the relevance of drinking to the productions of alcoholic and heavy-drinking writers. Going so far as to call the modern era the "Age of Literary Alcoholism," Gilmore draws a parallel between the effects of drunkenness and two leading characteristics of modernism, "radical dissatisfaction with commonplace reality and a consequent attempt to undermine conventional reality by greatly altering traditional states of consciousness." According to Gilmore, "the fundamental challenges to and ruptures of those states offered by heavy drinking may seem desirable from a modernist viewpoint."[31] Heavy drinking was no minor flaw in Faulkner's character, nor something that interfered with his living as he wished and doing what he wanted. Rather, it was absolutely indispensable to his sense of himself—as important as writing.

Intoxication and the painful shock of renewed sobriety appealed to Faulkner enormously. He once reacted, only partially in jest, to Jean Stein's pouring away some whiskey with this bit of hyperbole: "Deprivation never makes a saint; it only makes a minister. Think of all the work that went into that bottle of liquor. When man discovered the distillation of liquor, he raised the civilization of man above animals. Until then man had only made a few scratches on walls. Pouring out liquor is like burning books."[32] The cryptic association between books and whiskey is telling here. The finished products in Faulkner's imagination are the full liquor bottle, the scratches on the walls, and the books. Implicitly, drunkenness is somehow tied to the energy or state of mind which the book produces. The way liquor intoxicates is correlated here to the way a book challenges existence by its power to create alternative, or apocryphal worlds. The chaos of a drunken state of mind, and the eventual shock of a renewed sobriety, provides a neat paradigm for the jumble of perceptions and the chaos of sensations out of which the mind must make its "painfully fresh perception."[33] Whiskey drinking and the cycle of periodic alterations to reality—the play of apocrypha—are simply extensions and manifestations of Faulkner's impulse to experience the creation of meaning as among life's primary motifs. Only if we are willing to reshape completely the pieces and redefine the logic of association can we begin to attempt an assembly that is not dependent on prior example or established tradition. "Well, drinking," Faulkner mused in Japan in 1955, "I consider drinking a normal instinct, not a hobby. A normal and a healthy instinct."[34]

Faulkner believed meaning to be a plastic phenomenon created by the mind, transitory, dependent on circumstances, and always subject to revolution and alteration by the results of renewed revelation and fresh inspiration. Reality itself, as Faulkner liked to say, was continually in motion, a process intoxication did not distort, but actually validated and intensified and made clearer. Intoxication certainly allows us to experience life as *motion*. In his biography, this vision of the real resulted in his moving from Faulkner-the-farmer to Faulkner-the-writer and so on, and further served as expression of his refusal to accept a single image of himself as definitive. The process of the production of meaning was so satisfying to him that he sought to reproduce it physiologically by periodically erasing all connections between himself and his world, and returning, in all cases but one, to creative sobriety. Faulkner's drinking, then, was intimately tied to his understanding of knowledge and of creation. The metaphor of intoxication even has apocryphal validity, though it is impossible to say whether Faulkner ever imagined this. "He who thus is going to have knowledge knows whence he came and whither he is going," according to the gnostic *Gospel of Truth and the Valentian Speculation*. "He knows it as a person who, having become intoxicated, has turned from his drunkenness and having come to himself, has restored what is his own."[35]

In only one novel, *Pylon*, did Faulkner make alcoholic consumption a major motif. Significantly, though, the one novel about heavy drinking was written as a break from another novel, *Absalom, Absalom!*, with which Faulkner was having creative difficulty. It is almost possible to characterize *Pylon* as the "binge" that produced *Absalom, Absalom!* Even in *Absalom,* however, drinking is equated with storytelling. Throughout chapter seven, when Quentin is explaining how Sutpen told General Compson his story, it is clear that the telling was inspired by drink. The two men "drank some more of the whiskey and ate and sat before the fire drinking some more of the whiskey and he telling it all over" (247). When Sutpen decides to stop talking, he "looked at the whiskey bottle and said, 'No more tonight'" (256), thus conflating into one image the bottle and the story, as Faulkner would do years later to Jean Stein. Later in the narrative, Henry blurts out his fraternal love for Charles Bon "over the bottle one night," according to Shreve and Quentin, who have absorbed the connection between drinking and storytelling (315).

Faulkner, of course, was not oblivious to the darker side of heavy drinking, the destructive, killing effects of alcoholism which contributed to his own death. In *The Sound and the Fury,* Quentin, observing his dipsomaniac, self-destructing father, sees *"that liquor teaches you to confuse the means with the end* I am. Drink. I was not" (216). Quentin would not settle for a revolving obliteration, a confusion of means and end, but would achieve permanence instead. In fact, he dooms himself by his own intractability and by his insistence on absolute certainty, or sobriety. Nonetheless, his father, by refusing to be sober and to make "painfully fresh perception," drinks himself to death with the same finality as Quentin's suicide at Harvard. The fool figure, Jason, on the other hand, refuses both the alcohol his father craves and the uncertainty that plagues his brother.

This ambivalent presentation of alcoholic indulgence runs throughout Faulkner's fiction. In *Go Down, Moses,* whiskey accompanies the general nostalgia of the hunting rituals, but it also contributes to Rider's pathetic death. In *Requiem for a Nun,* whiskey plays a central role in the early economy and social order of Yoknapatawpha. The conquering Anglo-Saxon pioneer, "the tall man, roaring with Protestant scripture and boiled whiskey," arrives with "Bible and jug in one hand and (like as not) a native tomahawk in the other" (89) to finally dominate the land with his civilization's three great talismans: holy book, intoxicating drink, and weaponry. All three tokens act as whiskey does, as sources of strength and inspiration, and also as sources of death and obliteration. In *Sanctuary,* the novel *Requiem* intends to fulfill, it is the culture of *Prohibition,* of denying whiskey to those who crave it, that produces the evil which hangs over the sequence of events. On the other hand, the availability of bootleg alcohol during Prohibition puts into motion the events leading to Temple Drake's degradation. The apocryphal spirit is lifeless without these contradictions, and this is precisely the point. Through the representation of contradiction, Faulkner's apocrypha opposes orthodox finality and authoritarianism. Ordinarily, contradiction implies a lack of clear thought, just as inconsistency implies weakness. In Faulkner's apocrypha, these same qualities are the very stuff of human thought and creation. To deny them is to misrepresent the real as something permanent and intractable.

Faulkner's episodic binges of heavy drinking and his biographical plasticity are particularly salient aspects of the apocryphal writer's contradictory temperament, indicative of a personality that craved renewal and reformulation, and disdained static, definitive conceptions of self and place and time. In Faulkner there is a clear connection between the experience of intoxication and the will, or the need, to produce an apocrypha. There is also a clear connection between the various presentations of self and the practices of multiple vision, contradictory truths, and succeeding perspectives, which are the working principles of apocryphal texts. The biographical manifestations of Faulkner's apocryphal vision will contribute to an understanding of his two greatest productions, *A Fable* and the *Snopes* trilogy, works that are largely neglected despite their importance to Faulkner himself. Before getting to these novels, three more central points in the production of the apocrypha need to be explicated: the discovery of the figurative, in *As I Lay Dying;* the defense of subjective truth, in *Pylon;* and the role of rebellious intrusion, in *Intruder in the Dust.*

II The Discovery of the Figurative in *As I Lay Dying*

The production of meaning by Faulkner's characters resembles an interior drama, where the act of signification is central to the development of the fiction.[36] In fact, Faulkner's formal plots and storylines often emerge secondary to this epistemological drama, and the conflicts that provide tension and suspense in the typical Faulkner novel are as likely to be conflicts of meaning and epistemological projection as they are battles of will or intention. At least such struggles of will or intention are almost always demonstrated by Faulkner's narrative to flow directly from primary acts of conflicting signification. This dramatic production of meaning forms a motif throughout the major portion of Faulkner's work. Whereas most readers of Faulkner would say that *The Sound and the Fury* marks the turning point in his career from apprentice to master, I suggest that the turn was not completed until the Bundren family made its trip to Jefferson and laid the corpse of Addie to rest. When Addie is buried, simplistic notions of figuration and of the power of words are also put to rest, and Addie's mistaken "words are no good" is overcome by the triumph of Vardaman's emblematic "My mother is a fish." Vardaman, the youngest Bundren, emerges as the author-figure in the novel who will insist, as Faulkner would contend from *As I Lay Dying* onward, that his figuration, or his apocrypha, is real—as real an alternative as any to the literal, or to what often passes in fiction as realistic.

At the University of Virginia in 1957, Faulkner talked often about conflict, giving variations on this statement: "I'm interested primarily in people, in man in conflict with himself, with his fellow man, and with his time and place, his environment."[37] This trio of human oppositions—self and self, self and other, self and circumstance—faced by "people" suggests an intellectual as much as a physical series of polarities. First, man is "in conflict with himself," with the preconceptions and values he has inherited and carries with him, preconceptions and values that can blind him to reality and prevent independent or genuine reaction. Faulkner states this conflict best in "Smoke" from *Knight's Gambit*.

> But men are moved so much by preconception. It is not realities, circumstances, that astonish us; it is the concussion of what we should have known, if we had only not been so busy believing what we discover later we had taken for truth for no other reason than that we happened to be believing it at the moment.[38]

The drama of confronting historical events with peculiar vision and preconceptions is played out repeatedly in *Absalom Absalom!*, for example, where the beliefs and anxieties of the present inform the "realities" of the past and block the path to comprehension and communication.

Second, man is in conflict "with his fellow man." He is in eternal struggle with his fellows to communicate amid the cacophony of voices that in turn attempt to reach him. "We are like men trying to move in water, with held breath watching our terrific and infinitesimal limbs," Faulkner wrote in "Ad Astra," "watching one another's terrific stasis without touch, and without contact, robbed of all save the impotence and the need."[39] It is a battle of outward articulations, voiced and unvoiced, reflective of a jangle of human realities. In *As I Lay Dying,* voices compete in an effort to define just what reality amounts to and just what it is that is shared as "the real." Reality is repeatedly defied in Faulkner by the mind's capacity to delineate it and its power to configurate it. Finally, man is in conflict "with his time and place, his environment." He is the product of a particular set of historic circumstances with which he must struggle to form a world view independent of what is told or given to him, one that expresses his own vitality in reaction to the world and one that marks his place *in* that world. It is the failure to do this, or the perception that it is impossible to do this, that leads, or at least contributes to Quentin Compson's suicide, Isaac McCaslin's repudiation of his "inheritance," and Flem Snopes' ultimate stagnation. Conflict with "environment"—time, place, self, and circumstance—is the grounding for the apocryphalist ecology throughout Faulkner's work, and it provides Faulkner with his sense of drama.

The drama of meaning is a motif in Faulkner's fiction that flows directly from a particular view of the nature of reality and of human understanding of it. As conflict informs drama, so does it inform Faulkner's ontology. Throughout the Faulkner canon, meaning is not an external, fixed commodity *out there* to be consumed, but the product (and often the byproduct) of an eternal drama within and without the mind. It is a drama in which human understanding is created and projected by the mind, reflected in the structures and the products of social realities, overturned by human conflict with inherited meaning and value, and created again. Meaning, understood as a drama that engages the mind, is not fixed and established but elusive and subject to change. What is *real* in Faulkner is not external "reality," and neither is it any particular view of reality. What is real in Faulkner is the drama itself, the drama of meaning continually reasserted, continually denied, continually remade in eternal conflict with its source and signification. Meaning understood as a drama can no more exist independent of the mind than can the act on stage exist independent of the actor, the human subject and object of the drama.

This ontology leads clearly into polarity. On the one hand, it may serve to explain partially Faulkner's infamous asocial qualities and, perhaps, his capability for self-destruction. To hold to this view of reality is to hold to a kind of formal nihilism, where one would have to "know better" than to believe in anything fixed or eternal as true.

This is, for instance, Mr. Compson's position in *The Sound and the Fury*. Indeed, the best that a person might do in the midst of this drama is, as Faulkner liked to say, "endure." As he told Cynthia Grenier in 1955, what interested him was "trying to defy defeat even if it's inevitable." On the other hand, with "pity and honor and courage," to quote another Faulknerian signature, one might master the arts required by the drama and manage to leave one's "Kilroy was here" on the wall.[40] This is what occupied Faulkner throughout his career as a writer; this is what he said, in his Nobel Prize address, was "worth writing about."

Early in his career, during his own most intense period of production, Faulkner worked out the idea of the drama of meaning by demonstrating the way in which the drama is mastered. In *As I Lay Dying*, the meaning of death informs the epistemological drama and provides the basis for the trio of conflicts: between the self and the self, between selves, and between the self and its "time and place, environment." Harold Bloom has called *As I Lay Dying* "Faulkner's strongest protest against the facticity of literary convention,"[41] and it certainly is that. In this novel, more so, I think, than in its more famous predecessor *The Sound and the Fury*, Faulkner charted an aesthetic "discovery" of sorts, one that would call into question a number of assumptions about "realism" and "facticity."

Within the context of the drama of meaning, in other words, *As I Lay Dying* is *intensely* realistic. The realism, however, is of an apocryphal nature, and the reality projected in the novel comes into perpetual conflict with the reader's own "better" judgments. Nonetheless, the ammunition in this conflict is identified by Faulkner as consisting of a magazine of images, metaphors, and projections—of *figurations*—that characters volley at one another (and at the reader) in an effort to "know" what is happening to themselves, to each other, and to the environment. In *As I Lay Dying* and, I suspect, in Faulkner's own sense of his success as a writer of apocrypha, our role in the drama of meaning is largely determined by our mastery of the use of the figurative. There is no other way to enter into the conflict or to produce meaning.

The ontological concerns of *As I Lay Dying* form the core of Faulkner's lifelong meditation on the creation and nature of existence and knowledge. Even though there seems to be no limit to the ways in which critics effectively confront the novel, *As I Lay Dying* poses, and through its various monologues attempts to answer, a single, ontologically crucial question: Is life meaningless? The question of meaning and explanation permeates the novel, beginning with the basic motivation of the plot itself. Why are the Bundrens going to Jefferson? At first glance, the answer is obviously to bury Addie according to Anse's promise to her, but Anse is also going to Jefferson to buy new teeth. Dewey Dell is going in search of an abortion. Vardaman wants to see the toy train and get some bananas. Cash wants a "graphophone." Since he also wants to work on Tull's barn on the way back, he brings along his tool box. The only two Bundrens who do not have a personal motivation for the family trek are Darl and Jewel, but Darl goes crazy and Jewel never fully articulates his position, except to put Darl away. Even Addie has a personal stake in making the journey: to get even with Anse. It is the living, however, who triumph in *As I Lay Dying*, as Anse turns Addie's vengeance to his own purposes. Life, in Faulkner's early novel, is meaningless for those who cannot or will not give meaning to it, just as it is controlled by the dead and the meanings bequeathed by the dead for those who will not wrest control. Viewed from the outside, the Bundrens' trip looks like some absurdist joke, but when viewed from the inside—and here Faulkner's technique ceases to be "experimental" and should be understood ideologically—the trip is a demonstration of each character's relative struggle to wrest control by applying personal interpretation and value to his/her circumstances and predicaments.

If there is a "center" to *As I Lay Dying*, it is Addie Bundren, the woman who is dying, dies, and is buried in the course of the novel. Addie is the hub around which the monologue-spokes revolve, the "reason" carrying the Bundren wagon to Jefferson. Robert Dale Parker, in his analysis of "secrecy" in the novel, offers a perceptive "study of the individual secrets that Addie's secret inspires" and characterizes these mysteries as symptoms of "the primal indefinability in every one of us."[42] Mrs. Bundren, even if essentially unrevealable, is a bundle of contradictions, and her incongruities point to the novel's dominant epistemological concerns.

Addie says "words are no good" (157), but it is her "word" that compels the journey; it is her word, or request, that Anse bury her in Jefferson that moves the family. Addie knows that the reason for living (in addition to "staying dead for a long time") is "the duty to the alive" (155; 161), but the duty to the dead actuates the journey. Her attack on words, then, is essentially specious. She claims that words exist to take the place of real emotion or real things, but we see how Anse uses or takes advantage of his word to Addie to replace *her* with a new, improved (in the sense of being alive) "real" Mrs. Bundren. Thus, what Addie misses in her conception of words is that unless their user charges them with significance, they will remain what they are in the dictionary, simple potentiality.

The dichotomy between words and acts forms the basis of Olga Vickery's landmark essay on *As I Lay Dying,* but the dichotomy is, within the drama of meaning, a false one.[43] According to Vickery, "Awareness of the difference between empty and significant ritual, framed in terms of the word and the act, dominates Addie Bundren's dying thoughts." This is entirely true, but it is the source of Addie's failure, not her success; it is a misconception, not an "awareness." Vickery points out that Addie realizes that words have "repercussions in the world of experience" and so distinguishes between the "empty words of Anse" and "words that are deeds." Vickery, however, does not indicate that Addie's insistence on this fixed dichotomy blinds her to the interchangeable nature of words and acts. Words may or may not become deeds, may or may not communicate, but the transformation has nothing to do with the words or deeds. The actors in the drama determine through conflict which words will remain empty and which will be filled with significance. Addie, assuming the existence of a fixed dichotomy between empty word and significant act, dismisses Anse as ineffectual. Vickery concurs, describing Anse Bundren as "completely blind to Addie's intense desire for life and to her conviction that language is a grotesque tautology which prevents any real communication." This merely privileges Addie's eloquence over Anse's more muted speaking part in the drama. Nonetheless, Anse's "intense desire for life" is equal to Addie's and is fully communicated by his mouth full of new teeth and by his armful of new wife, both of which result from deeds informed by the filling up of Addie's words.

What Addie misses is the symbolic vitality of words. She bequeaths to Cash, her firstborn, her literal-minded approach to life, her ledger-book morality, and her sense of measured justice—all of which Cash converts into the principles of craftsmanship and physical productivity. Addie confuses symbols with "hard currency" (it took her three births to get from "Cash" to "Jewel") and expects words not to "mean" but to "be." As a result, she is disappointed by the apparent impotence, or falsity, of words. She lives by the dead and understands actions only, such as Cash's demonstration of love in building her the best coffin possible. It follows, then, that in order to understand sin, Addie must physically experience it by committing adultery. And if life is a struggle to create in the face of death, Addie will naturally pervert life into a simple preparation for death and will need to understand life and death only by living and dying. This is why her postmortem monologue is so fitting to her. Only after dying does Addie have anything to say. Addie, who actually loves death—when she tells Anse "I have people. In Jefferson" (157), she means dead people—is a woman born to die. She abhors life (after creating life by giving birth to Cash she realized that "living was terrible" [157]) and welcomes her death, all because she is unable to communicate and considers herself, as a consequence, completely isolated. "My children," she says of the products of her only "real" physical contact with others, "are mine alone" (160). If Addie stands for anything, or dies for anything, it is to demonstrate the absurdity of life without communication and the painfulness of repressed expression, in word *or* deed.

The ways in which the Bundrens cope with Addie's death reveal their relative abilities and methods of rendering life meaningful. Anse has a passive, consumer-oriented mastery of life: he simply replaces a used-up wife with a new one. Cash constructs a new physical place for Addie's body, maintaining a practical, literalist approach to life's complications. Darl finds it impossible to assimilate his mother's death because her death does not fit into his logical, ratiocinative—even if creative—understanding of phenomena. Jewel prefers either not to think about it or, as Addie's favorite, has repressed its meaning beneath anger. Dewey Dell's response is to avoid repeating her mother's fate by attempting to get off the cycle of feminine doom, that is, to have an abortion and not become a mother. Vardaman, finally, assimilates his mother's death by asserting her spiritual immortality, or rather her physical transubstantiation. He does this in his expression of the figurative "My mother is a fish," the culmination of the novel's celebration of metaphor as a method of controlling, appropriating, and communicating meaning.

A dialogue informs *As I Lay Dying,* one between Darl, who represents logic and rationality, and Vardaman, who stands for the symbolic and the figurative. Between the two is Cash, typifying precision and production. Their three successive chapters (67–74) early in the novel set up the dialogue between Darl and Vardaman, with Cash as a balancing influence. Darl's chapter ends with his meditation on being "emptied for sleep"; Cash's lists the thirteen reasons for making the coffin the way he did; and Vardaman's consists of the line about his mother being a fish.

Darl opens the novel with a monologue that is a precise, imaginative, and coherent narrative. His early observations are interesting—such as how to drink well water from a cedar bucket (9)—and penetrating, such as the "mis-matched eyes" on Jewel's horse and Anse's cramped, bent, and warped toes on his splayed feet (10). He has creative powers, such as when he "sees" Jewel cross inside the cottonhouse (3), knows about Dewey Dell's pregnancy by divination, and finds out about Jewel's paternity by watching his mother's attitude toward him in a crisis (122). Yet Addie's death throws Darl off that "path . . . straight as a plumb line" (3) on which he began the novel and into a realm where his ratiocinative powers can no longer satisfy him. His meditation on time and death comes on the first night he knows his mother is dead. In his thoughts, Darl tries to understand the passing away of his mother by comparing it to the lumber that is passing from one proprietor to another. The load of lumber, he thinks, "that is no longer theirs that felled and sawed it nor yet theirs that bought it and which is not ours either, lie on the wagon though it does," exists in a kind of limbo (72).

Darl's meditation here, and his similar concerns with time and space throughout the novel, reveal an effort to understand what has happened to Addie and to understand loss by purely ratiocinative means. The connection between what has happened to Addie and the selling of the lumber is found in the transformation of each from one state to another and from one definition to another over time. Yet even as ratiocination, it fails, because it considers time an absolute rather than a fluid quality. "Because if I had one," Darl says of his mother, "it is *was*. And if it was, it cant be *is*. Can it?" (89). Darl cannot accept his mother as both "alive" in the past, in his memory and emotion, and "dead" as a physical being. He does not see the past and future as "created species of time," in the Platonic sense, but as fixed entities. For him, time is not "a moving image of eternity"[44] but an absolute value or quality. Hence, his view of life and of the meanings that inform life is essentially static and constant, knowing nothing of the Faulknerian principle of epistemological drama, motion, and change.

Since Darl's is an either/or world and not one of becoming, his efforts to understand and communicate ultimately fall flat. He can articulate for others, and he can narrate effectively scenes that originate wholly in his imagination, such as the event of Addie's death, but he cannot, finally, make any sense of his observations because he never makes them his own and never pushes his impressions toward explanation. Darl demands, perversely, that his *idea* of things be proven externally, or logically. At the very basis of the novel, however, is the philosophic position that personal worlds exist and conflict with one another, and if there is a "center" of the universe, it shifts with the observer as the observers shift in *As I Lay Dying*. Darl's ratiocinative stance fails him because its reliance on logic leaves him unable to accept ultimate contradictions. He is creative and insightful, but his orthodox impulses to codify and order phenomena in the end drive him crazy. In his final chapter, he abandons his personal perspective entirely and speaks in the third person. Through his laughter, he says no to all of life—to the absurdities made emblematic by riding backward on the forward-moving train, to the family that has committed him to Jackson, and to himself— and does so by the paradoxical repetition of "yes yes yes yes yes." His is not a liberating laughter or a grotesque laughter that purifies him and absolves him, but one that disqualifies him from comprehension and removes him, as Cash says, from "this world."[45]

Cash assures the reader that Darl is "outside it too," just like "you," the reader of the novel, in his penultimate narrative (220). He believes it will be "better for" Darl to be in Jackson than in the family (221), just as he knew it was better for Addie to be in a good coffin than a shoddy one: everything in its place. Although Cash, the craftsman, is not about to pass judgment on the relative sanity of Darl or anyone else (221), he will insist on a good job where everyone is in his and her proper place and acting sane. Whether life is meaningful or not is really of little consequence to Cash, and his craftsman's attitude—his classic sense of the workings of things— tells him that a good job takes preference over the job's purpose. Cash will never challenge the way the world is defined for him, but he will master the definitions and skills handed down to him. "It's like it aint so much what a fellow does," he says, voicing the structural principle of the novel, "but the way the majority of the folks is looking at him when he does it" (216).

It is in the character of Vardaman Bundren that the novel's epistemological motif culminates, and through Vardaman that Addie's self-destructive nihilism is effectively counterbalanced and perhaps overturned. Vardaman's first monologue immediately follows Addie's death. He chases after her ghost and makes his first metaphoric observation: "The trees look like chickens" (49). His initial attempt to understand his mother's death is based on a Darl-like kind of logic of causation, and he blames Doc Peabody for killing her.

When this fails to satisfy, he simply denies she really died (60). He then makes a crucial connection between the fish he has caught and his mother. The fish, he says, "was laying right yonder in the dirt [and] now it's all chopped up. It's laying in the kitchen" now, he continues, "waiting to be cooked and et." Here he makes the imaginative, or associative, leap. "Then it wasn't and she was, and now it is and she wasn't. And tomorrow it will be cooked and et and she will be him and pa and Cash and Dewey Dell and there wont be anything in the box and so she can breathe" (60).

When Vardaman announces "My mother is a fish," he has discovered the figurative and entered the realm of the apocryphal production of meaning. Vardaman applies to his mother's death the principle of the fish's transformation from external part of nature to part of himself and his family; she is not dead but is a part of him now, and a part of everyone else she knew. Unlike Darl, who sees only things, or Cash, who sees only how things work, Vardaman sees how things change. He clings to his fish image throughout the novel, claiming it to be his own (89) and relying on it to maintain his important faith that the putrid corpse in the coffin has nothing to do with his mother (182). In the same way that Anse appropriates Addie's "word" for his own purposes, Vardaman has captured (or perhaps "caught") the principle of the appropriation and projection of knowledge.

Through Vardaman, Faulkner defines his apocrypha in a way that defends itself against the charge of being unrealistic or fantastic. The discovery of the figurative is the basis and supreme expression of the drama of meaning in human communication. It is not that "my mother is *like* this fish," or that the meaning I make is *like* the external world or reflective of it, but that my mother *is* a fish, my meaning *is* the world, my fiction *is* reality. All through *As I Lay Dying* characters try to explain and connect phenomena by saying things are "like" other things.[46] Tull says the house holds his wife "like a jar of milk in the spring" (125). Darl observes that Cash's head turns "like an owl's head" (95) and that the raindrops "are as big as buckshot" (68). He also compares Addie to "a handful of rotten bones" (44). Even the novel's title is a cryptic reference to something *else*. What is happening "as I lay dying," or what am I like "as I lay dying"? What is signalled by the "as" in this title?[47] The "as" immediately suggests that something is occurring "while" someone is dying. The temporal simultaneity, however, is complemented by the suggestion of a phenomenological simultaneity, based on the frequency of metaphor and simile in the novel. What is death *like?* Is it like the loss of word and deed, the drama's closed curtain, the end of conflict? Addie's post-mortem narration denies this. And for the other Bundrens, "as" Addie lay dead her words are transformed and the drama continues with someone else playing the role of "Mrs Bundren." Death seems to be what the living make of (and with) it.

It is never enough to describe one thing as being like another thing—Cash's head like an owl, Addie's body like rotten bones. True understanding, the kind that teaches and communicates, is achieved through figuration: applying the principle of what is understood of the owl, or the fish, or Addie the mother to phenomena that are problematic. Faulkner thus demonstrates the way in which the human mind constantly makes sense of the world—through association and metaphor—in a continuing dance with external reality, which amounts to the human drama of meaning at the core of Faulkner's apocrypha. What the discovery of the figurative adds to the drama, however, is *appropriation:* to transform the universe from something mysterious and "out there" to something in which the human mind is "at home." In this way, the external world of problematic phenomena (and of political phenomena, as will be seen in *A Fable* and *Snopes*) is *reived* by the mind and transformed into something known, something possessed and controlled, through the production of its significance. To say a thing is "like" something else, as many of the characters in *As I Lay Dying* actually do, is both to create a distance between the things to be comprehended and to maintain a distance between the knower and the thing known. Yet to depict one thing as if it were another thing, to say "My mother is a fish," is to digest it, as it were, and to make the problematic object a part of one's self. This is precisely what Vardaman does. As obtuse as the boy is, he is the only Bundren who has made the link between comprehension and the production of meaning. Vardaman creates a text of his own: "My mother," claims the author-Vardaman, "is a fish."

As I Lay Dying signifies the revelation and the articulation of Faulkner's apocryphal aesthetics. It marks as well the literal discovery of his apocryphal county and town, for he names "Yoknapatawpha" for the first time in *As I Lay Dying*. "They came from some place out in Yoknapatawpha county," mentions Moseley, who observes the Bundren clan, "trying to get to Jefferson" with Addie's corpse (188). Faulkner is on that journey as well, and when they all "get to Jefferson" old ideas about words and truth are buried in Addie's grave and new ones, like new teeth, take their place. Darl, the rationalist, is sent out of the apocrypha, and Anse, the man who challenges God's wisdom ("for who He loveth, so doeth He chastiseth. But I be durn if He dont take some curious ways to show it, seems like" [97]), emerges victorious and once again wedded, reiving from Addie's "revenge" his own triumph.

The name of the county was also appropriated in an apocryphal manner, reived from old maps of Faulkner's "postage stamp" on which "Yockeney-Patafa," the Chickasaw word for "water runs slow through flat land," marked the river to the south. The name was later abbreviated by whites to Yocona, the name by which Faulkner knew the waterway in his time. It was a significant act of appropriation by Faulkner. His river and county are not *like* Yocona and Lafayette; they *are* Yoknapatawpha. His Yoknapatawpha and Vardaman's fish are "postage stamps." They serve as means of conveyance, appropriation, and assertion, and of creating the thoughts and reiving the figures by which the world is produced as real.

III Excesses of All Kinds: *Pylon* and the Apocryphal Voice

It should not be difficult to see that apocryphal aesthetics, like whiskey, if taken in excess and without some sense of limitation or control or purpose, will not only intoxicate but will eventually produce a state of meaninglessness and of physical and intellectual incapacity and stagnation—the death of meaning and significance. The simile is wholly appropriate here because *Pylon* is about these two things juxtaposed: the uses and limitations of alcohol consumption, and the uses and limitations of the apocrypha.

Faulkner was having trouble with the manuscript of *Absalom, Absalom!* when he put it aside to write *Pylon*. Whereas *Absalom* is undoubtedly considered a masterpiece by contemporary standards, and it is a wonderful expression of Faulkner's apocryphal workings of mind and material, *Pylon* is more generally treated as a minor work, even as a kind of fluke in Faulkner's production. *Pylon* is, however, crucial to this study because it is about the problematics of apocryphal creation. (*Absalom, Absalom!*, for example, is a pure and confident work of apocrypha. Its map, reductive genealogy, and bald chronology all satirize with bogus historical realism the intensive acts of apocryphal production that form the novel and move it to heights of epistemological drama.) Before Faulkner could complete *Absalom*, however, he needed to work through certain problems in his aesthetics. Although *Pylon* concerns flying, the novel attempts to ground the apocrypha by setting the parameters of apocryphal accounts of the real.

If the mind creates meaning, what are the limits to what it might assert as "real" or significant? And, if the mind creates meaning, can it not then create machinery and technology that will aid it in the effort to supply meaning and significance to phenomena?[48] Can meaning and significance—*reality*—be objectified and controlled once and forever like a complex piece of machinery such as an airplane? *Pylon* characterizes the daredevil flyers as men and women who attempt the impossible because they need the money, the technology is there, and the public is hungry for titillation. In the same way, *Pylon* portrays those who run the newspaper (and other sources of *public information and knowledge*) as people who try the impossible because they too need the money, have the means, and the public is hungry for sensational news. Yet everyone fails in *Pylon*. Flyers are killed and scattered, and the Reporter never quite communicates what he sees. His editor, Hagood, cannot even read what the Reporter writes. "Can it be by some horrible mischance that without knowing it you listen and see in one language and then do what you call writing in another? How does it sound when you read it yourself?" (40). Is the apocrypha reaching a destination? Is its voice being understood or simply heard? Is that *English* which Mr. Faulkner claims as his postage stamp, his native language? What do you mean, your mother is a fish?

Everyone fails in *Pylon* because, as Quentin says in *The Sound and the Fury*, they *confuse means and end*. The flyers cannot continually venture life without losing it, or else the risk has no meaning. Neither can the objectifiers of knowledge and information continue to objectify without destroying their *subject*. *Pylon* mounts a powerful argument against objectivity by suggesting that although human beings make meaning, only a deluded human race would believe that meaning could be produced mechanically, independent of personal reflection and sublimation, and still be humanly significant. Newspapers and the other media in *Pylon* work not to extend and develop the human capacity to know, but to atrophy it and perhaps destroy it by muddling means and end, and by confusing, as Marshall McLuhan would write thirty years later, the medium with the message. In the same way, the airplanes in the novel are not the vehicles by which human beings exhibit bravery and courage or by which the spectators know something about human qualities. They are simply exhibitions of machinery, and thus of the objectification of mechanical thought. It is the *media*—the newsprint, the airplane—which are known, not the content they purport to communicate.

Faulkner made this clear in 1935 in a review of another book about flying. He referred to the attempt to create a "folklore" of "speed itself" in which airplanes exist "peopled not by anything human or even mortal but by the clever willful machines themselves carrying nothing that was born and will have to die or which can even suffer pain, moving without comprehensive purpose toward no discernible destination, producing a literature innocent of either love or hate and of course of pity or terror, and which would be the study of the final disappearance of life from earth."[49] The same reasoning can be applied to the newspaper and other mass media in *Pylon,* for they are "clever and willful machines" producing information "without comprehensive purpose toward no discernible destination" and manufacturing nothing very much of human consequence outside themselves. Flying concerns flying, not bravery, just as newspapers concern newspapers, not knowledge.

There are, of course, human beings in *Pylon* who fly the planes and report the news. The Reporter attempts to break free of his place chained to the newspaper machine by getting to know a group of flyers intimately. He wants to appropriate them (he even pays their way, buying them food and drink, and giving them a place to live) and understand them in order to write about them. Yet at the beginning of the novel, he sees only the machinery. He tells Hagood, his editor, that "they aint human like us," not seeing that the flyers *are* just "like him"—appendages to machinery.

What kind of transformation the Reporter makes in *Pylon,* if any, is still being debated. Some critics, most notably the French writer Francois Pitavy, argue that the novel's last chapter, "The Scavengers," is actually "written" by the Reporter and constitutes his transformation from reporter to Author.[50] Given the many abrupt changes in perspective in *Pylon,* this is highly plausible, particularly in the shift within "The Scavengers" from the Reporter sitting at his typewriter to the narrative of Laverne's abandonment of her son Jack (310). So many abrupt transitions also argues to the contrary, making the singling out of any one of them of dubious significance.[51] Regardless of such exegetic particularities, the point is that *Pylon* demonstrates an epistemological tension. Michael Millgate points out the Reporter's obsession "with the fact that he cannot be 'the Reporter' without also being the interpreter and suggests that the novel's "peculiarly clotted, congested effect" may be Faulkner's attempt to demonstrate the epistemological tension between fact and understanding.[52] Indeed, Thomas Perry concludes that the man we know "only as the reporter" is "an identity reduced to an epistemological function."[53]

The Reporter may be a lifeless living thing, as his appearance suggests to Jiggs. (Faulkner describes him as such throughout the novel.) All his drinking, his lust for Laverne, and his "air of worn and dreary fury" (46) resemble so many attempts to feel what it is to be alive. As such, he is what Faulkner intended him to be, "anonymous: he was every man,"[54] a kind of personified alienation. The Reporter's goal in life, however, is to communicate, not simply to write for the newspaper but to write "the great American" novel. His thoughts on this are emblematic of the "clotted, congested effect" of *Pylon* itself, "the great American in one billion printings slavepostchained and scribblescrawled: annotations of eternal electrodeitch and bottomhope" (63). By linking the Reporter's struggle to be a living thing with his quest to write "the great American," Faulkner again establishes the vital role of re-creation in his view of revolving life. Hence, in one sense the Reporter's recurrent vomiting is a kind of perverse symbol for his attempt to communicate what life is like inside of him: "life, sense, all, seemed to burst out of his mouth as though his entire body were trying in one fierce orgasm to turn itself wrongside out" (109). Yet he is no more successful at writing "the great American" than he is at holding his liquor. The story will not emerge because, as with his reaction to whiskey, there is something about *him* that will not hold it, appropriate it, and make it his own. The logic of the apocrypha assures that until he does, he will continue to vomit whiskey, lunch, news, all. Moreover, the reporter has no easy task because standing between him and his goal is a ton of machinery.

As they did in *As I Lay Dying*, Faulkner's characters in *Pylon* attempt to comprehend their world through metaphor and figuration. Unlike *As I Lay Dying*, which took its figures (fish, jars in a spring, rotten bones, et al.) from a premodernist context, in the modernist setting of *Pylon* metaphors have become, like news and speed, objectified—in a sense, reified—into consumer objects and tourist doodads. In the opening pages of *Pylon*, Faulkner demonstrates how the modern world exploits and parodies metaphor. In the shop windows Jiggs sees "pipes shaped like golfclubs," "drinking tools shaped like boots and barnyard fowls," and "minute impedimenta for wear on ties and vestchains shaped like bits and spurs" (4). We might also find a madonna in the shape of a fish in some other shop window context. This is clearly an excess of figuration, burlesquing into trivialities aprocryphal transfigurations of reality by mass-producing them into consumer objects. In this context of trivialization (perhaps idolatry is a more precise term) Faulkner attempts to capture the airplane in an allusion to the natural world, as he does in the opening paragraph when he calls it "a species of esoteric and fatal animals not trained or tamed."

Metaphors permeate *Pylon*, and a great many of them invoke comic and burlesque images, implying that Faulkner had more than simple mimetic accuracy in mind.[55] The effect of the often outrageous metaphorization (for example, when the aviators get on the bus, "the scene began to resemble that comic stage one where the entire army enters one taxicab and drives away" [15]) is to satirize Faulkner's own apocrypha and demonstrate the effects of the "inebriated" narrative. The reader is alienated from much of the novel because it is simply too much. In *Pylon* the metaphors run wild like an airplane out of control. They fail to communicate anything but a sense of futility in anticipation of the inevitable crash. Figuration in *Pylon* purposefully falters because it is accomplished mechanically, without reflection but as mass-produced excess, so that the form is no longer individually significant and is reduced to a disposable commodity. In fact, a mechanical, mass-produced apocrypha ceases to challenge the social and political configurations of the orthodox world and becomes a source of diversion, a form of entertainment. A mechanized apocrypha becomes a daredevil flying show, as trivial and meaningless as it is dangerous and wasteful. As another consumer object in the shop window, the apocrypha is burlesqued. It resembles an idol devoid or drained of its ideological significance.

The way in which the modern world unnaturally conjoins images ("pipes shaped like golfclubs" and "drinking tools shaped like boots") is mirrored and intensified by Faulkner's persistent manufacture of "unnatural" word formations. Things such as a "windowbase," the "countrylife," "confettispatter," and "engineparts" may give an autonomous definition to the facts of human environment, but a "stillopen" door or an "alreadypacked" car reflect a tension in the environment. We sense an acute alienation from the "blacksplotched" newspaper in the elevator or the "iowacorncolored" hair on Laverne's head. In *Pylon*, Faulkner's language is thickest when he deals with manufactured reality, such as in this description of the city: "The ten thousand inescapable mornings wherein ten thousand swinging airplants sippleprop the soft scrofulous soaring of sweating brick and ten thousand pairs of splayed brown hired Leonorafeet tigerbarred by jalousied armistice with the invincible sun" (291–92). It is the least thick when he describes human emotion and comprehension, as in the description of the Reporter's response to Laverne's personal history. "When he came out of the booth, back into the light, he began to blink again as if he had a little sand in his eyes, trying to recall exactly what eye moisture tasted like" (250). What is "alien" in *Pylon* is not the human race but the environment manufactured by the race to serve it.

The environment in *Pylon,* as George Bedell comments, resembles Kierkegaard's description of the modern age, "an age without passion," which "has no values," and where "everything is transformed into representational ideas" or metaphors for something else. This era is one largely created by "the Press, which in itself is an abstraction." According to Bedell, the individual "loses his identity" in this milieu "and is overwhelmed by the power of a monstrous abstraction, an all embracing something which is nothing, a mirage—and that phantom is *the public. Pylon* is set within such a society."[56]

Most important in *Pylon* is the distance between the mind and its object of study, the environment. Very little is known firsthand in *Pylon;* most of one's information about the world is received from the media. The "public" learns about itself from the newspaper, but what it learns has no human content or significance, which produces a feeling of isolation in the reader, the individual component of the public. The city editor's idea of news is "an accurate account of everything that occurs out there . . . that creates any reaction excitement or irritation on any human retina" (48), or in other words, pure sensation. The newspaper in *Pylon* remains a "fragile web of ink and paper, assertive, proclamative, profound and irrevocable if only in the sense of being profoundly and irrevocably unimportant . . . the dead instant's fruit of forty tons of machinery and an entire nation's antic delusion. The eye, the organ without thought, or amaze" (110–11). In this environment, the abstract and illusory "public" is fostered and catered to as if it were alive, leaving the individual man or woman alienated by his or her own emotional responses—responses that are triggered by images and thereby cheapened, falsified, and numbed. The result is that even human emotion is removed from its human context as the press becomes adept at "manipulating" public reaction.

If aviation is representative of modern society in *Pylon,* then the airfield announcer, the public address system, is emblematic of the media's control and use of information in that society. In the modern world, *information* is among the factors of the environment. Like the machines, information is created by human beings, and yet it is scarcely comprehended by them. At the airfield, the announcer's "masculine and disembodied" voice fills the air "in a running commentary to which apparently none listened, as if the voice were merely some unavoidable and inexplainable phenomenon of nature like the sound of wind or of erosion." It is "as if the voice actually were that natural phenomenon against which all manmade sounds and noises blew and vanished like leaves" (23). Actual events— things human beings do—exist for the benefit of the voice, while the voice, the medium, assumes an authority over reality unmatched even by human sensibility. Actual events are not considered real until they are processed by the medium empowered to report or mediate them: "And here is the official clocking of the winners of the two hundred cubic inch race *which you have just witnessed . . .*" (25; emphasis added).

The public address system in *Pylon* has an even greater significance. It is "the voice" in the novel. The man behind this voice actually resembles Faulkner. He wears "a tweed jacket even a little oversmart," as Faulkner was known to sport, "with the modest winged badge of a good solid pilots' fraternity in the lapel," as Faulkner himself was known to wear. Once amplified, according to the text, the voice becomes "apocryphal, sourceless, inhuman, ubiquitous and beyond weariness or fatigue" (36). It seems clear that in *Pylon,* Faulkner examines the limits, and the excesses, of his own fictional program. In the same way that the airfield voice mediates events, the apocryphal author *sublimates* them to the apocryphal. As author and narrative voice, Faulkner establishes himself as *singular authority* in the text itself, an act antithetical to an apocrypha. To overcome this, he divides his voice into numerous pieces, contradictory and conflicting, as he often did in his fiction. But can there be such a thing as an apocryphal author with a growing list of titles? Or was Faulkner attempting something as futile as "the living breath" of news when he persevered in writing fiction? Behind the airplanes and the newspapers and the whiskey, Faulkner struggles in *Pylon* with no less than his own authorial voice, the voice of the apocrypha. The sound of engines, the starting gun, the pylon race itself: all these events are "mere insignificant properties which the voice used for emphasis as the magician uses his wand or handkerchief" (23).

The public address voice tells the public what and where to watch so that each person stays "informed." It describes events (in the play-by-play) that are plain to see, and it adds commentary to make reality more interesting or more dramatic. Hence, the voice *informs* action and reality by directing all the "meaning-makers," the individual consciousnesses from *As I Lay Dying*'s formulation, to its own conceptions and interpretations. As it is suggested in *Pylon,* modern society itself is a mirage, a meaningless airplane race, unless "the voice," or the media, is there to explain what is significant about the mirage to what it views as a passive, sensation-seeking mass. When the newsboys cry out the evening headlines on the streets of New Valois, voice and newsprint fuse together as media. "The familiar black thick type and the raucous cries seemed to glare and merge faster than the mind could distinguish the sense through which each had been received" (53). Information and forced meaning in the form of events, descriptions, and "news" are the natural environment of *Pylon.* Similarly, the reader of the text is forced to confront a thick and cluttered prose style that seems intent on confusion. Consequently, the reader mimics the dilemma of the modern human being in the effort to sift through a jumble of images and information in order to find out what is going on in the text, or the world, just as the airfield audience listens to the voice and follows the official program in order to find out what it sees in the sky. In *Pylon,* however, the "authoritative voice" is garbled; the narrator is not doing his job.

The function of the airfield announcer and the newspaper, and of the media in general, in Faulkner's novel is to manufacture a common view of the world based on objective observation and accomplished by neutral reportage, but the newspaper, in the Reporter's opinion, tells nothing. He sees in the newspaper "the same boxheading, identical from day to day—the bankers the farmers the strikers, the foolish the unlucky and the merely criminal—distinguishable from one day to another not by what they did but by the single brief typeline beneath the paper's registered name" or by the day's date (212). Receiving knowledge about human affairs in this way reduces human complexity and individuality to a false and manufactured set of sterile, repeatable images: "FARMERS REFUSE   BANKERS

DENY   STRIKERS DEMAND   PRESIDENTS YACHT
ACREAGE REDUCTION   QUINTUPLETS GAIN" and so
forth (110). What Hagood demands of the Reporter, that he deliver
"the living breath of news" (39), becomes a contradiction in terms. The
news is a dead form of knowledge, just as the emblematic Reporter
(who only gets a capital *R* when critics talk about him) is a "dead"
form of human life, "something which had . . . escaped into the
living world" (17). The "living breath" of airfield news would be the
story of the aviators as sensual human beings, not as air cowboys or
as subhuman or even superhuman creatures. Yet this is not what
Hagood wants because it creates no "reaction excitement or irritation on any human retina." In fact, the "living news" is usually
imperceptible by the organs of the media. The character of Roger
Shumann provides exemplary evidence of this.

Schumann is not understood as a fleshy creature in *Pylon* but is
presented as "single-purposed, fatally and grimly without any trace
of introversion or any ability to objectivate or ratiocinate, as though
like the engine, the machine for which he apparently existed, he
functioned, moved, only in the vapor of gasoline and the filmslick of
oil" (174). The way Roger Shumann chooses to die—he decides to
crash into the lake rather than into the grandstand—belittles this
portrait. By concentrating on objects such as airplanes and newspapers, *Pylon* shows that *subjects* are diminished into types or extensions of the media. Identified by association with the objects that
serve them, the human race in Faulkner's novel exists as raw material
for the strengthening of the authoritative positioning of the news
media. Faulkner's task in *Pylon* is to chart a way out of this strong-
hold.

The Reporter's journey in *Pylon* is one away from his supposed
calling of journalism and toward subjectivity. Early on in the novel
he ceases to "report" on the aviators and attempts to live as one of
them, buying his way into their society by "paying" for them in a
literal sense. When information is an object for consumption, experience can be bought and paid for. The reporters pay for information
and then sell it to the public as news. On his buying spree, the
Reporter's primary fixation is Laverne (he assumes she is a whore,
that is, a woman for sale), who changes, in his perception of her,
from fantasy figure to tragic human being during his flight from
objectivity.[57] After Laverne repudiates him ("God damn you to hell!
Get away from me!" [240]) after Shumann's death, the Reporter is
jarred from his journalistic, detached coldness and into subjective

involvement. Ironically, only after Laverne expels him from his "fellow-traveller" aviator status does he begin to feel a compulsion to "explain" rather than report. "Let me explain it to you," he begins to say repeatedly to fellow reporters, "you dont understand. Let me explain it to—" (244). There are two obstacles the Reporter must overcome before he can begin to understand the aviator group. One is the flippant notion that they "aint human"; the second is that they can be bought. Both of these assumptions are equally characteristic of an objective reading of the Reporter himself. He is repeatedly portrayed as a corpse or a lifeless scarecrow, and he continually is placated by and accepts Hagood's charity toward him. Hence, the two things that he cannot seem to get past in his appreciation of the aviators are two aspects of his own outward personality. This makes any understanding he may hope to achieve wholly subjective and makes any change in perspective dependent on a realignment of his self-perception.

Faulkner explains the Reporter's shift from objective delusion to subjective involvement as an "alteration of purpose." When he refuses a drink offered by a fellow journalist in the airfield bar, "it was as though his throat and the organs of swallowing had experienced some irrevocable alteration of purpose from which he would suffer no inconvenience whatever but which would forever more mark the exchange of an old psychic as well as physical state for a new one, like the surrendering of a maidenhead" (246). When the Reporter rejects the drink, moreover, he symbolically accepts sobriety and prepares himself for "painfully fresh perception" and the process of creation.

Following this episode, the Reporter makes what could well be the transformation to "author," and there is no question that he begins to see beyond the "aviator" label that the newspapers use to "objectivate" the fliers. He is visibly moved by Laverne's history, and he "sees" the scene where Jiggs delivers the toy airplane to Laverne, Jack, and Holmes. It is now "himself who was the nebulous and quiet ragtag and bobend of touching and breath and experience without visible scars" (289). Due to his illumination, the Reporter cannot listen to the chatter of the other reporters who discuss Shumann's death in the diner. Their callous and disinterested perspective is as false and "objective" as the Reporter's was at the beginning of the novel. "But it aint for money" that the aviators fly, according to one of the journalists. "It's because they have got to do it, like some women have got to be whores. They cant help themselves" (300). To the Reporter, these "voices might have indeed been the sound of the cards or perhaps leaves blowing past him" (298). When the journalists question him about Shumann, the Reporter feigns ignorance and refuses to "sell" the information. The narrative then moves to his questioning Jiggs about where Laverne has taken her son, and then to the critical writing scene and the account of the abandonment of Jack. This marks a definitive transition from the deluded understanding of authoritative objectivity to the more authentic comprehension (and composition) of subjective, or apocryphal involvement. Whether the Reporter also makes the transition is secondary to the textual shift, and whether he can sustain his realization is secondary to the fact of his at least momentary illumination. "So I feel better," he tells himself as "living breath" enters this Lazarus figure for the first time. "Oh God, I feel better! I feel better! I feel! I feel!" (309).

The newspaper is the modern repository of fact. It chronicles what's going on, and it serves as the authoritative repository of what people, as the cliche goes, "need to know." Often called the daily bible, it is the supreme reminder of the primacy of non-fiction, and it purports to represent reality in an (ironically) *immediate,* up-to-date manner. As such, it stands in opposition to an apocrypha because it has no interest in sublimating the actual, but instead it reports it. *Pylon* objects to the authority of the newspaper to know much of anything. In *Pylon,* newsprint's bogus stance of objectivity, which is presented as no more than a series of meaningless, repetitiously manufactured images differentiated in form only by the date at the top of the page, lends an authority to meaninglessness which acts to atrophy the human ability to recognize and comprehend anything authentic. In other words, any phenomenon that cannot be represented in the "symmetrical line of boxheads" will fall between the cracks of the media's prefabricated system of communication. Hence, the men and women who operate the newspaper are themselves, like the Reporter, lifeless and mechanical, mere appendages to a process of manufacturing. Similarly, the aviators "aint human" because they operate those mysterious "creatures imbued with motion though not with life and incomprehensible to the puny crawling painwebbed globe" (25) and therefore must be lifeless "scarecrows," too. The most life-threatening aspect of mechanization is not that human beings live and die by machines but that they confuse the characteristics of the creation with those of the creator. This gives the newsprint and the airplane an authority over the reporter and the flyer, when it is the reporter who must act as the "medium" of communication and the flyer who must operate the airplane. Thus, the media—newspapers, airplanes, all of humanity's creations— threaten to deprive human beings of that very authority by which they manufactured the media in the first place, the authority of the human imagination and creation.

The technological environment of *Pylon* is far from the "pinewiney" ruralism of Yoknapatawpha, but the aesthetic and political concerns of the apocryphal program are present with equal, if not more urgent, forcefulness. In *Pylon,* human beings confront not just the thought and actions of other human beings but also the mechanized extensions of their minds: automobiles, buses, airplanes, disembodied loudspeaker voices, newspapers. In *As I Lay Dying,* a person simply battles with other voices; in *Pylon,* the competition for expression involves a far more complex and objectified environment. The environmental excesses of the modern world, however, are not signs of an excess of meaning—an apocrypha out of control—but rather the converse. The attempt to objectify information and knowledge about the world in a daily newspaper is as ludicrous and redundant as the loudspeaker's narrative of events in plain sight and the aviators' attempts to demonstrate courage by operating a machine designed to fly in mid-air. These are manufactured situations, not responses to problematic phenomena, inspired by the media themselves and not by the need to explain or to act significantly. When the Reporter (and the narrative) shifts from news toward the creation of an apocrypha, the move is away from operation within a pre-structured medium and toward the making of an autonomous creation. His "literature," if he manages to accomplish it, will not be published in the daily bible but will have to find its way to print in some other context.

The narrative strategy and thematic implications of *Pylon* point to a single, vital apocryphal conception that serves to undergird Faulkner's understanding of the way in which reality is represented truthfully. The novel contains an objection and a contention. The first relates to the claim that objectivity is a significant kind of knowledge which deserves to be privileged. Objectivity, in *Pylon,* looks more like redundancy. At best, the newspaper is spectacle. More often, however, it represents knowledge about itself only or about itself as medium, and communicates little in the way of the "living breath" of anything vital. As such, newsprint ought to be harmless, but because the newspaper commands attention as a single authoritative source of what is important, it becomes a substitute for knowledge and communication. Furthermore, as the Reporter's experience indicates, it replaces personal interaction and direct understanding of the environment. *Pylon* makes the contention, then, that only subjective involvement fosters comprehension. The Reporter begins to "feel" once he removes himself from his role as vicarious, objective mediator and begins to see past the machines—his own newspaper and the flyers' airplanes—to the flesh-and-blood human beings around him. Only after he sublimates information into apocrypha, into something of his own making beyond "mere provable information," does he place himself in a position to know and to communicate. In the novel, Faulkner likens this realization to the onset of sobriety which follows inebriation, the rush of feeling and, perhaps, the overwhelming need to know and to explain. The Reporter sips whiskey just before the narrative shifts to Laverne's abandonment scene, but the liquor has no effect on him. "It tasted, felt, like so much dead icy water" (310). On this morning of fresh perception, "that brisk-up-and-doing sobriety of Monday morning" (307), it is apocrypha, not whiskey, that intoxicates.

Pylon claims that knowledge cannot be objectified and flown about like airplanes around a pylon. The apocryphal voice, unlike that of the airfield announcer, knows that truth cannot be standardized (or canonized) or frozen into some fixed medium, technology, or bible—or made portable. When this is attempted, the human capacity to know itself or its time or its place is atrophied, numbed. When Faulkner returned to *Absalom, Absalom!*, he did so with a renewed faith in his apocryphal aesthetics. He would append to *Absalom, Absalom!* a standardized genealogy and chronology that contained all the narrative's information about what happened to Sutpen and his progeny. This "objective" appendix to the novel is ludicrous and actually acts as a parody to what is accomplished in the book. For example, the bare factual entry, "1820 Sutpen ran away from home. Fourteen years old," cannot begin to suggest the reasons for or the importance of Sutpen's initial flight. Neither can "1866 Sutpen becomes engaged to Rosa Coldfield, insults her. She returns to Jefferson" account for the magnitude of that event in Rosa's imagination and the long shadow that hangs over her, and therefore the reader's impression of Sutpen. To understand truly what the chronology contains, the reader must reach a point where the chronology is essentially meaningless and outrageously insufficient. In other words, the reader must paradoxically learn that "the facts" will tell nothing in order to begin to comprehend fully what the facts mean. The chronology added to the back of *Absalom, Absalom!* is equivalent to the newspaper and the airplane in *Pylon,* a mechanical appendage to human thought, but not thought itself. The chronology may represent the desire for order, the newspaper a desire for community, the stunt airplane a desire for courage, but these media are no substitutes for the qualities themselves, qualities of character that are hardly fulfilled and are actually muted by these structures.

The apocrypha maintains that any valuable kind of knowledge, as opposed to "just information," must come from productive engagement with self and time and place, and not with mere passive consumption. Faulkner's apocryphal voice is saved by its decision to abjure objectivity as inherently false and deluding. In *Pylon,* the apocryphal voice announces itself as "some unavoidable and inexplicable phenomenon of nature like the sound of wind or erosion" (23), not authoritative but ephemeral, subject to change and alteration. Faulkner clearly views knowledge not as a consumable product but as *production,* where truthfulness can only be recognized as something which contains in it the capacity to be remade, reformulated, and restructured as something else. When the Reporter sits down at his typewriter and Faulkner's narrative shifts to Laverne's abandonment scene (310), it is impossible to determine authoritatively whether the episode is created by Faulkner or by the Reporter. It is difficult to determine whether the scene "really" happens or whether it reveals the Reporter's imagination finally taking shape. As such, the author, as authority, disappears from the text, for he is no longer final authority. The scene is as real as it is unreal, as true as it is false. This, finally, is the "authoritative" voice of the apocrypha.

IV *Intruders* All: The Apocrypha as Political Stance

In the 1950s, Faulkner realized, or perhaps finally articulated, the political implications of his apocrypha. While *A Fable* and the *Snopes* trilogy are his two major political projects, this chapter has attempted to chart the aesthetics of the apocrypha out of which those two works were produced. The novels studied in this chapter were chosen for their particular, landmark contributions to the apocryphal vision. For the sake of space and the reader's patience, however, any number of early novels could have been presented here as further evidence of the expanding scope of Faulkner's apocrypha.

The very technique of *The Wild Palms,* for example, lends itself to an analysis of radical juxtapositioning of materials. The failure of Joe Christmas to see his own life, his time and place, as a "production" for which he is finally responsible makes him a kind of Christ in search of a cross in *Light in August,* one of Faulkner's earliest meditations on the apocryphal self. Throughout Faulkner's work we find an engagement with the political realities, the ideologies, of time and place. The ideologies of racialism, of sexuality, of historical narrative, of bourgeois escapism: all these systems of belief and social order are confronted separately or in some combination in *Light in August, Sanctuary, Absalom, Absalom!, The Unvanquished, The Wild Palms,* and *Go Down, Moses,* as well as in the novels discussed in whole or in part in this study.

In the acclaimed masterpiece *Absalom, Absalom!,* historical narrative is presented without apology as a blatantly ideological art form. The narrators in *Absalom* engage in historical narration not to tell about the past but to justify or lament the political and social arrangements of the present. Quentin, for example, wishes to justify to Shreve why he lives there, in the South, and does not "hate it." Faulkner's most radical assertion in the novel is what *Absalom* takes as given: that the "facts" of any historical narrative are always sublimated to the narrator's own particular social and political (and economic and sexual and racial) position in the present. In this sense, there is no such thing as a problematic history in *Absalom, Absalom!*; there is only the struggle for authority in the present. Historical narrative, then, is always mediated by ideology (or if unconscious, by presupposition). The commonplace understanding of a present informed or predetermined by the past is reversed in *Absalom, Absalom!* The necessities and compulsions of present social and political arrangements determine the past. Faulkner is probably among the most politically radical of all those whom America's literary establishment privileges as its major authors. And yet for some ideological reason, he is more often thought of as the great mythmaker, the fabricator of the nostalgic legends of the South. In the historical canonization of Faulkner's writings, the literary academy has stripped his work of its essential power as apocrypha.

One novel stands out as an anomaly in Faulkner's *oeurve,* one that is more than likely to be ignored in assessments of his career after all the "non-Yoknapatawpha" novels have been excluded. *Intruder in the Dust* (1948) is Faulkner's most politically realistic work, that is, the actual materials "sublimated" to the apocryphal lay quite close to the surface. Unlike *Go Down, Moses,* which also deals with race relations but does so primarily at a safe, historical distance, *Intruder in the Dust* takes place contemporaneously within its own time period and concerns issues that, in 1948, were receiving increasing national attention. Critics have found the novel very odd and perhaps even embarrassing, and have treated it as they do *The Reivers,* but without the inevitable pathos that hangs over Faulkner's "last" novel. *Intruder* is like *The Reivers,* however, in at least one respect. It is far less simplistic than it appears, although its rather indulgent prose style has misguided many readers into taking the congenital liar at his overwrought word.

No matter what Faulkner may have said or what critics may echo and explicate, *Intruder in the Dust* is no murder-mystery story.[58] It is not even a failed or a bungled one because, essentially, there is nothing mysterious about the plot development. From the first pages it is clear that Lucas Beauchamp is innocent of any crime. If a mystery *is* involved, it is whether and how Beauchamp, unlike many falsely accused black men before him, will be exonerated. It is a mystery whether the authorities, specifically Gavin Stevens, will take the time to investigate the murder. Yet these are not aspects of a *murder*-mystery; they are aspects of a racial-mystery. Without racism, the novel makes no sense. All Beauchamp has to do is tell Stevens what he knows, make his accusation against Gowrie, and the problem is solved. Beauchamp will not do this because he is a Negro in Mississippi in 1948 and cannot accuse a white man of a crime. *That*'s the mystery in *Intruder in the Dust:* how this state of human affairs came to be, and why "in God's name" it is perpetuated. It was not the first time Faulkner had raised the issue. He did so concerning sexual politics in *Sanctuary* and the intersection of both racial and sexual politics in *Light in August.*[59]

Faulkner attempts to solve the "mystery" in *Intruder* through an initiation tale setting, similar to the one he would employ in *The Reivers.* Whereas *The Reivers* concerns stealing horses and automobiles, *Intruder* centers on stealing bodies—the appropriation of dead bodies as well as the appropriation of one's own body as a political, or in this case specifically racial emblem. In its initiation motif, the novel charts the maturation of Charles Mallison's white body, beginning with its early "baptism" in the creek near Beauchamp's house, where Mallison confronts racism not as an idea but as a physical reality. Beauchamp's home is described as "a postage stamp in the center of an envelope" (8)—literally on white Edmonds' land—and that "postage stamp" conveys to Mallison the very structures of his society which perpetuate racial antagonism. Standing naked before Beauchamp, Mallison learns that his white skin is itself a "postage stamp," a medium of expression, something he can use or not use depending upon his time and place. When Mallison offers to pay Beauchamp for the food he has eaten, he acts within his learned code of white, paternalistic propriety; and likewise, Beauchamp's refusal of the money is done with the code of his *self-produced* refusal to be defined by that code. This is the baptism which Mallison must either accept or reject in the novel, the choice to admit or deny Beauchamp's "refusal to be a nigger" (18, 24).

The next time Mallison removes his clothes is to wash his body, near the end of the novel. This time the dirt on his self is a kind of "postage stamp" for the dirt he has experienced in his community. Now he stands before a white man, his uncle Gavin Stevens, and the question is whether he can cleanse himself of the actions of "his people," the white community. "Some things you must always be unable to bear," Stevens tells him. "Injustice and outrage and dishonor and shame. No matter how young or how old you have got" (206). In his view of things, Stevens exemplifies that understanding a problem has little to do with affecting its solution, and as usual, his rhetoric far outdistances his actions and capabilities.[60] It is Mallison who has done far more than comprehend and intellectually "refuse to bear" injustice and shame, while Stevens mostly talks. Significantly, Mallison cuts off their conversation here with an attempt at levity, thus ending the discussion.

In *Intruder in the Dust*, it is the powerless, not the powerful men such as Gavin Stevens, who affect significant change. "Young folks and womens, they aint cluttered," Ephraim, an old black man, tells Mallison. "But a middle-year man like your paw and your uncle, they cant listen. They aint got time. They're too busy with facks" (71). As in *The Reivers* and as in *Snopes* and *A Fable*, the powerless are the sources of creativity and political insight in Faulkner's apocrypha. The powerful men (and they are all men, all white men) are too invested in reality, in "facks," in established structures and beliefs to see alternatives. One established "fack" that middle-year men have is a respect for the dead and for the sacred idea of the grave. Stevens tells Mallison that he would just as soon shoot another of Gowrie's sons than "to dig his boy's body up out of the ground it had been consecrated and prayed upon," *especially* not "to tell him the reason was to save a nigger from being lynched" (80). The facts of a "consecrate and prayed upon" dead body outweigh, in Stevens' socially tuned mind, the living emblem of racism and injustice in his world. Here, Mallison realizes the depth of his baptism. The "respect" for dead white bodies—as memories, as symbols, as ancestry and heritage—serves to perpetuate the same evils men like Gavin Stevens claim they wish to see overcome. To succeed where Stevens will obviously fail, Mallison must break out of this structure.

As is so often the case in Faulkner's apocrypha, meaningful reform of the conditions of social existence is preceded, in *Intruder in the Dust,* by rebellion. Beauchamp's "refusal to be a nigger" sets the example by which Mallison's unwillingness to acquiesce passively to structural racism is accomplished. He refuses to take his uncle's advice because he recognizes it for what it is. "Until now [his uncle] had had no more trouble than he believing things that all other grown people doubted for the sole reason that they were unreasonable" (72), but now the uncle had failed, and the nephew must see the failure. Mallison's "irrevocable moment" of commitment to his act of stealth—exhuming a corpse—occurs when he leaves his parents' home without permission, "the irrevocable moment after which there would be no return" (84). When he sneaks out he begins his defiance of home, of the beliefs and values of his parents and uncle, and of the limitations of his elders. *Intruder in the Dust* is, in fact, filled with rhetoric about growing up, including Gavin Stevens' stories about playing football and the refrain about a mother resenting her child's self-sufficiency, all of which both enforce the motif of the child taking control of life and form the thematic backdrop to Mallison's defiance of parental claims to authority. When Mallison does act, he finds allies among the powerless: his black friend, Alek Sander, Mrs. Halbersham, and "young folks and womens."

Critics have recognized the symbolism in the act of digging up a corpse. Patrick Samway explains that "digging up Gowrie's grave . . . disturbs the normal patterns of existence in Jefferson," for example, and Joseph Gold equates the act of exhumation with "an examination of the past."[61] When the past is exhumed in *Intruder in the Dust,* more than simple facts come to light. What is revealed about the past and about the object of the community's respect and the source of its heritage is a set of complex relations not all of which are entirely worthy of consecration and prayer. What Mallison digs up in particular is white fratricide, swindling, and deception, all of which is accomplished in hopes that everything will be covered up by scapegoating a black man.

Mallison literally "intrudes" in the dust to exhume the grave and asserts the authority of his own living body over that of the dead bodies buried below him. Although it is Gowrie's grave which is exhumed and Gowrie's body which is missing, all through *Intruder* it is *Mallison's* body which is the object of scrutiny by Mallison. The re-examination of dead bodies leads him to reconsider the significance of his own. His body, in Faulkner's apocrypha, means more than one thing: it is the body of the adolescent boy, the white male, the son, the nephew. Each successive context betrays competing, often contradictory meanings. Twice in the novel Mallison stands naked before an audience of one man, first a black man and then a white one. Before Beauchamp, he is white and Other, and the racism apart from which "he could not even imagine an existence" permeates the atmosphere like an "odor." He believes that "he had smelled it forever, he would smell it always," and that it was as real as his own body and his own smell (12). He partakes in this reality in the same way he partakes in Beauchamp's "nigger food," and it—food and atmosphere—is "accepted and then dismissed also because it was exactly what he had expected" (13). When he acts within this context, however, he is embarrassed by his own profound ignorance, "standing with the slow hot blood as slow as minutes themselves up his neck and face" as he attempts to pay Beauchamp for the food (15). His body here compels him to re-examine the definitions by which he comprehends and acts in this confrontation.

When Mallison stands practically naked before Gavin Stevens, near the end of the novel, he again comes to terms with physical reactions to human behavior. Again he feels shame, "the hot hard blood burn[ing] all the way up his neck and face" (205). This time the shame is not for his *own* act but for the actions of the white community as a whole. Before Stevens, he is not white Other but white Same, and he must consider himself as part of a socially dominant and historically powerful and abusive group. After dressing, he again eats and thinks that by eating "did he actually enter the world, get himself into the world" (207). This time, however, he eats white food, and he must listen to Stevens, not Beauchamp. Beauchamp told him to pick up his money and go on; Stevens also tells him to "pick up" and go on despite his alienation from his race. In both cases, Mallison's nakedness signals a re-examination of himself as symbol or emblem in the racial complexities of his time and place. The question for Mallison then becomes what he will be. He never does tell Stevens what he thinks as he stands undressed before him, and as usual, Stevens' inability to stop talking precludes his finding out what Mallison wants to say. Mallison has left Stevens behind by this point in the narrative. Significantly, however, Faulkner does not plainly articulate where Mallison will go or what he will do with his thoughts. *Intruder* may be a "talky" novel, and many readers have objected that it says too much, but most of what it says actually amounts to very little. Its chief "spokesman," Gavin Stevens, is a blowhard, and he blows dust into the eyes of those who will not see through, or perhaps intrude, into the novel's "secret" or apocryphal significance. The two most important utterances in the novel, what Beauchamp knows about the murder and what Mallison learns about racism, lie buried in the dusty narrative, while Stevens keeps talking.

Mallison exhumes Gowrie's grave and finds another body there, and later, when he returns, he finds no body at all. This is similar to his first exposure to Beauchamp, in which he finds "another body"—a young racist—in his place, and to his second exposure to Stevens, in which he finds that he wishes to efface himself from association with whites. Both the exhumations and the self-confrontations are parts of the larger re-examination at stake in the novel, the "exhumation" of the structures by which Mallison has been taught, or fed his racism. Once he understands himself (and understands the grave, or the past) apocryphally, that is, as the result of a revolving series of productions, a complex set of potential significations dependent upon self and time and place for meaning, does Mallison free himself from the definitions imposed upon his body by his community. Only then does he also free himself of the destructive belief in the permanence and inevitability of his own and of his community's racism. Once "he was free" (30, 34) of any fixed behavior, free not only of racial determinism but also of the determinism of his age and "respect" for his elders, the dead, and the past, Mallison can violate the repressive structures of race, age, parental authority, and the sanctity of both grave and heritage. Faulkner does not make clear at the end of the book where Mallison will go with his knowledge because the narrative direction of the novel has already accomplished his arrival.

With *Intruder in the Dust*, Faulkner challenged the contemporary political scene with his apocryphal interpretation of reality. Unfortunately, the novel (like *The Reivers*) has been read too literally. Too often are Gavin Stevens' windy attempts to "explain" the South taken as creditable, and too often is the novel considered and then dismissed as a bad murder-mystery. Once seen as apocryphal sub-limation, the realism of *Intruder* must be eyed with particular scru-tiny and suspicion. The real situation of the novel is sublimated and then *exhumed*, torn from the ground and made into something else. Racism, like Mallison's body, is stripped naked in *Intruder in the Dust* and exposed as historically produced (supported by "con-secrated and prayed upon" graves), structurally reinforced (by re-pressive systems of authority), and entirely subject to revolution as well as perpetuation. The seeds of the solution to the novel's greater mystery, the mystery of racism, lie in the twin refusals of Lucas Beauchamp and Charles Mallison. Beauchamp's "refusal to be a nigger" will cost him his life unless it is matched by Mallison's parallel refusal to be many things—loyal son, respectful nephew, law-abiding citizen—among the structures that feed and sustain his racism, and will eventually demand a display of the same attitudes from him. This is what is sublimated in *Intruder in the Dust* beneath the "actual" plot of a cozy (and bad) murder-mystery and beneath the racialist pontifications of Gavin Stevens. By "sublimating the actual into the apocryphal," Faulkner freed himself to address issues which the facts and the realities of his place and time precluded. As apocrypha, Faulkner's novel would place rebellion and refusal at the core of his solution to the great mystery of racism.

---

1. *Faulkner in the University*, p. 189.
2. *Faulkner: A Biography*, p. 105.
3. *Ibid.*, p. 1088. As a further presentation of himself, Faulkner retained the original spelling of his family name, "Falkner," in his farm dealings. On the ledger book for his farm business he wrote, "Falkner, Wm" over each page of transactions. See p. 1091.
4. *William Faulkner of Oxford*, p. 217. Faulkner expressed the sentiment to Harrison Smith in 1932 as well. "I am going cold-blooded Yankee now; I am not young enough anymore to hell around and earn money at other things as I could once. I have got to make it at writing or quit writing." See *Selected Letters*, p. 60.
5. William Faulkner, *Essays, Speeches and Public Letters*, edited by James B. Meri-wether (New York: Random House, 1966), p. 35. The vagabond or "tramp" image dates back to Faulkner's youth. In 1920, he told friends who were concerned with his dishevelled appearance, "All I want to do is write. . . . Who knows, someday you may see a headline in the newspapers, 'Tramp Becomes Famous.'" See *Faulkner: A Biography*, p. 292.
6. Gilbert Rhyle, *The Concept of Mind* (New York: Barnes and Noble, 1949), p. 61.
7. Stephen Longstreet, "William Faulkner in California," *Orange County Illus-trated* (May 1964), pp. 30–31.
8. *Faulkner in the University*, p. 268.

9. Longstreet, "William Faulkner in California," p. 31.
10. James G. Watson, *William Faulkner; Letters and Fictions* (Austin: University of Texas Press, 1987), pp. 1–28. The quotation is on p. 21.
11. Joseph L. Blotner, "The Sources of Faulkner's Genius," in Doreen Fowler and Ann J. Abadie, *Fifty Years of Yoknapatawpha* (Jackson, MS: University Press of Mississippi, 1980), p. 249. The one conclusion Blotner makes is that Faulkner's "great talent times time spent" accounts for his genius, p. 268.
12. David Minter, *William Faulkner: His Life and Work* (Baltimore: Johns Hopkins University Press, 1980), pp. 76–77.
13. *Ibid.*, p. 116.
14. For example, in a 1931 letter to the *Saturday Evening Post*, Faulkner chastized the magazine for rejecting eight stories "by this Faulkner. Let this be a warning, that the Post is unwittingly in the way of falling from that high place in letters to which [Faulkner's admirers] (including the aforesaid Faulkner) raised it." See James Meriwether, "Faulkner's Correspondence with the *Saturday Evening Post*," *Mississippi Quarterly* 30 (Summer 1977), pp. 461–76. In his introduction to the Modern Library edition of *Sanctuary*, Faulkner wrote: "So I told Faulkner, 'You're damned. You'll have to work now and then for the rest of your life' " *Essays, Speeches and Public Letters*, p. 177. In 1937, Faulkner indicated to Maurice Coindreau that his writing often even surprised him. "You see, I usually write at night. I always keep my whiskey within reach; so many ideas I can't remember in the morning pop into my head." As for a particular passage the translator had questioned, "I must have had something in mind, but I can't tell you what" *Faulkner: A Biography*, p. 960. Blotner claims that Faulkner "always had this curious attitude toward his finished work, as though it was something completely outside himself " *ibid.*, p. 1817.
15. One example should suffice here. Carvel Collins refers to Faulkner's "extreme emotional disturbance" following his having missed Helen Baird in Europe in 1925, leaving the reader to wonder whether he means that Faulkner began drinking. Collins goes to great lengths to prove that Faulkner was not a "womanizer," saying that Meta Carpenter had said so and that Joan Williams agreed. This causes the reader to wonder why the protection is necessary and how these two women could say anything other than that Faulkner was not and still maintain their self-respect. Similarly, Collins claims that Faulkner never went to brothels except to get a drink and to talk with friends. Finally, he says that Faulkner liked to recite the Shakespeare sonnet "The Phoenix and the Turtle" during "times of trouble." It is clear that "times of trouble" were when Faulkner began to drink heavily. See Collins, "Introduction," in Faulkner, *Helen: A Courtship*, pp. 28, 64, and 101.
16. Quoted in Paul Gardner, "Faulkner Remembered," in *A Faulkner Perspective* (Franklin Center, PA: Franklin Center Library, 1976), p. 23.
17. Bezzerides, scriptwriter, *A Life on Paper*, pp. 9–10.
18. A good exploration of this point is in Andrew Pfeiffer, "Eye of the Storm: The Observer's Image of the Man Who Was Faulkner," *Southern Review* XIV (October 1972), pp. 763–73. According to Pfeiffer: "The problem lies in trying to plumb the depths (or sometimes merely the surface) of the man of many masks, for Faulkner legends arose during his long career because of the myths about his biography that he himself helped to fabricate, and because of his intense private solitude with its accompanying facade of simplicity and disdain for recognition. The masks Faulkner wore made him appear paradoxical and enigmatic to his champions and Janus-faced to his antagonists. There was Faulkner the legendary Anti-Intellectual: the non-working Count 'No-'Count,' who postured a World War I nobility; the hunter turning down a visit by a foreign noblewoman to keep a coon-hunting date; the Rabelasian drinker once quoted as saying that civilization started with distillation. . . . There was Faulkner the Oxfordian: the Mississippian who could be courteous or rude, noble or crude; the schoolmaster, air-raid warden, carpenter, and farmer who also was a neo-

Oxfordian resembling an English nobleman, tweedy and aloof in a bowler hat. There was also Faulkner the Southerner, too liberal for his neighbors, too moderate for the Northern liberal, possessing a love-hate relationship for his South like Quentin Compson, simultaneously identifying with elements of the past and trying to keep up with changes," pp. 766–67.

19. Robert Coughlin, *The Private World of William Faulkner* (New York: Harper and Row, 1954), p. 21.

20. Dorothy Commins, *What is an Editor?: Saxe Commins at Work* (Chicago: University of Chicago Press, 1978), pp. 202, 204, 217.

21. Maurice Coindreau, "The Faulkner I Knew," in *The Time of William Faulkner,* p. 92.

22. Stephen B. Oates, *William Faulkner: The Man and the Artist: A Biography* (New York: Harper and Row, 1987), p. xiii.

23. Robert N. Linscott, "Faulkner without Fanfare," *Esquire* 60 (July 1963), p. 36.

24. Pagels, *The Gnostic Gospels,* p. 22.

25. *Lion in the Garden,* p. 14.

26. According to Blotner, *Faulkner: A Biography,* p. 1220, Faulkner once told the Oxford pharmacist in regards to the jukebox in the drugstore, "it looks like all the people of this world must have a lot of noise around them to keep them from thinking about the things they should remember." In 1951, he told Edward Kimbrough that "I like silence. . . . Silence and horses. And trees." He also said that there is nothing one can do for eight hours a day but work. "What else are you going to do? . . . You can't drink eight hours a day. Or make love. Work's about the only thing a fellow has to do to keep from being bored" *Lion in the Garden,* p. 64. He said much the same thing about work to Jean Stein. "One of the saddest things is that the only thing a man can do for eight hours a day, day after day, is work." He also told Stein that "I prefer silence to sound, and the image produced by words occurs in silence" *ibid.,* pp. 249, 248. Malcolm Franklin, Faulkner's stepson, refers to Faulkner's "silent days" at Rowen Oak, when Faulkner might be writing. "On such days you could not be sure whether he was writing or not. It was all very quiet. No telephone, no radio and no door bell! These were forbidden items." *Bitterweeds: Life with William Faulkner at Rowen Oak* (Irving, TX: The Society for the Study of Traditional Culture, 1977), p. 33.

27. Coughlin, *The Private World of William Faulkner,* pp. 24–25. In context: "His was not a split personality but rather a fragmented one, loosely held together by some strong inner force, the pieces often askew and sometimes painfully in friction. It is to ease these pains, one can guess, that he escapes periodically and sometimes for periods of weeks into alcoholism, until his drinking has become legendary in the town and in his profession, and hospitalization and injections have on occasion been necessary to save his life. After one of these episodes he returns for a relatively long period to an existence of calm sobriety: he is not an alcoholic, but perhaps more accurately an alcoholic refugee, self-pursued."

28. Coindreau, "The Faulkner I Knew," p. 49.

29. Linscott, "Faulkner Without Fanfare," p. 36.

30. Hodding Carter, "The Forgiven Faulkner," *Journal of Inter-American Studies* XXXIV (Summer 1949), p. 140.

31. Thomas P. Gilmore, *Equivocal Spirits: Alcoholism and Drinking in the Twentieth Century* (Chapel Hill: University of North Carolina Press, 1987), pp. 15, 170. Gilmore's use of the term "Age of Literary Alcoholism" is, as he admits, offered with reservations, in the same spirit that one might call the Romantic period the "Age of Literary Opium Addiction." Unfortunately, Gilmore does not discuss Faulkner's career.

32. Quoted in *Faulkner: A Biography,* p. 199n.

33. The phrase is from Hyatt Waggoner: "Faulkner's fiction breaks up and reconstitutes the conventional and expected elements and patterns and feelings of experience, imposing on us the burden of painfully fresh perception." *William Faulkner: From Jefferson to the World* (Lexington: University of Kentucky Press, 1959), p. 251.

34. *Lion in the Garden*, p. 149.

35. Barnstone, *The Other Bible*, p. 292.

36. Much of the material in this discussion of *As I Lay Dying* has been published previously. See my essay, "William Faulkner and the Drama of Meaning: "The Discovery of the Figurative in *As I Lay Dying*," *South Atlantic Review* 53:2 (May 1988), pp. 11–23. I would like to thank *SAR* for permission to reprint the essay here.

37. *Faulkner in the University*, p. 19.

38. *Knight's Gambit* (New York: Random House, 1949), pp. 24–25.

39. *Collected Stories* (New York: Random House, 1950), p. 407.

40. *Lion in the Garden*, p. 253.

41. Harold Bloom, ed., *William Faulkner: Modern Critical Views* (New York: Chelsea, 1986), p. 3.

42. Robert Dale Parker, *Faulkner and the Novelistic Imagination* (Chicago: University of Illinois Press, 1985), p. 49.

43. Olga Vickery, *The Novels of William Faulkner: A Critical Interpretation* (Baton Rouge: Louisiana State University Press, 1964), pp. 53–54.

44. The quotation is from Plato's *Timaeus*; see Plato, *The Collected Dialogues of Plato, Including the Letters* (Princeton, NJ: Princeton University Press, 1963), p. 1167. Faulkner's comments in Virginia about "the mystical belief that there is no such thing as *was*" echo the language of the *Timaeus*, *Faulkner in the University*, p. 139.

45. Compare Mikhail Bakhtin: "Laughter purifies from dogmatism, from the intolerant and the petrified; it liberates from fanaticism and pedantry; from fear and intimidation, from didacticism, naivete and illusion, from the single meaning, the single level, from sentimentality" (123). Darl, however, is *driven to* laughter, not liberated by it.

46. Joseph Reed, in *Faulkner's Narrative* (New Haven: Yale University Press, 1973), p. 93, suggests a thematic function. "The catalog [of metaphors and similes] adds up to less than one might want it to, perhaps, until one realizes the rather unpredictable function of all these metaphors, the emphasis of grotesque distance, corresponding to the tension between our subjective empathy with the Bundrens which leads to a perception of tragedy and our objective ridicule which leads to a sense of them as comic." Calvin Bedient also stresses the primacy of the simile in the novel in "Pride and Nakedness: *As I Lay Dying*" in Leland Cox, ed., *William Faulkner: A Critical Collection* (Detroit: Gale Research Pub., 1982), pp. 219–20.

47. The significance of the "I" in the title is not entirely clear. For example, Melvin Bachman, "Addie Bundren and William Faulkner," in Glenn O. Carey, ed., *Faulkner: The Unappeased Imagination: A Collection of Critical Essays* (Troy, NY: Whitson Publishing Co., 1980), p. 22 claims that it may refer to Faulkner himself, "the threatened artist." Lynn Gartrell Levin, *Faulkner's Heroic Design: The Yoknapatawpha Novels* (Athens: University of Georgia Press, 1976), p. 111, cites the source of the title as taken from book eleven of the *Odyssey*, a speech made "to denounce the cruelty of Clytemnestra and of all women in general."

48. Reading *Pylon* with Marshall McLuhan's *Understanding the Media: The Extensions of Man* (New York: McGraw Hill, 1964) in mind sheds a great deal of light on Faulkner's thinking in that novel.

49. *Essays, Speeches and Public Letters*, p. 192.

50. Cited in Hugh M. Ruppersberg, *Voice and Eye in Faulkner's Fiction* (Athens: University of Georgia Press, 1983), p. 78. Ruppersberg does not agree with Pitavy.

51. I think any of three interpretations are valid regarding the Reporter's "trans-

formation" to Author: 1) he writes the abandonment scene, in which case he has made the transformation to apocryphal production; 2) he writes only the newspaper copy (in the last pages of the novel), which the copyboy finds, in which case the Reporter actually regresses to melodrama; or 3) he does both. In the end it does not really matter, because the final chapter effectively demonstrates the difference between a reporter's "understanding" and an apocryphal "understanding." Faulkner makes a case once again for re-creation.

52. Millgate, *The Achievement of William Faulkner*, p. 147.

53. Thomas Edmund Perry, "Knowing in the Novels of William Faulkner," doctoral dissertation, University of Rochester, New York, 1974.

54. *Selected Letters*, p. 301, letter to a reader in March 1950.

55. A few examples: Jiggs puts his hand in his pocket, and it looks like "the ostrich in the movie cartoon swallow[ing] the alarm clock," p. 10; Jiggs walks "like a mechanical top that has but one speed," p. 11; Jack Holmes' "bleak humorless handsome face . . . like the comedy young bachelor caught by his girl while holding a strange infant on a street corner," p. 36; the six of them on their way to the Reporter's apartment "in a tableau reminiscent . . . of the cartoon pictures of city anarchists," p. 81; the aviators "worked quiet and fast, like a circus team, with the trained team's economy of motion," p. 130.

56. George C. Bedell, *Kierkegaard and Faulkner: Modalities of Existence* (Baton Rouge: Louisiana State University Press, 1972), pp. 210–11.

57. For a good reading of *Pylon* that places Laverne at the center of analysis, see Joseph R. McElrath, Jr., "*Pylon*: The Portrait of a Lady," *Mississippi Quarterly* XXVII (Summer 1974), pp. 277–90.

58. In 1948, Faulkner told his agent, Harold Ober, that his new novel was "a mystery-murder though the theme is more relationship between Negro and White." *Selected Letters*, p. 262; Walter Taylor, *Faulkner's Search for a South* (Urbana: University of Illinois Press, 1983), pp. 162–63, for example, claims Faulkner "could not pay enough attention to the conventions of the mystery to make his novel credible" as a "murder mystery" and that the book is simply "a thin subterfuge" for Faulkner's "polemics."

59. See my essays, "Temple Drake's Truthful Perjury: Rethinking Faulkner's *Sanctuary*," *American Literature* 55:3 (October 1983), pp. 435–44, and "Menstrual Blood and 'Nigger' Blood: Joe Christmas and the Ideology of Sex and Race," *Mississippi Quarterly* 41:3 (Summer 1988), pp. 391–402.

60. In this Gavin Stevens parodies subsequent actions Faulkner himself would take. The film version of *Intruder in the Dust* was made on location in Oxford, and on one occasion the entire MGM cast and production crew were invited to Rowan Oak for a party. The Faulkners, however, could not invite Juano Hernandez, the Puerto Rican actor portraying Lucas Beauchamp, without inviting the Oxford black family with whom he was staying. To avoid violating local strictures on interracial social gatherings, the party was held for the entire crew making the film about racism—minus Hernandez. What Faulkner could accomplish in his apocryphal county he dared not attempt in actuality. See Blotner, *Faulkner: A Biography*, one-volume edition, p. 503.

61. Patrick H. Samway, S.J., *Faulkner's Intruder in the Dust: A Critical Study of the Typescripts* (Troy, NY: Whitson Publishing Co., 1980), p. 252; Gold, *William Faulkner: A Study in Humanism*, p. 87.

3. The Spirit of Apocrypha
A Fable

TWENTY-SEVEN YEARS before *A Fable* was published, Faulkner's Major Ayers, in *Mosquitos* (1927), observed that World War I had "made war so damned unpopular with the proletariat" that the authorities would not be able to "have another war right off." The rank and file, Ayers continued, "would get all their backs up and refuse to go again." The problem with the war was that the authorities "overdid it," Ayers concluded. "Like the showman who fills his stage so full chaps can see through into the wings."[2] Two ideas voiced by Major Ayers in Faulkner's second novel germinated over the course of the author's career and emerge as central assumptions in his sixteenth and perhaps greatest work. The first, that the masses have the power to stop war, is at the root of the regimental mutiny, or rebellion that precedes the plot of *A Fable*. The second, that warfare is an artificial struggle "staged" by Authority in order to maintain and reinforce its control over the people, is the anti-authoritarian assertion upon which the novel so powerfully insists.

A Fable is more important, however, as Faulkner's supreme articulation of his apocryphal production. Critics have attacked the novel for its heavy-handed symbolism and for its reliance upon the structure of Christ's life for its "allegory" and plot development. This criticism misses the point entirely and misreads the novel. The corporal in *A Fable* is not a *symbolic* Christ, nor is the story an *allegory* based in the life of the historical Jesus. The reason critics find that the symbolism does not work in *A Fable* is because there is very little symbolism in it. In the spirit of a gnostic gospel or other New Testament apocrypha, *A Fable is* Christ's life, not symbolically or allegorically, but apocryphally. In the novel Faulkner, inspired by accounts of Christ's life he had read, meditated on, and wrote about throughout his career, recreates the life of Christ in his own time—in a World War I setting. This is a point which no reader will overcome without fully understanding the meaning of Faulkner's apocrypha, an understanding finally liberated from the New Critical straitjacket in which Faulkner had been placed prior to completing *A Fable*. The corporal is not *like* Christ and the story is not *like* that of the historical Jesus any more than Vardaman in *As I Lay Dying* meant to say that his mother was *like* a fish. Rather, the corporal *is* Christ, and the story *is* the story of His last days on earth—not the historical Christ, but an apocryphal Christ. Just as a gnostic Christian would claim to have witnessed the resurrection centuries after its historical occurrence, Faulkner claims in *A Fable* to witness and narrate a recasting of the challenge, passion, and condemnation of the Child of God, or the Son of Man, as he calls the corporal. In orthodox terms, *A Fable* is heresy. In New Critical terms, the novel is a massive failure. In terms of what Faulkner was attempting to articulate in the late 1940s and throughout the 1950s, however, it is the very spirit of the apocrypha.

As is generally known, Faulkner got the idea for *A Fable* while working in Hollywood. During a story conference in late 1943, producer William Bacher said he wanted to do a film about Christ's return to earth during World War I and his second crucifixion. "Faulkner, always notorious for his calm, was sufficiently moved to say," according to Tom Dardis, "that it 'could be a pretty interesting thing'" and began work on the project "immediately," producing a "ten thousand word screenplay adaptation" of the idea.[3] Faulkner could not get to work on a literary treatment of the idea, however, unless he was released from his Warner Brothers contract. With the support of Random House, Faulkner negotiated a three-month leave of absence from Warner Brothers and an advance of one thousand dollars from Bacher to work on the idea.[4] From the beginning *A Fable* represented, in Dardis' words, Faulkner's "passport to freedom" from Hollywood. It would also be his "passport to freedom" from his "mythical county" and toward a clear statement, which is not to say a clearly *understood* statement, of the logic of his apocrypha. Random House would continue to support the project long after Bacher lost interest.[5]

Faulkner was back in Oxford in the fall of 1943 and at work on the synopsis for Bacher. He considered the idea powerful enough to serve him in more than one way. In November 1943, he told his agent, Harold Ober, that he had plans to write not only a film synopsis but also a magazine story, a stage play, and "a novelette-fable."[6] Faulkner was so set on the synopsis that he refused to take on a project Ober wanted him to do, a short piece on the Mississippi River, on the grounds that he could not write something " 'cold,' without that speck of fire, that coal, from which a book or picture should burst almost of its own accord."[7] Right through the beginning of *A Fable,* this was Faulkner's understanding, based on his own experience, of how a novel or any work of art is completed. Through a "burst" of creative energy Faulkner had completed such works as *As I Lay Dying, Pylon,* and after a temporary snag, *Absalom, Absalom!* In the winter of 1943–44, it seemed to Faulkner that this new project would be no different. He wrote an enthusiastic letter to Random House editor Robert K. Haas in January 1944, explaining the point of his new novel in terms of re-creation, not symbolism.

> The argument is (in the fable) in the middle of that war, Christ (some movement in mankind which wished to stop warfare forever) reap-peared and was crucified again. We are repeating, we are in the midst of war again. Suppose Christ gives us one more chance, will we crucify him again, perhaps for the last time.
>
> That's crudely put; I am not trying to preach at all. But that is the argument: We did this in 1918; in 1944 it not only MUST NOT happen again, it SHALL NOT HAPPEN again, i.e., ARE WE GOING TO LET IT HAPPEN AGAIN? now that we are in another war, where the third and final chance might be offered us to save him.[8]

Faulkner's work on "the fable" was interrupted in February 1944 when Warner Brothers called him back to Hollywood. In April he wrote Ober. "I dont know when I shall get back at" the manuscript, Faulkner said. "War is bad for writing." He expressed disillusion-ment and a sense of powerlessness before the face of a second world war. Perhaps he felt that his fable, as strong an idea as it was to him, was a useless weapon against the war machines. "It's too bad I live now though," he continued in his April letter to Ober. "Still too young to be unmoved by the old insidious succubae of trumpets, too old either to make one among them or to be impervious, and therefore too old to write. . . . I have a considerable talent, perhaps as good as any coeval. But I am 46 now. So what I will mean soon by 'have' is 'had.' "[9]

In December, Faulkner was back in Oxford, and in January 1945 back at work on the manuscript of his fable. "I will carry on with this fable," he told Ober.[10] With financial support from Random House, he worked on the manuscript until June, when he returned to Hollywood for what would be his last stint under the Warner Brothers contract. In 1946, Robert K. Haas and Harold Ober worked to secure his release from that commitment, freeing Faulkner to devote full energy to what had become, in his words, "a novel now and not just a lot of rhetoric."[11] Describing the project as "a novel" probably indicates an act of possession on Faulkner's part and not a genuine aesthetic judgment, for Faulkner was never comfortable for long with calling the manuscript a novel. Yet the project was all his now and not just rhetoric, a movie script, or a plot synopsis. When Faulkner was finally free to write *A Fable*, however, his troubles with the manuscript were just beginning. In March 1946, he told Ober "I cannot do the book in three months" and expressed concern over going further into debt with Random House, which had been sending him regular advances. In April he expressed doubts that Random House would continue to "underwrite me" for as long as it would take to complete the novel. Faulkner told Ober that "this is going to be a lot of book, something new for me, really not a novel. It may go slow at times; it may take me two years to get it right. I shant release it until it is right." A month later, he wrote much the same thing to Random House and mentioned plans to return to Hollywood to make money. He also gave Haas reason to continue to advance money to him. "To repeat," Faulkner wrote, "I think it is all right. It may be my best. It is not a novel at all. I think it's more than just a fable."[12] It may have been that Faulkner's problems with the writing of *A Fable* stem from the fact that it was not a novel but a Christian apocrypha, and even he may have blanched at the audacity of such a production in the twentieth century.

During Faulkner's 1944 stint in Hollywood he was approached by Malcolm Cowley. While Cowley was piecing together his *Portable Faulkner* legend of Yoknapatawpha, Faulkner was immersed in what he considered to be the most mature and most important project of his career.[13] Cowley's interest in Faulkner did succeed in rescuing him from the disillusion he had expressed ("War is bad for writing"), but the way Cowley viewed Faulkner's purposes only fueled the author's interest in this important departure from Yoknapatawpha and the American South. Although he was extremely pleased with Cowley's accomplishment (he ordered a dozen copies for himself), when *The Portable Faulkner* was published in 1946, Faulkner was declaring renewed interest and confidence in his fable.[14] In June he told Haas of his personal faith in the project. "I believe now it's not just my best but perhaps the best of my time." He promised to send the manuscript to Haas piecemeal to assure Random House, no doubt, that it was getting its money's worth. "I believe I see a rosy future for this book, I mean, it may sell," Faulkner concluded, "it will be a War and Peace close enough to home, our times, language, for Americans to really buy it." Then he tempered his hard sell. "You understand this is a confidential letter to the firm, the House; dont quote me outside please."[15]

Writing *A Fable*, whatever the level of enthusiasm, was never easy for Faulkner. He had recurring doubts about its relevance and whether the book would be understood.[16] He also continued to do painstaking revisions and rewrites, sometimes calling back whole sections of the manuscript from Random House. In the spring of 1947, he accused the "trash and junk writing" he had done in Hollywood as responsible for his slowed pace now but voiced confidence in his progress. In August he took time from the manuscript to write "a complete novelette," which would become the "Notes on a Horsethief" portion of the novel. By then, however, the book had again escaped Faulkner's control, and he could not even "guess how much longer" it would take to finish it when he wrote to Ober in October.[17] As the writing of *A Fable* dragged on, Faulkner became increasingly anxious over Random House's money, which he felt he was not earning because he was not finishing anything. For this reason he took three months off in the beginning of 1948 to write *Intruder in the Dust*[18] and later, between 1948 and 1951, spent time on such projects as *Knight's Gambit* (1949), *Collected Stories* (1950), and *Requiem for a Nun*. Faulkner would never let his difficulties in finishing *A Fable* convince him that he could no longer create.

When Faulkner finally did complete the manuscript of *A Fable* in 1953, he told Saxe Commins, "I love the book, gave ten good years of my life to it." He also wrote to his mother from New York, in a tone reminiscent of his letters to her and his Aunt Bama in the 1920s, that "I believe the book is a good one. All the people here like what they have seen of it."[19] The book had taken Faulkner a long way in his career and a long way in his understanding of himself and his literary purposes. During the writing of it, he witnessed his career move from that of an out-of-print, "Southern" writer whose name was "mud" in publishing circles and who was compelled to work in Hollywood to pay his bills and support his family to a Nobel Laureate, a member of the American Academy of Arts and Letters, a recipient of the National Book Award and the Pulitzer Prize (for *A Fable*), and an author whose novels were becoming valued commodities in Hollywood. Nonetheless, the writing of the big book never became easy nor did Faulkner ever regain the original fire. Toward the last months of work on *A Fable*, Faulkner wrote "by simple will power." His "initial momentum ran out" in 1953, he said, and the writing was "getting more and more difficult, a matter of deliberate will power, concentration, which can be deadly after a while."

The composition of *A Fable* was indeed something of an epic journey for Faulkner. "Am so near the end of the big one," he told Commins in August 1953, "that I am frightened lightning might strike me before I can finish it. It is either nothing and I am blind in my dotage, or it is the best of my time."[20] In some ways, the *A Fable* experience represented a microcosm or a miniature of Faulkner's career pattern through 1954: an initial creative surge, followed by the regretful loss of that first heat, and a gradual settling into deliberate and self-driven work. "But it's nice to know that I can still do that: can write anything I want to, whenever I want to, by simple will, concentration, that I can still do that," Faulkner wrote to Joan Williams in 1953. "But goddam it, I want to do it for fun again like I used to: not just to prove to bill f. that I still can."[21]

What Faulkner did in *A Fable*, however, was not at all like what he had done before. What were often considered minor and unsuccessful departures from the Yoknapatawpha setting in *Pylon* and *The Wild Palms*, and even the pre-Yoknapatawpha settings of *Soldier's Pay* and *Mosquitos*, hardly indicated to critics that Faulkner would write something like *A Fable*. The fact that Faulkner worked so long and with such conviction on this particular project throws into question assumptions about his literary purposes and ambitions, and it certainly disputes the relative importance of the Yoknapatawpha setting as Faulkner's aesthetic ordering principle. The themes and concerns that emerge from the pages of *A Fable* are pure Faulkner and reverberate in the novels that precede and follow the work, but they have nothing to do with Yoknapatawpha, Southern mythmaking, or legend. *A Fable,* however, is certainly apocryphal. The novel might be characterized as a meditation on the trinity of human life: as flesh, a sensual creation destined to oblivion; as mind, capable of defining and ordering the natural world and all of reality; and as spirit, marked by rebellion and forever in a struggle with the doomed flesh and the unquiet mind. This same trinitarian meditation would emerge central to the *Snopes* trilogy. In 1947, Faulkner told Haas that he could not tell if *A Fable* was "perhaps the last book I'll write and I am putting all of it into it, or 2. It may contain the germs of several more books."[22]

A Fable is the "big one," the "magnum o," the masterpiece of Faulkner's career. The place of the novel as something of an anamoly in the Faulkner canon is only partially due to its difficulty, for it is no more strenuous to read initially than *Absalom, Absalom!* or parts of *Go Down, Moses.* The failure of critics to integrate *A Fable* adequately into an understanding of Faulkner is more likely due to the novel's divergence from how "Faulkner" had been critically understood when he wrote the book. The novel is impossible to read with the political blindspot of New Criticism. It is equally impossible to read in the context of social realism or of naturalism. The novel is not satisfying either as a political novel or as a proletariat novel in the leftist sense. Finally, it wholly challenges the Cowleyan interpretation of Faulkner as mythmaker and demands, though the demand is seldom met, that readers think again about their understanding of Faulkner and that they take seriously his creation of an apocrypha.

According to Joseph Blotner, Faulkner was "seized with" an "anxiety" to make people understand *A Fable.* He would explain the book to his wife and daughter, going into detail as he had never done before with his work. This concern about being understood led him to do something he had refused since *Sanctuary* to do with his books, that is, write an explanatory note or preface.[23] Faulkner wrote the prefatory note just before the novel was published. His editor, Saxe Commins, disagreed with Faulkner's stated aims and interpretation of the novel and considered the preface inappropriate for use in either publicizing or explaining the novel. Instead, Commins wrote his own description of the novel and printed it on the book jacket. Once again, Faulkner's own words to describe his work would be suppressed by an editor attempting to construct and produce a certain, less volatile image of the writer.

It is not surprising that in 1954, Commins would act to censor Faulkner's interpretation of *A Fable* and suppress his aims in writing the novel. The statement is astounding and inflammatory, and is difficult if not impossible to reconcile with a Cowleyan or New Critical portrait of Faulkner as mythmaker or conservative moralist. On the eve of an American decade of civil disobedience and passive resistance to intransigence and authoritarianism at home, on the heels of a war in Korea, and in the midst of the Cold War with the Soviet Union, Faulkner advocated armed citizen resistance against any further calls for war by any government anywhere in the world. "This is not a pacifist book," Faulkner began in the first paragraph of the suppressed preface to *A Fable*. "On the contrary, this writer holds almost as short a brief for pacifism as for war itself, for the reason that pacifism does not work, cannot cope with the forces that produce wars." Faulkner hoped that readers would see in *A Fable* that "something more powerful than war and man's aptitude for belligerence" is needed to end human strife. In fact, Faulkner asserts, "man may finally have to mobilize himself and arm himself with the implements of war to put an end to war." The mistaken assumption we have operated under until now, Faulkner continues, is that one nation or one ideology battling another nation or ideology might actually end war once and for all. This belief, he says, is baseless and false. We must recognize who it is that makes war and why it is that wars are fought, and then "the men who do not want war may have to arm themselves as for war" in order to "defeat by the methods of war the alliances of power which hold to the obsolete belief in the validity of war." This is an incredible statement coming from a man considered to be a "conservative" or "traditionalist" writer, the literary voice of America's new cultural hegemony. The statement argues not pacifism or love to end war but armed insurrectionary struggle on the part of the rank and file soldiering classes. In the statement, Faulkner disavows any faith in "nations or governments or ideologies" as defenders against war or as tools through which wars might finally end. Rather, he implores "simple human beings vulnerable to death and injury," the ones who "will be the first to be destroyed," to become conscious of their power to confront and overrun the warmakers.

Faulkner's statement was surely inappropriate for America's Nobel Laureate, and Saxe Commins was no doubt attempting to protect Faulkner from inevitably hostile responses to this highly potent interpretation of his work. Claiming "that pacifism does not work" and calling upon citizens to "use the fire itself to destroy the fire" are far from what is expected of national spokespersons or canonized authors. What did Faulkner mean? Was he speaking abstractly? Are "war" and "fight" and "destroy" on the same level of meaning as "honor" and "pity" and "compassion"? That idea seems unlikely, especially given the actual content of *A Fable*.

When Commins censored the prefatory note, Faulkner did not insist on it. Rather, he allowed the statement to find obscurity and never again referred to its inflammatory contents. It is a pattern Faulkner would repeat in the years ahead. In his art, Faulkner was bold and confrontational. In his life, however, when he realized that his ideas were too radical to be heard or accepted, he simply withdrew. His writing is aggressive, challenging, and relentless—and *A Fable* may be his most aggressive, most challenging, and most relentless novel. Yet the man William Faulkner always preferred privacy to challenge, and he would back down or even reverse himself verbally rather than force a confrontation. He was no authoritarian and was uneasy even with the literary authority conferred upon him by the Nobel Prize. These qualities made Faulkner the survivor that he certainly was, and they also opened him to charges of hypocrisy or weakness. As he often said, however, his single ambition was to write, not to lead a mass movement or to be a public spokesperson. To write, he needed the privacy secured by being nonconfrontational and withdrawn. I suspect, then, that the prefatory statement to *A Fable* was written in desperation, the kind Joseph Blotner describes when he says that Faulkner was "seized with" anxieties to make others understand the novel. The prefatory statement represents a moment of weakness, in a sense, when Faulkner let down his authorial guard and laid his cards on the table. He then picked them up quickly. In the second paragraph of the same statement, Faulkner retreated to a safe distance from the implications of his novel. Even Saxe Commins found something to salvage from this half when he wrote his dustjacket copy.

In the second part of the prefatory statement to *A Fable*, Faulkner outlines what he called "the trinity of man's conscience" as it is presented in *A Fable* by Levine, the Quartermaster General, and the Runner. Levine, according to Faulkner, "symbolizes the nihilistic third" of conscience which, like Quentin Compson, "sees evil and refuses to accept it by destroying himself." The Quartermaster General "symbolizes the passive third." Like Harry Wilbourne, the Quartermaster General sees evil and grieves for it, but his grief leaves the world unchallenged. Finally, there is the "active third" of conscience, the rebellious third. The Runner, whom Faulkner calls "the living scar," says in the last scene, " 'I'm not going to die—never.' i.e., there is evil in the world and I'm going to do something about it." Faulkner never paraphrased the first part of the suppressed statement, but he would often in the years ahead employ the "trinity of conscience" explanation when called upon to discuss the statement in public. In fact, it became one of what Stephen Longstreet would call Faulkner's "lines."[24] It was a good line. It met the criteria of Faulkner's image as created and perpetuated by leading critics of his era and certainly met the criteria of a Cold War culture bent on *being* the "active third" in a world divided into three parts: capitalist, communist, and developing. Amputated from the paragraph that precedes it, however, the line is a gross misunderstanding of the novel. As early as 1943, Faulkner had expressed fears that his fable, "an indictment of war perhaps, and for that reason may not be acceptable now," would be misunderstood.[25] His fears proved well founded.

In 1954, war was known to bring death home and destruction abroad, but it was also associated with prosperity. Moreover, limited war had proved necessary to contain communist aggression. A permanent war footing and a growing military and corporate partnership were becoming the acceptable price to pay to balance power with the nation's adversaries and to assure the American way of life. Faulkner's anti-authoritarian and insurrectionist stand on war would find no audience, not even with the man editing his novel about authoritarianism and insurrection. It was heresy, and it was suppressed. Rather than challenge Commins and personally dispute the cultural and critical hegemony against which he wrote, Faulkner yielded. He repeated the more abstract, acceptable portion of his statement and survived to continue writing.

In the first half of his "preface" to *A Fable,* Faulkner clearly sees the novel as a model of rebellion, insurrection, and anti-authoritarianism. He chose the Christ story as the vehicle to express these models because he believed that human potentiality is the message of Christ. The Christ story preceded the writing of the novel, after all, so what we have in *A Fable* is Faulkner's meditation on the significance of the life of Jesus Christ, in essence, his personal Christian apocrypha. One biblical scholar has asked whether to write "a Gospel for our time, in which Christ speaks to us directly in our present situation, is that not perhaps even laudable?" Per Beskow recounts numerous apocryphal accounts of the Christian savior, including stories of Christ as vegetarian, nature healer, magician, homosexual, and woman. There are no limits to the "inventions," Beskow announces, that have followed the official, Gospel inventions we have come to accept as canonical. Beskow addresses the issue of retelling Christ's story today, and his conclusions are particularly applicable to Faulkner's Christian apocrypha.

> The objection that this would be an inauthentic Gospel is somewhat difficult to uphold, if we consider how the exegetes used to dismiss parts of our canonical Gospels as "congregational theology," "creations by the primitive church," "secondary insertions," and "redactional framework." If the primitive Church was allowed to make inventions about Jesus within good conscience, why are we forbidden to do it?[26]

Following the novel's publication, Faulkner explained his use of the Christian story as "one of the best stories that man has invented, assuming that he did invent the story, and of course it will recur."[27] Faulkner's understanding of Christ is close to a gnostic conception, one in which Christ's life exists not *historically*—not in some completed past—but eternally and presently. What mattered to gnostic Christians was not the literal vision of Christ historically but the spiritual vision of Christ experienced in the present. Inventions inspired inventions, and they were absolutely necessary to place the Christ story in a recognizable context. Faulkner's setting was that of war because warfare, it seemed, was becoming his culture's primary means of expressing and understanding itself. The Christ story was the "best" story by which to articulate his fable of man's existence, "a good one that people could understand and believe, in order to tell something that I was trying to tell."[28]

Faulkner's apocryphal Gospel, however, has remained as misunderstood and obscure as Faulkner apparently believed the story of Christ remained in his time. The authorities, the "lords and proprietors" of civilization, have generally cited Christ's emblematic suffering and emphasized a passive, pacifistic message as among Christ's greatest gifts to humankind. Faulkner, on the other hand, chose to stress Christ's vitality as a model for rebellion and insurrection against authority.[29] In the ten years over which he wrote *A Fable*, the United States emerged as a world power on a permanent war footing, wielding the threat of atomic weapons in order to secure a militaristic global peace. If anything, the situation that gave rise to the fable of Christian civilization only worsened as he wrote the novel—a protracted state of war contributing, perhaps, to a protracted effort to sublimate the actual situation facing the world into an apocryphal Christian Gospel. "Perhaps some unknown authors will create something new about Jesus in the future, and in a form unknown to us," writes the speculative Beskow. "The time of myths is not ended, and perhaps in the future people will be filled with a new Jesus vision that will make our present faith seem powerless and impoverished."[30] This is precisely what Faulkner attempts in *A Fable:* to renew our faith in our "best story" by supplanting Christ as a figure of authoritarian control and by replacing the martyr with the rebel. *A Fable* is Faulkner's most blatantly anti-authoritarian and anti-establishmentarian novel. It defines the human spirit as that dimension of the human experience that rebels against limitation and definition. It is Faulkner's "Gospel for our time," a time when global existence is threatened by the degeneration of Christianity into authoritarian structures of repression, death, and destruction.

◆ Articulations and Allegories

A Fable is not about a mutiny or a failed attack during World War I. This action takes place prior to the events of the text itself. Instead, it is about human reaction to such an event. The text opens with the mass reaction of the Paris citizenry to news of a rebellion in the ranks, and successive perspectives shift from infantry to aviators to officers and generals, and to the kinfolk of those involved in the rebellion. Even the Christian apocrypha is but one more reaction to or interpretation of the event—this time it is the author's—one more way in which a person might respond to such a fantastic episode. The actual event, the mutiny, is told over and over again. The story is narrated, quoted, and allegorized until *A Fable* emerges as a meditation on rebellion. As the Runner says, "we dont know what and we are not going to know what" happened at the Front when the regiment refused to fight. "Besides, it doesn't matter what happened. What matters is, what happens afterwards" (65). Through their thoughts on the event, various characters reach conclusions and formulate interpretations, some fatal, as in the case of Levine, and others reinforcing, as with the Old General. *A Fable* clarifies Faulkner's position that it is not human events that move people, but how those events are interpreted and fit into the pattern of historical memory. The novel works against literalism and literal interpretations, for instance. It challenges General Gragnon's refusal to believe in the characters of the book he is reading ("besides being in another country and long ago and therefore even if they had been real, they could never impinge, affect, the course of his life and its destruction" [40]) and supports the position that as symbol nothing dies, nothing is irrelevant. The Arch of Triumph, for example, is understood to be "invincible and impervious, to endure forever not because it was stone nor even because of its rhythm and symmetry but because of its symbolism" (367). In *A Fable,* Faulkner is concerned with symbolism, but not the kind of symbolism invested in public monuments. Indeed, *A Fable* concerns itself, on a much grander level than *Intruder in the Dust,* with the symbolism of bodies and of human beings: what they stand for, why they act as they do, and who they think they are. In this sense *A Fable* is not a work that *contains* symbols. Rather, it is a work that sees human life itself as symbolic. To say, then, that the Corporal is a Christ symbol is a redundancy.

The Old General speaks directly to the novel's narrative, or figurative strategy, when he says to the Corporal that "we are two articulations, self-elected possibly, anyway elected, anyway postulated" (294). In *A Fable*'s vision of the modern world, human beings are not human beings so much as they are embodiments of offices or classes, postulations of particular purposes or positions, articulations of entrenched arguments or advocacies. When the crowd considers General Gragnon, for example, they do not blame him for the failed attack, even though he is "the postulate of their fear and instrument of their anguish." They absolve Gragnon because he was not only just doing his job, he *believed* in his office. Gragnon was "not only a French soldier, but a brave and faithful one, he could have done nothing else but what he was doing, believed nothing else except what he believed, since it was because of such that France had endured this long" (113). Meditating on Gragnon's devotion, the crowd, as Faulkner articulates their collective position, realizes the significance of Gragnon's dilemma. He is "a soldier: that not only his honor and that of his division, but the honor of the entire profession of command, from files and squads and armies to groups of them, had been compromised" by the rebellion in his ranks (113).

It is the rank and office of the human being that speaks and moves human history in *A Fable,* not the man himself. *A Fable* presents a definitive hierarchy in human affairs, using the military and warfare as its setting because nowhere else is the human hierarchy so well defined and so unmistakably articulated. The ethic of this world is professionalism. When the Runner thinks about the

Sentry, he postulates the modern professional creed, which applies, in principle, to all the "good soldiers" in the novel. "He has ethics," the Runner thinks, "like a banker, not to his clients because they are people, but because they are clients. Not pity: he would bankrupt any—all—of them without turning a hair, once they had accepted the gambit; it's ethics toward his vocation, his trade, his profession. It's purity" (123). Ideology is articulated in *A Fable*, the ideology of bureaucratic professionalism, of hierarchy, of authority, and of corporate control over human behavior.

The military establishment is fruitful ground on which to build a "fable" of power and authority because, like any good fable, its principal, or metaphoric content can be transferred easily to one's own confrontation or experience with power and authority. The meaning of *A Fable*'s bureaucratic allegory is clear. We do not encounter human beings in the modern, corporate environment but articulated offices, each with a pre-established purpose and a pre-defined range of authority. This is why, for instance, there are almost no names given to the office holders in the novel and why most are identified by the name of their job: the Runner, the Sentry, the Quartermaster General, the Corporal, and so on. The man whose precise authority is unknown, who may be omnipotent for all we know, has more than one title but still no name: the Old General, the Generalissimo, the Supreme Commander. The exceptions to the rule of anonymity in *A Fable* are also important. Division Commander *Gragnon*, for example, loses his office in the course of the novel, as his office is used by his superiors for their own higher purposes. Since Gragnon's superiors force him to question his official capacity and to confront the issue of who controls whom, his humanity, in all its confusion, triumphs over his office. The same is true for Levine, who sees though the artificiality of the war itself, and for Marthe, who refuses to believe in the integrity of any man's office. The Reverend Sutterfield, of course, comically changes his name to mimic homophonically the name of his office, and "Tout le Monde" becomes "Tooleyman."

The characters of *A Fable* are, as the Old General says, articulations of their particular places in the human hierarchy or of particular roles in the human drama. The question raised, then, is to what extent human beings are trapped in their "official" capacities and to what degree and for what purposes is escape possible. Even the Corporal, despite his central role in the rebellion, acts through his office. When Pierre Bouc is on his knees, the Corporal urges him to

get up. "Be a man," the Corporal says, but Bouc stays down. "Be a
Zsettlani," but still Bouc will not get up. "Be a soldier," the Corporal
finally says, and Bouc responds (301). The Corporal, like Christ,
goes willingly to his death in accordance with the law of the established order rather than betray his place in that order, despite the fact
that his execution is for the crime of rebelling against that established
order. As such, *A Fable* might be read as a pessimistic book, from the
point of view of advocates of change in the world order. Keen
Butterworth, for instance, interprets *A Fable* as refusing to "condemn those who fight the war, nor those who direct it, in good faith
for just cause. The novel recognizes that violence and conflict, no
matter how regrettable, are unavoidable as long as man remains
man."[31] Such fatalistic readings of *A Fable* are wholly understand-
able given the strength and realism with which Faulkner paints his
dark picture of the forces of authority in the world. *A Fable* acknowledges that there are powerful forces that act against the liberation of
man from his place—his office, his position, his class—but it also
defines with precision the rewards of the struggle against authority
and against fatalistic resignation of the delusion of predetermination.

◆ The Spirit's Antagonist: Authority

In wartime, Faulkner says in *A Fable,* the machinery of civil authority
reveals its true capacity and purpose. "The politicians, the lobbyists,
the owners and publishers of newspapers and the ordained ministers
of churches, and all the other accredited travelling representatives of
the vast solvent organizations and fraternities and movements which
control by coercion or cajolery man's morals and actions and all his
mass value for affirmation or negation—all that vast powerful terror
inspiring representation which, running all democracy's affairs in
peace, comes indeed into its own in war, finding its true apotheosis
then, in iron conclave" (196). Wartime, then, affords a kind of civic
lesson on the principles of authority and obedience which underlie
democracy. As Heinrich Straumann has pointed out, warmaking
and peacemaking must remain in the province of the authorities "lest
the whole significance of the military hierarchy and its concepts of
honor break down."[32] By extension, the basis of all civil authority
depends upon the "proper" and hierarchical execution of the war.
"Because there are rules," the Corp Commander explains to Gragnon. "Our rules. We shall enforce them, or we shall die" (45). The
rules, including "the immutable hierarchy of War" (115), are more
important in *A Fable* than any ideological or territorial struggle

between nations. "Cant you understand," the Corp Commander insists, "either of us, without the other, couldn't exist?" (24). Adversaries though they are in war, the Corp Commander says, the French and German commanders have more in common with each other than they do with their own rank and file. Authority is understood to be transpolitical and transideological.

If what the Corp Commander says is true, and the events in the novel support him, then *A Fable* suggests that the ideological struggle among nations is a false construction fabricated by the authorities in the various nations in order to maintain control over their civil populations. It is not difficult to see why Faulkner found this statement of such vitality in the immediate postwar period— post-Second World War—and also, perhaps, of such obscurity in the early 1950s. It must have been particularly disillusioning to work at perfecting the novel during the latest red scare in America and during the Army–McCarthy hearings. In Faulkner's imagination, his "fable" was being played out on the American national scene. At all costs, the Corp Commander explains, the masses must not suspect that the real power lies with them, not with their leaders. "They may even stop the wars, as they have done before and will again," he says, "ours merely to guard them from the knowledge that it was actually they who accomplished the act. Let the whole vast moil and seethe of man confederate in stopping war if they wish, so long as we can prevent them learning that they have done so" (45). The Corp Commander's principle of leadership in the modern state has particular relevance to the American demobilization in Vietnam, one calculated to avoid the appearance of being dictated by the domestic anti-war movement and being instead wholly under the control and timing of the American Commander in Chief.

The principles of authority in *A Fable* and the maintenance of hierarchy precede, in importance and priority, the needs and interests of those who are, in theory, represented or defended by the authorities. Simple entrance into the military establishment teaches the individual these priorities. Even the common criminal, Lapin, knows that once in uniform "you were free of cops and civilians and the whole human race" (304). The civilian population becomes, in the eyes of the authoritarian military establishment, an obstacle and a complication. The Sergeant–Major, for example, has spent twenty years as a soldier and views the civilian world from his position of "unchallengeable immunity, with a sort of contempt as alien intruders" (8). He knows that by joining the military "he had sold his

birthright in the race of man" (9). There is in *A Fable* something
inherently dehumanizing in exercising authority by virtue of office,
something in the authoritarian act which alienates the person from
the spirit. The higher in rank a person rises in the military hierarchy,
moreover, the further he is removed from the human experience.[33]
The Runner observes "that the biped successful enough to become a
general has ceased to be a German or British or American or Italian
or French one almost as soon as it never was a human one" (267). In
a universe where a human being is the articulation of an office, it
follows that the greater the office and the louder the postulate, the
more muted will be the human spirit beneath the uniform. When the
German General responds to the Generalissimo's offer of "an alternative to chaos" (279) and breakdown of authority, he acts in the
interests of his office. During the meeting of the adversary generals,
the German articulates the principle of authority which *A Fable*
presents as responsible for so much injustice. "Because I am a soldier
first, then a German, then—or hope to be—a victorious German.
But that is not even second, only third. Because this," and he points
to his uniform, "is more important than any German or even victory" (260), and more important, presumably, than even the "I," or
whoever this man is.

The exercise of authority in *A Fable* is equivalent to the traditional conception of "losing one's soul" or trading it to some demon.
Delmore Schwartz has argued that the Old General has convinced
himself, in order to rule supremely, "that human beings are worth-
less" and displays an "inexhaustible contempt for everything truly
human."[34] Despite criticism to the contrary,[35] the textual evidence
in Faulkner's novel supports Schwartz's contention that the Old
General is an evil force against which good human forces ought to
fight. Whether we view the Old General as Satan or as God or as
some dualistic, fatalistic Both depends not so much on our understanding of theology but of authority. The Quartermaster General,
for one, describes the Old General as a recurring product of democracy when he tells him, long before his ascension to power, that his
day will inevitably come. "It will be a new time, a new age, a new
century which doesn't even remember our old passions and failures,"
the Quartermaster General explains. The General, he says, will return and take power after he, and the authoritarian principles he
represents, will have seemed to have disappeared from the world. By
that time, "those who feared you once will have watched you pass
out of enmity to amazement: to contempt: to unreality, and at last

out of your race and kind altogether, into the dusty room of literature" (222). Out of that "dusty room of literature" Faulkner took *A Fable* and placed it in fearful opposition to fixed authority and against the denial of humanity by the hierarchies and established orders that dominate the human spirit. As Marthe says to the Old General, "In you is something which all earth had better beware and dread and be afraid of" (241).

The Old General is to be feared and dreaded because he knows human nature so well and despises it so deeply that he is perfectly suited to trampel upon it and enslave it. The Quartermaster General fears the Old General himself but will not, or does not know how to stop him. When he realizes that his failure to act against the Old General is in reality acquiescence to the Generalissimo's principles, he offers to resign. The Old General regains his support, temporarily, with his own placative fatalism when he tells the Quartermaster General about Polcheck and the inevitable betrayal. This fatalism informs the whole of the Old General's beliefs and accounts for his having "won the right to believe in nothing whatever save man's deathless folly" (196). This fatalism—as good a synonym as any for "evil" in *A Fable*—also leads the Old General to describe war as "a vice so long engrained in man as to have become an honorable tenet of his behavior and the national altar of his love and bloodshed and glorious sacrifice" (291). The strategy with which the Old General subdues the Quartermaster General is turned on the Corporal with equal effectiveness, but this time it is not fatalism so much as careful manipulation of the Corporal's principles that gives the Old General his rhetorical victory. The Generalissimo's statement to the Corporal is so convincing and has such a ring of truth to it because it is, as Faulkner was doubtlessly aware, a skillful presentation of idealistic and humanistic principles by an authority figure intent on undermining their significance. In other words, the Old General takes the Corporal's position as defender of man and turns it around to serve the purposes of man's continued subjugation. He insists, for example, that the two realms which he and the Corporal represent ("this mundane earth" and "man's baseless hopes") "can even exist side by side together" had not the Corporal's "interfered" with his (294). This does not stop the Old General, however, from offering to join forces with the Corporal in order to rule the world more completely. "You will be God, holding him forever through a far, far stronger ingredient than his simple lusts and appetites," which is the basis of mundane authority such as that which the Old General wields, but "by his triumphant and irradicable folly, his deathless passion for being led, mystified, and deceived" (295).

What the Old General really means, then, when he tells the Corporal that man "is capable of enduring and will endure" (293) is that man can endure *authority*, and when he says that man will "prevail," he means survive even his reign. As Supreme Commander, the Old General must believe that man will "endure" him, or else he would have to question his own position. He will make a martyr out of the Corporal, as he tells the Quartermaster General, because he knows the importance of martyrs in keeping strong the capacity of man to endure authority. The Old General realizes that he maintains his ruling position by strategic command, but he also reserves a leader's healthy respect for the capabilities of his subjects. "I dont fear man," he tells the Corporal. "I do better: I respect and admire him. And pride: I am ten times prouder of that immortality which he does possess than even he of that heavenly one of his delusions" (299). The strength and the entrenched nature of the Old General's authority is such that he will successfully incorporate the Corporal's rebellion and make it serve his own purposes. He welcomes the rebellion as a test of his authority and of his subjects' vitality; he crushes it as an exercise and demonstration of his power and, and, this is the truly remarkable aspect, as evidence of man's immortality. The leadership in *A Fable* successfully defuses challenges to its authority by taking the language of the rebel and the life of the martyr—of the Christ—and turning them back on the masses, actually using them to justify the authority of the ruling powers.

The rhetorical vacuity of the Old General's statements ("Because I believe in man within his capacities and limitations," for example, is not faith but cynicism) is matched only by his redundancies. "I not only believe he is capable of enduring and will endure," the Old General pronounces, "but that he must endure, at least until he himself invents evolves produces a better tool than he to substitute for himself" (293). What the Old General actually says here is that man "must" be immortal because if he is not, he will die away. In other words, he "must" endure because if he does not, he will not. Through the representation of the Old General, Faulkner gives a supreme example of the ideological double-talk and windy rhetoric common to modern authoritarian hyperbole. It is a rhetoric that adopts for its own purposes the words and phrases which ordinarily would signify the very opposite of what the authority represents. In doing so, the authority trivializes the words he uses by divesting them of meaning, as the Old General does with his pontifications, and actually uses the words as weapons against those who maintain a faith in human communication. It is no peculiarity that the Old General, in meeting with the Corporal, does all the talking. No words can affect the Generalissimo because he uses words as he uses everything else at his disposal: as tools to maintain his own authority. Impervious to rebellion, he is equally immune to the meaning of words. In the Old General, Faulkner has created a prototype not of the modern demagogue but of the modern politico, who is in office to maintain not some principle or in the name of some consituency, but to maintain the authority necessary to remain in office. The Generalissimo is the "apotheosis" of the democratic system.

♦ The Spirit's Protagonist: Rebellion

Standing in opposition to the Old General is not so much the Corporal, who does counter the Old General's cynicism, as it is the Runner. Where the Old General is Supreme Commander, the Runner is wholly anti-authoritarian. He wants to be rid of the single pip that would give him some authority over other men. Where the Old General despises all things human but professes admiration for man, the Runner loves humankind but professes disdain and wants to be free of humanity (51). His disdain is false, however; it is only a mask for his vulnerable faith in man's potential. When he meditates on the mutiny, he knows "it would not matter whether Authority knew about it or not, since even ruthless and all powerful and unchallengeable Authority would be impotent before that massed unresisting undemanding passivity" (57). What turns this faith sour is the Runner's knowledge that man has powers he does not use. When the old private tells the Runner that "all we ever needed to do was just to say, Enough of this" (56), it sinks in profoundly. The Runner thus realizes Christ's message: *"All you have to do,"* he thinks, *"all He ever asked and died for eighteen hundred and eighty-five years ago"* (61).

The Runner's awareness of man's potentiality leads him to his act of rebellion, and through his rebellion comes, in Camus' words, "the sudden, dazzling perception that there is something in man with which he can identify himself, if only for a moment."[36] This perception—which, in Faulkner's apocryphal Gospel, we might call the recognition of the spirit—is shared by the cynical Sentry, who, until his involvement with the Runner, had been blind to his own humanity. When the Sentry sees the British and German soldiers being murdered by their respective artillery, he yells, "No! Not to us!," which Faulkner identifies as "the first time in his life probably" that "he had said 'we' and not 'I' " (271). The Runner's anti-authoritarian attitude is undaunted by the defeat of the second mutiny, and his "They cant kill us! They cant! Not dare not: cant," is the second strongest expression of rebellion in the novel. When the Runner later flings the Corporal's medals into the Old General's coffin, his anti-authoritarianism reaches a powerful crescendo. "You helped carry the torch of man into that twilight where he shall be no more; these are his epitaphs," and the Runner voices the respective war slogans of France, "They shall not pass"; of America, "My country right or wrong"; and of Britain, "Here is a spot which is forever England" (369). These slogans, the "patriotic nonsense" of the authorities who waged the effort which destroyed man's spirit, are all that is left of the spirit they were to embody. It is here that the rebel claims his immortality, not be offering an epitaph to rebellion but by denying entirely the death of the spirit. His rebellion, born of "a prolonged protest against death," in Camus' formulation, "a violent accusation against the universal death penalty,"[37] is expressed, finally, as the Runner's appeal to the human spirit: "I'm not going to die," he testifies. "Never" (370).

The radicalization of the Runner—who, when we first meet him, says he abhors man—is the motivation behind the telling of the long story known independently as "Notes on a Horsethief."[38] Although, as Faulkner said himself, the story "is really one single adjective clause describing a man,"[39] the Sentry, the story does have a profound effect on the Runner. It is true that Sutterfield tells the Runner the story of the three-legged horse to explain his connection to and interest in the Sentry. Through the story of the racehorse, however, the Runner realizes the significance of the Corporal's mutiny. "The horse is thus a stupendous narrative metaphor," according to Delmore Schwartz, "since he is the cause of belief and nobility in other human beings just as the illiterate corporal is"[40] As such, the "Notes on a Horsethief" metaphor is testimony to Faulkner's profound belief in the power of the tale and of the importance of fabulation and figuration to human intelligence. Through the telling of this particular tale a bond is formed between the Runner and Sutterfield. When the Runner is ready to make his move into "radical politics" and follow the Corporal's example of rebellion, he knows he can count on Sutterfield's support. In turn, both men are confident that with a little prodding the Sentry will be with them in their efforts to disrupt the war further.

Faulkner's employment of "Notes on a Horsethief" displays his belief in the power of human "fables" to provide the bonds of faith and confidence necessary to promote human action. It explains as well his attraction to the story of Christ (civilization's "masterpiece" [219]) as the basis for his most radically anti-authoritarian novel. The way we understand our most widely told story, Faulkner implies, will determine to a large degree the range of action we believe is available to us. If God's Child represents rebellion, for instance, the world might appear differently from the way it does if the Child represents sacrifice or submission. In this sense *A Fable* is unmistakably Faulkner's attempt to redefine, not refer to, the significance of the life and death of Jesus Christ.[41]

When Sutterfield begins to tell the Runner the story of the crippled racehorse, the Runner immediately knows why he must listen to the tale. "A protagonist," he says. "If I am to run with the hare and the hounds, I must have a protagonist" (127). In other words, if the Runner is going to become involved in any kind of human action, particularly a rebellious one, he must believe in something. This story, this "love story" as Faulkner describes it in the text (127), will provide the Runner with a basis of faith. The tale of the three-legged horse is descended, Faulkner tells us, from "man's own legend beginning when his first paired children lost well the world and from which paired prototypes they still challenged paradise" (129). From the beginning of time, human beings have exchanged stories about lost worlds, stories that "challenged paradise" and formed bonds among them. The existence and repetition of these stories, including this one about the racehorse, prove the existence of a human spirit which transcends the physical body. Through the tale the spirit is transmitted, "the doomed glorious frenzy of a love story, pursued . . . by its own inherent doom, since, being immortal, the story, the legend," Faulkner asserts, "was not to be owned by any one of the pairs who added to its shining and tragic increment, but only to be used, passed through, by each in their doomed and homeless turn" (129). Human beings may all suffer the "universal death penalty,"[42] but their belief in the possibility of adding to the "shining and tragic increment" of the legend, or the history of human endeavor, props them up in life. Until the Runner has a "protagonist," or a view of human events in which someone like himself can be effective, he does not have the faith necessary to act.

The "protagonist" of the Runner's radicalization comes in the form of the crippled racehorse. The horse was a "champion," Sutterfield tells him, "it never belonged to no man" but rather inspired "things and people" to belong to or believe in it (126). Its crippled and abused body never maimed its spirit. Those who stole the horse likewise did so in the name of its spirit, not its body. "The reason was so that it could run," the deputy explains, "keep on running, keep on losing races at least, finish races at least even if it did have to run them on three legs, did run them on three legs because it was a giant and didn't need even three legs to run them on but only one with a hoof at the end to qualify as a horse" (137). In stealing the racehorse, the three grooms deliberately break a property law in the name of a higher law, which is, by *A Fable*'s definition, the mark of freedom. "The mark of a free man," Faulkner narrates, "was his right to say *no* for no other reason except *no*" (145–46). Sutterfield, however, does not define his "higher law" as God's or anything ethereal or esoteric but simply as "man's" interest. He bears witness, he tells the lawyer, not simply to God but more importantly, to his fellows. "To man," the Reverend Sutterfield says. "God dont need me. I bears witness to Him of course, but my main witness is to man" (152). By these words he answers the Old General's cynicism about man's delusive faith in God's salvation with a brand of activism which assumes that God expects men to act, not merely to pray or to hope.

Sutterfield's tale and his affirmation that rebellion is "the mark of a free man" provide the Runner with an understanding of human history and a faith in human potentiality. He departs Sutterfield's office knowing what he needs. "To believe," he tells himself. "Not in anything: just to believe." He leaves Sutterfield wanting to "believe"—the crucial first step towards faith, as Faulkner expressed it in *Requiem for a Nun*. "Do you know what the loneliest experience of all is?" he asks Sutterfield. "But of course you do: you just said so. It's breathing" (171–72). From his desire to believe in man's ability to affect history—his belief in the spirit—and from his consciousness of man's ultimate self-reliance is born the Runner as Faulknerian rebel. When the Runner learns about the blank shells in the staged attempt to "shoot down" the German General, he is moved, finally, to act. Faulkner effectively and realistically indicates the powerful forces of authority which outnumber the Runner by ending the Runner's anti-war action in a barrage of artillery fire from both sides of the barbed wire. The Runner does survive, of course, as does his story—the story of a rebellion inspired by a "love story" and modelled on a man's (a Christ's) conspiratorial rebellion against the warmakers. In the Runner is something which the Old General, to borrow Marthe's words, "had better beware and dread and be afraid of."

♦ The Spirit's Potential: The Masses

If there is a sin or a failing among human beings portrayed in *A Fable*, it is their tendency to suppress their need to act in futile hoping.[43] It is "the baseless hoping which is the diet of weaklings" (19) or, as the Runner says, "that sort of masturbation about the human race people call hoping" (51) which is responsible for the widespread hopelessness in the world. Organized religion, Faulkner argues, only enforces the lethargy of the masses. Christ's "poetic metaphor" about building His church, or "airy faith," upon a rock, or "unstable unconstant heart," has been perverted into a mandate for an established church. The priest, in his meeting with the Corporal, explains that the church represents "an *establishment*, a morality of behavior. . . . Not *snared* in that frail web of hopes and fears and aspirations which man calls his heart, but *fixed, established*" (308). Clearly, in Faulkner's terms, a faith that is "fixed" and not in motion, "established" and not in constant change, is no living thing. Faith in the hands of the established church turns into authority, living not for man's spirit in the name of the Child Christ but established for the control of men in the name of the Lord, Ruler Christ. All that is left to the faithful under these circumstances is hope, the baseless, masturbatory delusions of a regimented people. Against this gruesome reference Faulkner's *A Fable* presents its Christian apocrypha.

A Fable begins with a minor but decisive confrontation between the mob in Paris and the military, and the military wins. In the opening scene, the crowd confronts the cavalry, led by the Sergeant–Major, in its effort to find out what is going on with the mutinous regiment. The Sergeant–Major is unable to stop the advancing mob, for his orders were issued "too late: the crowd had already underswept the military" (4). The cavalry loses ground, but the Sergeant–Major moves forward, "into and through the moving crowd" in an attempt to assert his authority. The mob simply keeps surging toward the boulevard, flinging aside the cavalry. In the boulevard, however, the crowd meets up with "a whole battalion" dispatched there to control it, "armed except for packs . . . led by a light tank with its visor closed for action." These forces push and cajole the crowd "until at last the whole boulevard . . . was clear and empty again between the two thin lines of bayonnetted rifles" (5). In the very first scene of *A Fable* the mass of humanity is portrayed as forced, regimented, and controlled by powers which represent authority and order.

The forces of authority depend upon the malleability of the masses to assure their continued domination. Although Faulkner portrays the crowd as "almost orderly, merely irresistible in the concord of its frail components like a wave in its drops" (4), the military representatives in the boulevard must impose their own definition of order on the mob so that the military's purposes—the arrival of the allied commanding generals—will run unimpeded. "It is man who is our enemy," the Corp Commander tells Gragnon, "the vast seething moiling spiritless mass of him." The Corp Commander calls the mutiny an "occupational hazard" of exercising authority. "In one more little instant," he explains, the rebellious regiment "might have changed the world's face. But they never do. They collapse, as yours did this morning. They always will. But not us," he concludes, expressing the confidence of authority. "We will even drag them willy-nilly up again, in time, and they will collapse again. But not us. It wont be us" (25). The Corp Commander's shrewd and cynical observations contribute to the aura of gloom which threatens to overshadow the meaning of *A Fable*. He tells Gragnon that the authorities must enforce the belief among the masses "that tomorrow they will end it; then they wont begin to ponder if perhaps today they can." It is baseless hope, he suggests, which must be maintained in the masses to keep them submissive. "Tomorrow," the Corp Commander continues, miming the prayers of the people. "And still tomorrow. And again tomorrow. That's the hope you will vest in them" (46).

Against this grim portrayal of human hopelessness Faulkner presents his own faith in the "weary and indefatigable" masses, "indomitable in their capacity not alone for endurance but for frenzy as well" (111). In "Notes on a Horsethief," Faulkner's belief in the resiliency and the resistence of "the crowd" is presented through the meditations of the lawyer, who thinks that what appears to be passivity among men and women is, in fact, potentiality. "They are just watching, waiting for something," he thinks. Realizing that there exists "some bond between or from man to man" (139) which is stronger than his common subjugation to authority, the lawyer sees "that on his own feet and in motion, he is terrible." He is humbled and proud of his humanity when he envisions "the mass of him moving of itself in one direction" and with a single, binding purpose. One of the functions of the "Horsethief" story is to remind us of the capacity for mass action.

There is no question, however, that in *A Fable* the human spirit is under siege. Although the possibilities for mass action remain, they are increasingly curtailed by the forces of authority which regiment behavior and thought. In a crucial passage, the lawyer offers this meditation on man:

> Threatful only in locomotion and dangerous only in silence; neither in lust nor appetite nor greed lay wombed the potency of his threat, but in silence and meditation: his ability to move *en masse* at his own impulse, and silence in which to fall into thought and then action as into an open manhole; with exhaltation, too, since none know this better than the lords and proprietors of his massed breathing, the hero-giant precentors of his seething moil, who used his spendthrift potency in the very act of curbing and directing it, and ever had and ever would (157–58).

The "masses" exist in *A Fable* as the embodiment of the spirit's potential. This potential is both good and evil, as Sutterfield explains to the Runner. "Evil is a part of man, evil and sin and cowardice, the same as repentence and being brave." Believing in the human spirit means believing that "man is capable of all of them, or he aint capable of none" (171). The "lords and proprietors" know this, and for that reason keep a constant vigilance over the masses to ensure their positions of authority and command. For this reason even silence must be filled with the reminder of external authority. In silence, individuals—such as the Runner—contemplate and prepare to act. To accomplish complete control over men and women, "the silence must be conquered too: the silence in which man had space to think and in consequence act" (158). Significantly, the "lords and proprietors" know that in order to control the masses, individual thought must be limited to responsiveness.

It is in the name of silence that Faulkner made his strongest plea for the vitality of the human spirit. Characteristic of his faith in man, Faulkner does not address "the masses" in *A Fable*, nor does he puff up any more delusive beliefs about the natural benevolence of the mass of humanity. In *A Fable*, Faulkner works against such naive and simplistic illusions. Similar to his disdain for lectures and his approval of dialogue, Faulkner's radicalism comes not in a mass appeal for rebellious action but in a quiet challenge to the reader through his text. One of the reasons *A Fable* is so difficult to read is that it has among its narrative strategies the regeneration of thought and reflection about human circumstances. Effective action against domination and endless war begins, for Faulkner, not with the trading of one mass delusion for another or one set of redundant and simplistic platitudes for another set of slogans and aphorisms about Humanity and Peace and Jesus. It begins, instead, with the purposeful action of men and women to challenge authority. The "masses" simply do not exist in *A Fable* unless they are massed together to do something—charging the boulevard in Paris, refusing to make war at the Front, supporting the horsethief in Mississippi. Hence, it is not true that Faulkner "disliked, even despised humanity acting in mass"[44] but that he did not *believe* in the masses as anything other than groups of purposeful individuals. To address human beings as "the masses" is to take an authoritarian stance with the assumption, as voiced by the Corp Commander, that the masses can and ought to be controlled. To address human beings as individuals—as individual manifestations of the human spirit—is to take a subversive stance with the assumption, as voiced by the Runner, that the individual can and ought to consider him or herself the hinge on which the human drama depends. With this kind of faith, a man might actually believe, as the Runner did, that he can succeed where his predecessors had failed. It is precisely this kind of faith which moved Faulkner throughout his career and informs his fiction.

◆ Legacy: *A Fable* in Context

In *A Fable*, a Christian apocrypha is imposed on a World War I tale and published in the political era of post-World War II America. The book is primarily concerned with the "Again" of warfare and of ideological rivalry, an "Again" which Faulkner experienced in his own lifetime. *A Fable* was written about World War I, but it is addressed to the common experience of World War II. It makes war a preposterous undertaking, since the massive, impressive, inexhaustible capacity of humanity to organize, regiment, and sustain mass action is perverted into thoroughly destructive and spiritually voided ends. When the Old General looks into the future in his monologue to the Corporal, he sees the present scene in 1954 as Faulkner understood it. In the atomic and then the nuclear age, technologies will do battle, the Old General predicts, and the atmosphere will be "filled with the inflectionless uproar of the two mechanical voices bellowing at each other in polysyllable or verbless patriotic nonsense" (299). This is the scene to which Faulkner utters the "no" of *A Fable* and against the artificial international rivalry which emerged in the post-war world as "an alternative to chaos." After the war a man asks the soldiers, "Isn't the war over?" to which the Sergeant–Major replies, "But not the Army. . . . How can you expect peace to put an end to an army when even war cant?" (329).

The most sustained speech of protest against militarism, hierarchy, and authoritarianism in general comes from Marthe, the Corporal's half-sister. Her speech to the Old General amounts to an articulation of feminist hostility toward, and protest against, the masculinist rapine and anger that define civilization. Her indignation is aimed at the patriarchal prerogative represented by the Old General, a man who fathered a child by her mother and had no obligation to either the mother or the child. The Old General, with the power to create and destroy but not the obligation to sustain and nurture, embodies, in Marthe's eyes, all that is repressive and cruel in her civilization. Her rage is consciously withheld from the Generalissimo personally ("Because, that's not enough," she says [242]) and is unleashed on the self-serving power he represents.

What the Old General represents, to Marthe, are the events and "circumstances" which kept her mother, and keep Marthe in her turn, oppressed by outside forces. The Old General seems to have been "sent there," to her mother's world thirty-three years before "to find that beautiful and fateful face." Her mother was not "weak in pride and virtue, but rather doomed by that face from them" (242). Because Marthe's mother had something that the Old General, or Authority, wanted, the woman's life and the lives of her children are wholly disrupted. What so often appears as "fate" to people of little or no political power, Faulkner suggests, is merely a manifestation of their dispossession. Marthe's mother had nothing but her "beautiful" face to call her own, but no possession is immune from the "lords and proprietors" of the state.

Marthe's protest to the Old General expands into a feminist challenge to the masculinist interpretation of the Christ story.[45] The Generalissimo arrived in her mother's life, Marthe says, "to create a son for one of you to condemn to death as though to save the earth, save the world, save man's history, save mankind" (242). This is the same perspective from which Temple Stevens asks in *Requiem for a Nun* what kind of God would sacrifice a child to save a soul. It is an articulation of an objection to Christian patriarchy, asking not simply what kind of God would create life to extinguish it in the name of salvation, but what kind of God would also destroy the Son to preserve the Father's authority. "You will never believe, perhaps you dare not risk it, chance it, that he would have never made any claim on you," Marthe says to the Old General (254). The Generalissimo, as Supreme Commander, cannot risk believing that "people are really kind, they really are capable of pity and compassion for the weak and orphaned and helpless," Marthe continues, because he "cannot, dare not believe that: who dare believe only that people are to be bought and used empty and then thrown away" (246). Through Marthe, the Old General is portrayed as the embodiment of all the structures of Authority: religious, political, social, and sexual. Marthe recognizes him, furthermore, as an authority figure whose primary interest is the perpetuation of his authority.

Marthe's bravery before the Old General is a model of that courage of which the Corporal himself speaks when he tells the Generalissimo, "Dont be afraid. . . . There's nothing to be afraid of. Nothing worth it" (297). This statement, which has been referred to as the novel's "only true affirmation,"[46] is the Corporal's one significant rebuttal to the Old General's doomsday monologue. It at once denies the authority of Authority and postulates the immortality of the human spirit. When he refuses to "take the earth" (294), as the Old General offers, the Corporal claims he acts out of loyalty to his fellow rebels. What he is really saying is that it is not worth it. The Corporal's short life in opposition to all that the Old General represents is worth more than a prolonged mortality as his ally. The Old General has faith in nothing, as Faulkner narrates, "with a face wise, intelligent, and unbelieving, who no longer believed in anything but his own delusions and his intelligence and his limitless power" (11). The Corporal's faith lies in the immortality of the rebellious spirit; furthermore; his faith assures him that his life will not be wasted as long as his story is told. The weight of *A Fable* argues against fear, and for human confidence and the courage to face the day when man "has finally realized" that his fiercest enemy "is not another frail and mortal dissident to his politics or his notions of national boundaries," as the Old General says, "but the very monster itself which he inhabits" (299). The Old General's apocalyptic sermon on the mount is the frightened voice of a leadership incapable of breaking with a tradition which even it recognizes is leading clearly to annihilation. The Corporal's simple affirmation of courage is the insistent voice of the human spirit which will always say no to the apocalypse, will always deny the authority of the Old General as anything but artificial, and will continue to defy death by its rebellion.

1. Albert Camus, *The Rebel: An Essay on Man in Revolt*, translated by Anthony Brewer (New York: Random House, 1956), p. 72; Camus explains how rebellion "lures the individual from his solitude" toward an appreciation of community, where suffering and oppression are common bonds.

2. William Faulkner, *Mosquitos* (New York: Boni and Liveright, 1927; Dell Publishing, 1962), pp. 60–61.

3. Tom Dardis, *Some Time in the Sun: The Hollywood Years of F. Scott Fitzgerald, William Faulkner, Nathaneal West, Aldous Huxley, and James Agee* (New York: Penguin, 1981), p. 138.

4. *Faulkner: A Biography*, p. 1149.

5. Dardis, *Some Time in the Sun*, p. 147.

6. *Selected Letters*, pp. 178–79.

7. *Ibid.*,p. 187.

8. *Ibid.*, p. 180.

9. *Ibid.*, p. 181.

10. *Ibid.*, p. 189.

11. *Ibid.*, p. 192

12. *Ibid.*, pp. 230, 233, 234.

13. See, for example, *ibid.*, p. 188, letter to Cerf and Haas in January 1945: "I am doing a thing which I think is pretty good. Unless I am wrong about it . . . I have grown up at last. . . . Well, I'm doing something different now, so different that I am writing and rewriting, weighing every word, which I never did before; I used to bang it out like an apprentice paper hanger and never look back."

14. See *ibid.*, pp. 233–34.

15. *Ibid.*, p. 237.

16. Comments like these were common: "If the book can be accepted as a fable, which it is to me, the locale and contents wont matter. But then you might not want to publish it," in a letter to Haas in March 1947, *ibid.*, p. 247.

17. *Ibid.*, pp. 248, 253, 256.

18. On Faulkner's monetary anxieties, see his letter of October 1947 to Haas, *ibid.*, p. 258. In February 1948, he wrote Ober that he had "put the big book aside" to begin *Intruder in the Dust*, as yet untitled, *ibid.*, p. 262.

19. *Ibid.*, pp. 361, 355.

20. *Ibid.*, pp. 344, 345, 352.

21. *Ibid.*, p. 344.

22. *Ibid.*, pp. 254–55.

23. The preface is quoted in full and briefly discussed in *Faulkner: A Biography*, pp. 1493–95. It is also included, with a brief note about Commins' reaction to it, in James B. Meriwether, ed., *A Faulkner Miscellany* (Jackson: University Press of Mississippi, 1974), pp. 162–63. Meriwether notes that the explanatory statement was intended not as a formal preface but as "dust jacket copy" or for publicity purposes.

24. See, for example, *Lion in the Garden*, p. 247; and *Faulkner in the University*, p. 62.

25. *Selected Letters*, p. 178

26. Per Beskow, *Strange Tales About Jesus: A Survey of Unfamiliar Gospels* (Philadelphia: Fortress Press, 1983), p. 109.

27. *Faulkner in the University*, p. 117.

28. *Lion in the Garden*, p. 100.

29. For one alternative in support of Faulkner's Christ, see S. G. F. Brandon, *The Trial of Jesus of Nazareth* (New York: Stein and Day, 1968; Scarborough Books, 1979). Brandon argues that Christ was executed for sedition by Roman officials in cooperation with Jewish authorities who saw him as a threat to their control. Christ gathered apostles from among the Zealots, Brandon says, a group "nourished on the Maccabean tradition of holy war against the oppressors of Israel" (141). According to

Brandon, "Jewish leaders were primarily concerned with Jesus as one who menaced the existing social and political order, and not as a religious heretic. His activities in the last few days, especially his attack on the Temple establishment, convinced them that he was a subversive force, for whose suppression the Romans would hold them responsible" (92).

30. Beskow, *Strange Tales About Jesus,* p. 109.

31. Keen Butterworth, *A Critical and Textual Study of Faulkner's A Fable* (Ann Arbor: University of Michigan Research Press, 1983), pp. 15–16. See also Albert J. Guerard, *The Triumph of the Novel: Dickens, Dostoevsky, Faulkner* (New York: Oxford University Press, 1976), pp. 66–67: "The novel is an eloquent pacifist and anti-establishment tract, and a pessimistic one too, which suggests man can learn nothing from history."

32. Heinrich Straumann, "An American Interpretation of Existence: Faulkner's *A Fable,*" in Frederick J. Hoffman and Olga W. Vickery, eds., *William Faulkner: Three Decades of Criticism* (East Lansing: Michigan State University Press, 1951), p. 338.

33. Compare Isaiah Berlin, *The Hedgehog and the Fox: An Essay on Tolstoy's View of History* (New York: Simon and Schuster, 1966 [1953]) p. 17: "The higher soldiers or statesmen are in the pyramid of authority, the farther they must be from its base which consists of those ordinary men and women whose lives are the actual stuff of history; and consequently, the smaller the effects of the words and acts of such remote personages, despite all their theoretical authority, upon that history."

34. Delmore Schwartz, "Faulkner's *A Fable*" (1955), in Donald A. Dike and Davis H. Zucker, eds., *Selected Essays of Delmore Schwartz* (Chicago: University of Chicago Press, 1970), pp. 298–99. Schwartz is on to the Old General's deviousness. "He affirms repeatedly at great rhetorical length that he believes in mankind and admires human beings, a claim which is quite false. . . . It is thus the way in which the general articulates each of the temptations that demonstrates his essential contempt for all human beings including the corporal and himself. . . . Though the general is not a foolish man, he becomes foolish as the interview continues and he must contend with the corporal's simple desire to be faithful to his followers and to himself."

35. See, for example, Straumann, "An American Interpretation," in Hoffman and Vickery, eds., *Three Decades of Criticism,* p. 340, where the Old General is seen uniting "in himself qualities which can lead to the best as well as the worst. He has Godlike as well as satanic traits."

36. Camus, *The Rebel,* p. 14.

37. *Ibid.,* p. 100.

38. "Notes on a Horsethief" was rejected by the *Partisan Review* for publication in 1947 because, according to Blotner, it "read like a first draft—it just wasn't ready for publication." The rejection only added to Faulkner's anxiety about *A Fable* and his taking money from Random House. See *Selected Letters,* pp. 261–62. *Notes on a Horsethief* was published in 1951 by Hodding Carter and Ben Wasson of Levee Press in Greenville, Mississippi; these two men are cited in the acknowledgments to *A Fable.*

39. *Selected Letters,* p. 260, letter to Ober in November 1947.

40. Schwartz, "Faulkner's *A Fable,*" in Dike and Zucker, eds. *Selected Essays of Delmore Schwartz* p. 295.

41. Compare John W. Hunt, *William Faulkner: Art in Theological Tension* (Syracuse, NY: Syracuse University Press, 1954), p. 175: Faulkner "finds the Christian story itself needs to be reformulated"; and Noel Polk, *Faulkner's Requiem for a Nun: A Critical Study* (Bloomington: Indiana University Press, 1981), p. 233: "So in a real sense, perhaps we *do* need sacrifices like the corporal's . . . as symbols of our own freedom to rebel."

42. Camus, *The Rebel,* p. 100.

43. An early formulation of this argument against "hoping" can be found in "The

De Gaulle Story," which bears a number of resemblances to *A Fable*. For example, Georges tells De Gaulle that the Free French "must do more than just hope. . . . Just to wait and hope is not enough, we must do more." Faulkner, *"The De Gaulle Story"*, p. 51.

44. Butterworth, *A Critical and Textual Study*, p. 23.

45. It is significant that Faulkner should cast Marthe, the female, in the role of articulate protest against orthodox hegemony in this apocrypha. Pagels, *The Gnostic Gospels*, p. 68, points out that one result of orthodox centralization of power in the early Christian church was to remove "virtually all the feminine imagery for God" from the canon and all references to the authority of women from the Christian tradition.

46. Schwartz, "Faulkner's *A Fable*," in Dike and Zucker, eds., *Selected Essays of Delmore Schwartz*, p. 303.

4. At Home with the Apocrypha
The Logic of Localism

♦ *Requiem for a Nun:* The Politics of Permanence, Creativity, and Survival

A Fable is Faulkner's answer to the slick, digestable view of his work represented by *The Portable Faulkner.* He had to journey far from Yoknapatawpha and far from his established range of fictional subject matter to make his statement and to gain, perhaps, greater perspective on his own literary purposes. There is no question that "the big book" establishes the parameters and significance of the apocryphal vision. What lay ahead for Faulkner was the application of that clarified vision to Yoknapatawpha. When he completed *A Fable,* he began almost immediately to think about matters closer to home—Mississippi and the South, the *Snopes* trilogy—and about the role of the apocryphal writer in the local community.

A Fable is dedicated to Faulkner's daughter, Jill. In 1953, Faulkner addressed her graduating class and began his speech with the idea of the incomplete world. "What's wrong with the world is, it's not finished yet," he said. "It is not completed to that point where man can put his final signature to the job and say, 'It is finished. We made it, and it works.'" This idea of the unfinished universe is crucial to understanding Faulkner's conception of the world and the way he thought. Also central to his thinking is the conviction that human beings have it within their power to continue to shape the world. "Because only man can complete it," he stated in his Pine Manor Junior College Address. "Not God, but man. It is man's high destiny and proof of his immortality too, that his is the choice between ending the world and effacing it from the long annal of time and space, and completing it."[1] These ideas were very much a part of Faulkner's thinking in 1953, the year he finished *A Fable*. They are also, however, apparent in Faulkner's conceptualization of existence at least as early as his first major novel. In *The Sound and the Fury*, Faulkner confronted the tragic illusion which, as he saw it, leads human beings to attempt to find some kind of completion or resolution to the myriad tensions of life. As early as 1929, Faulkner suggested that the life process was more accurately understood and characterized by incompletion, and that the endeavor to achieve resolution was futile, perhaps even destructive. In *The Sound and the Fury*, Faulkner demonstrates that the only possibilities for resolution in human affairs are aesthetic. The most one could accomplish would be to set the components of one's own surroundings into a controllable pattern, "each in its ordered place."

Faulkner's insistence upon the unfinished world, based as it must be on the principle of the ever-changing, unfinished body,[2] has led some critics to view Faulkner as a man obsessed with defeat. Walter Slatoff has called the author's career a "quest for failure," claiming that Faulkner places a "higher value upon the effort to do the *impossible* than upon accepting human and artistic limitations," and measures "the effort by the extent of the failure" rather than, presumably, the success.[3] There are good reasons for conclusions such as these because the idea of failure is common in Faulkner's comments and observations about himself and his work. He told Robert Coughlin, for example, that his career had "brought a sense of failure" to him because, according to Coughlin, "he has not succeeded in originating a true and great American kind of writing."[4] Similarly, Faulkner repeatedly characterized himself not as a prose writer but as a failed poet who wrote fiction as some sort of consolation.[5] He would also explain his books as successive failures. "The work never matches the dream of perfection the artist had to start with," he said in 1955.[6] The consistency with which Faulkner made statements about failure makes him appear, out of context with his fiction and other clarifying statements, as obsessed with some kind of perverse humility. This "failure line," however, is a signal for a more complex principle in Faulkner's imagination.

All of Faulkner's pronouncements about failure are merely inversions of his principle of the incomplete universe, which informs his work and his attitude toward it. A closer look at one of the failure lines makes this evident. In 1955, he explained to a Japanese audience why he must keep on writing. "Because as I see it, one never does tell the truth as he views it. He tries and each time he fails. And so he tries it again. He knows the next time will not be good either, but he tries it again until he does, and then he quits."[7] The presupposition behind this statement is that nothing is ever "done," that completion is not a part of the life process. Under these terms, the artist only "quits," as Faulkner did, when he dies. The only completion known to the life experience is the end of the life process itself. In Faulkner's imagination, then, the life process was characterized by a "failure" to resolve the tensions of living. Hence, to accept failure was to "succeed" at living, and paradoxically again, the greater the failure the greater the life. If one succeeds, that is, if one finds some resolution—by repetition, by escape, by giving up—then the life process is perverted. Benjy Compson, in clinging to repetition and familiarity, unwittingly represented a perversion of the life process; Quentin Compson did so by negating it; Temple Stevens, as Nancy says in *Requiem for a Nun,* did so by "quitting." To accept the life process for what it is, as an unfinished, ever-changing, ever-creating, eternally moving phenomenon, is to accept, on Faulknerian terms, the glory of human failure.

In Faulkner, the human spirit dwells in a body that is ever-unfinished and in a universe that is never completed, where the possibilities for creation and change are limited only to the human ability to imagine alternatives to inherited reality. In his Pine Manor Address, Faulkner moved logically from the principle of incompleteness to the human capacity to effect change. The artist, he claimed, "can only remind us that we are capable of revolt and change. They do not need, we do not need anyone to tell us what we must revolt against and efface from the earth if we are to live in peace and security on it, because we already know that." Despite the principle of incompletion, much of the world *appears* to be fixed and impervious to change. This is why the impulses of the human spirit are so often manifested in rebellion against that which is characterized not by life but by death, defined not by the living generation but by its forebears. What the artist can do, Faulkner continued, is "remind us that man can revolt and change by telling, showing, reminding us how" to do so.[8] The human spirit, as Faulkner characterized it, is defined by a resistence to completion—its impulse is to move the living, not defend the dead—and by a resistence to death. (Even Addie Bundren, as ready to die as she was, realized at one point in her life that the reason for living was not "to stay dead" but was "the duty to the alive.") All that is complete, established, and fixed in the universe is abhorrent to the human spirit. The very notions of "success," of "achievement," and of "completion" are denied by Faulkner because they are associated with the end of life, not with the process of life. Therefore, the spirit is innately rebellious; its impulse is to disestablish, overturn, and redefine. In his Nobel Prize Acceptance Speech, Faulkner claimed he wrote out of "the materials of the human spirit," that is, out of the conviction that to live is to attempt change, and to attempt change is to rebel against what precedes life in existence. In the unfinished universe, rebellion is more "natural" than establishment, and saying no more lifelike than saying all right.

The principle of the unfinished world provides a link between *A Fable*'s universal concerns and the local concerns that would occupy Faulkner immediately after the publication of that novel. Despite the principle of incompletion, human beings do accomplish and build structures with an eye toward permanence, and these structures tend to contradict or impede subsequent creation. When Faulkner turned his attention away from the cosmos and back toward home and community, he faced this contradiction and found it immovable. His first attempt to articulate the contradiction appears in *Requiem for a Nun*, the novel he wrote before finishing *A Fable*.

The experience of the individual member of the human community, as Faulkner understood it, was characterized by a profound schism, or a set of competing tensions that reverberated throughout society. In 1933, Faulkner defined "the South" as a community "in the sense of the indigenous dream of any collection of men having something in common, be it only geography and climate, which shape their economic and spiritual aspirations into cities, into a pattern of houses and behavior."[9] In *Requiem for a Nun*, however, when Faulkner tells the story of the foundation and evolution of Jefferson, Mississippi, the forging of "a pattern of houses and behavior" is no ideologically neutral thing. In the Courthouse essay, for example, there is a tension between the urge to create from nothing and the impulse to preserve and maintain what has been established. Creation is clearly within the province of the actions of free men; the founders of Jefferson, whatever their motives, act willfully in creating their town. As they construct the physical institutions of their community, the French architect assures them that they will succeed in creating a town because, as he says, they are acting creatively and originally, having "nothing to copy from" and be corrupted by (33). The architect also presciently forewarns the founders that they "will never be able to get away from" their creation (34). Permanence and order, Faulkner demonstrates in the Courthouse essay, will soon conquer and extinguish the creative spirit of the founders, and it will become more important to have every civic institution and structure "each in its ordered place" (34) than to have each continually renewed, revitalized, and reconstructed. Indeed, when the townspeople are free to change the name of the town from Jefferson, a name accepted in order to bribe a federal official, to something more organic to the community, they refuse in the name of tradition. Even the Courthouse itself, symbol of the town's vitality in *Requiem for a Nun,* is immovable and fixed. Every few years, Faulkner explains, county officials would attempt to modernize the Courthouse, and they would always be stopped. The fate of the Courthouse is that of the community in general. "Because its fate is to stand in the hinterland of America," Faulkner exhorts, "its doom is its longevity; like a man, its simple age its own reproach, and after the hundred years, will become unbearable" (41). Creativity, in the Courthouse essay, is a rare and valuable commodity in the town. The community's instinct is to rest upon the creations of others, particularly those of its forebears, celebrating permanence over change, longevity over adaptation, reorder, and redefinition.

The life process itself, however, implies perpetual change, and Faulkner often defined it in terms of motion, modification, and movement. The establishment of a community, on the other hand, depends upon institutions and "patterns of houses and behavior" that are intended to last more than a lifetime. If human life is identified with creation, motion, and change, then the only authentic life experiences in the community occur at the community's founding. If the community is viewed not as a fixed value, however, but as something wholly within the individual's—or the collective individuals'—province to change, then "authentic" human life is, on Faulkner's terms, possible in the community. The tension remains, nonetheless, between the impulse to create new things and the desire to preserve old ways, which accounts for the contradictions in

Faulkner's view of the human community. It also explains the contradictions, for example, in the ways in which critics have characterized Faulkner's "politics."[10] Because he embodied both extremes, sometimes speaking to the individual's right to stand alone against an intransigent community, sometimes speaking to the individual's duties and responsibilities within the community, Faulkner appears to be unsystematic in his thinking at best, and careless in his formulations at worst. On the one hand, Faulkner recognized the healthy community as characterized by the kinds of changes and evolutions that distinguish the life of the human body; on the other hand, he saw the perpetual life of institutions and traditions as among humanity's more impressive accomplishments. The struggle between the individual's will to create and "leave a mark" and the community's will to maintain itself and control its constituency would always reveal, in Faulkner's imagination, the schism in the human experience between disestablishment and establishment, or between, for example, a view of history as oppressive and a view of history as progressive.

At the end of the Courthouse essay, Faulkner offers two views of temporal progression, one which characterizes history as moving forward but burdensome, and the other which presents it as continually re-experienced but eternally terrifying. The pigeons in the belfry, Faulkner explains, cannot get used to the Courthouse bell's hourly bong because to them, "the hours instead of merely adding one puny infinitesimal more to the long weary increment since Genesis had shattered the virgin pristine air with the first loud ding-dong of time and doom" (42). If each bong merely adds "one puny infinitesimal more" to history's unrelenting progression, then institutions and foundations must, at all costs, be preserved and maintained so something of human significance can be postulated in the face of the endless tomorrows. But if, instead, each bong of the Courthouse bell is "the *first* loud ding-dong of time and doom," then each moment in history is a renewed opportunity for creation—and human creation and change must, at all costs, be protected from historical encroachment. In Faulkner's imagination, the ding-dong of the bell does not chime out two *alternative* views of time and history, but rather it rings out a fundamental tension in the human experience, a tension that characterizes life itself. The tragedy of the human community, according to Faulkner, is that human beings experience both impulses simultaneously.

The tension between establishment and change, between canonization and apocrypha, provides the general mood and narrative purpose to the requiem in *Requiem for a Nun*. Superficially, the novel might be viewed as an effort to lay to rest the violent and disturbing events of *Sanctuary* (1931). *Requiem for a Nun* does tell us what happened to Temple Drake after "the season of rain and death," and if sequential resolution is any comfort, then the novel does settle things. Spoiling its simple function as a sequel, however, *Requiem for a Nun* raises issues that far from resolve matters. In fact, the "sequel" strongly suggests that the past, if it is to be of any use to Temple, must remain *unresolved* and a source of perpetual tension in her life.

If Temple is to be "saved," in the language of the novel, she must not forget ("fumigate") her violent personal history.[11] Faulkner demonstrates this point in her own story and reinforces it as historical principle by retelling the story of American civilization in its local, postage stamp setting of Yoknapatawpha. The sustained metaphor of the Holy Mass, or Requiem, attaches to history more than a secular significance or even an ideological significance, but rather an apocryphal one. In the human capacity to create and narrate history is the evidence of the miracle of life and proof of the existence of the eternally rebellious spirit.

A requiem celebrates the resting of departed souls, but the actual Mass, like any religious ritual, consoles the living. The Mass retells and defines again the basic parameters of faith. What is being celebrated in *Requiem for a Nun* is not the sacrifice and salvation of Nancy Mannigoe, who is hardly an important figure and merely a useful narrative tool, but the regeneration of Temple Drake Stevens. The story of Temple Drake is laid to rest, finally, by Temple Stevens' ability to narrate her past, the "history" of her soul. When Temple realizes that she has a soul and that her soul, or her story, is not just hers but is the "protagonist" of all human history, the groundwork of her salvation is established. It is precisely this attitude which Faulkner must have shared and which gave him the confidence (some will say the arrogance) to create the apocryphal Gospel and the apocryphal county, and to see in himself and his spirit the whole history of his civilization. That history and civilization, according to the narrative logic of *Requiem,* is what produced Temple Drake, and it is well within her power to in turn tell the story of that process as a means of appropriating what is hers. By doing so she reclaims her past and her soul. By setting the telling of her story against the broad sweeps of the apocryphal prefaces, Faulkner reclaims (and pro-claims) what is his.

The terms of Temple's regeneration are simple: she must accept the place of faith in her story. What Faulkner means by "faith," however, is highly problematic. The despair that tempts Temple away from faith and away from the burden of living is that same despair that was ultimately stronger than Quentin Compson. When Gowan leaves the Governor's office in the middle of the night, Temple fears that he might wreck the car again in his fragile emo-tional condition. "Oh God. Again," she cries, voicing Quentin's saddest of all words. "Tomorrow and tomorrow and tomorrow" (177). Yet Gavin brings the conversation around to where Temple can see faith's answer to Quentin's despair. There is a certain miracu-lous nature to the progression of human events, she implies, or to the *use* of time and alteration for human purposes. "So good can come out of evil," Temple concludes, to which Gavin affirms, "It not only can, it must."

To believe in the necessity of evil, Faulkner suggests here, implies a transcendent acceptance of the vitality of defeat. He urges, again by narrative implication, the will to make the transference of evil into good, a production process that demands human participation, human will, and human rebellion against limitation, all of which define human spirituality in the apocrypha. When Temple Stevens realizes that Temple Drake is valuable, that no matter how repugnant the memory, something good can be produced of it, she articulates, on a personal level, the meaning of apocryphal faith. Until Temple saved her soul—saved her history, *appropriated* it—she was doomed to live in a world of "tomorrow and tomorrow and tomorrow" in the endless repetition of a life with a fixed and established past pointing to a predetermined, equally sordid future.

Temple Stevens is no twentieth-century anomaly, Faulkner makes clear. Her historical paralysis is symptomatic of her time. The twentieth century, as Faulkner presents it in "The Jail" preface, is not simply "a new century and a new way of thinking, but of acting and behaving too" (207). Temple is the product of a civilization whose founders' "mouths were full of law and order" instead of justice and where "all men's mouths were round with the sound of money; one unanimous golden affirmation ululated the nation's boundless immeasurable forenoon: profit plus regimen equals se-curity" (93). Coming out of this tradition of establishmentarianism and material security, Nancy Mannigoe's canonical faith in an ineffable God and a spiritual salvation means nothing to Temple; it is, in fact, irrelevant to her world. When Nancy tells her to "believe," Temple, the product of a capitalist and authoritarian tradition, can only respond, "Believe what?" For much the same reason, Temple cannot put her faith in "the man" Nancy calls Jesus because she has relied too much on "men" as it is. Temple surely holds "Him," the masculinist deity, responsible for her suffering continually at the hands of those created in His image. Nancy Mannigoe's submissive Christianity, moreover, is repugnant to Temple and of no use to her. Yet Temple has no alternative, and this is why she is so lost in the novel. The terms of understanding spiritual existence that Temple needs are apocryphal ones: redefinition, re-creation, and re-invigoration of Nancy's worn-out terms "Believe" and "Jesus." Nancy Mannigoe is a dupe of her "Jesus" and a dupe of the state and of Christian orthodox hegemony. She killed a child to save Temple's faith, just as the orthodox Christian God sent his Child to be killed in order to found a Christian empire on earth and to save (establish) humanity's faith in God. It is a repressive and murderous logic which Nancy follows blindly. Nancy is the fool's martyr, and in her deadly act she extinguishes not only human innocence but also the coming generation who ought to rise and mock her.

The twentieth century's constricted understanding of Christianity and its total lack of apocryphal engagement are what make Nancy's faith inapplicable to Temple's experiences. Moreover, the logic and challenge that inform the questions Temple asks of Nancy are similar to the kinds of questions raised about orthodoxy in the Christian apocrypha. When the Old Testament God claimed that "I am a jealous God, and there is no other God beside me," asks the *Secret Book of John*, "what did he mean? [By] announcing this he indicated to the angels that another God does exist; for if there were no other one, of whom would he be jealous?"[12] Temple asks questions in the same spirit. "What kind of God is it that has to blackmail his customers with the whole world's grief and ruin?" (241). The language in which Temple's question is cast— "blackmail," "customer"— reflects a need on her part to understand God and Christ in a personally inspired context, or to know Christianity apocryphally. What Temple lacks is *the will to apocrypha*, the will to create out of her own story and her own experience a salvational understanding. The only example of Christian faith made available to her is that of the pathetic martyr Nancy. The force and structure of the novel itself, however, exists to counter Nancy's "hopeful," "masturbatory" faith and to provide Temple the model she needs to make her own salvation.

Faulkner demonstrates the parameters of willful faith in the human spirit in "The Jail," the final preface. The jail is presented as the community's chief witness. As the first institution, the jail testifies to the inherent failure of law to regiment human beings, to the triumph of the community for its recognition of that failure, and to the perseverence of the community to make the effort nonetheless. Crime signals the inadequacy of law to demand and receive obedience; the jail marks the community's faith in its power to defy its own failure and to make an institution of that defiance. This primal institution, the jail, indicates that all human endeavor is steeped in failure, and that failure is implicit in human affairs. Yet human endeavor, which transformed the wilderness into "a community: a settlement: to a village: to a town" (184), is the spirit's insistent denial of, or rebellion against this inevitable doom. On the faces of all human beings who left behind them something they made themselves is the look anyone should recognize, "provided there is will enough," as reflecting the "knowledge of anguish and foreknowledge of death, saying no to death . . . asking still the same old unanswerable questions" that are always asked (185). This approaches the essence, once again, of the apocrypha. The futility and doom that enslave living human beings today have oppressed the spirit throughout history, Faulkner argues, and the building of civilization is testimony to the spirit's insistent refusal to capitulate to meaninglessness. From "the vast weight of man's incredible and enduring *Was*," the living ought to find inspiration to create what *will be*. This is the faith of the apocrypha: the nearly arrogant, wholly confident belief (and demonstration) that the world, because it has been created in the past, can be made new in the present.

The present drama of *Requiem for a Nun* is written in play form to underscore this point structurally. As drama, the struggling of the living generation in the novel is a kind of Platonic embodiment of the eternal struggle of existence, of Being. As "requiem," however, Faulkner attempts to invest the present with the significance it is deprived by *progressive* ideas of history. As a Holy Mass, the present is understood not as culmination but as a *re-enactment* of history's essential meaning. This same view of history allowed Faulkner to recreate Christ's story in a Gospel "for our time" in *A Fable*. In *Requiem for a Nun*, the apocrypha is set in "our time" *and* place—in Yoknapatawpha—and the principles of apocryphal production are

applied to personal and community history. Temple might be saved
if she accepts her life as a drama, that is, as a present, living re-
enactment of the human spirit's rebellious struggle to create significance in the face of the sureness of failure and death. The past may
produce the present, but the present also conjures its future out of
the past. In this way, history is understood not as the burden of the
past upon the present (because its meaning is never fixed) but as
something always subject to re-examination. Temple re-examines her
past and Faulkner re-examines the history of her place and time in
the prefaces. History, in Faulkner's apocrypha, represents the human
capacity to act in significant ways. Retelling history does not *determine* the present but liberates it as long as the retelling is understood
to be in itself a human creation.

"The past is never dead," Gavin says without realizing the significance of his words. In the novel the past *is* never dead. It is continually resurrected to justify something someone wants to do in the
present.

Faulkner tells Yoknapatawphan "history" with the purpose of
defending his apocryphal position. When the living read where
Cecelia Farmer "inscribed . . . her paradoxical and significantless
name" (199–200) on the jailhouse kitchen windowpane, the spirit
of that "frail anemic girl" (197) touches the present with its defiance
of death. Stared at, the inscription moves and demands attention for
the simple reason that its maker once breathed life. *"Listen stranger,"*
as Faulkner emphatically interprets Cecelia's inscription, *"this was
myself: this was I"* (225). In "The Jail," Faulkner expresses a supreme
faith in the redemptive power of apocryphal understanding and
offers an interpretation of spirituality based not on the mysteries of
orthodox faith but on the power of apocryphal re–creation. Cecelia
Farmer's defiance and her quiet determination to make her mark on
the world, however brief and "significantless," embodies "the will
and hope and dream and imagination—of all men" who live (224).
The spirit survives when its essence is communicated defiantly, free
of its physical cage and free of the temporal and factual constraints
that imprison bodies in the present, "the rubbledross of facts and
probability, leaving only truth and dream" (225). The spirit,
Faulkner concludes, exists in the stories of men's and women's lives
as they are re-created and re-enacted in the imagination of the living
generation, "so limitless in capacity is man's imagination" (251), and
on the pages of the printed books men and women write.

In an attitude which Faulkner describes as "quiet amazement,"

Temple realizes that the simple telling of her story might save her. It is the salvational function of personal experience that keeps the tales of departed souls alive. Through the telling of her own story, Temple demonstrates the cathartic and regenerative nature of self-confrontation and re-examination. Simply by telling her story, the narrative suggests, Temple might save herself, and others as well from the resignation that life might really be insignificant, a meaningless futility full of sound and fury. "For no more than that," she says to Gavin. "For no better reason than that. Just to get it told, breathed alive, into words, sound. Just to be heard by, told to, someone, anyone, any stranger none of whose business it is, can possibly be, simply because he is capable of hearing, comprehending it" (78). Just to get the story told: the individual tale of the individual life becomes in *Requiem* the material by which the rebellious human spirit achieves immortality and communicates across the ages the community of defiance. To save herself, Faulkner suggests, Temple ought to look not to Jesus or to the Governor or to Gowan, but to herself and to what she can create. When she ceases to rely on the authority of others—church, state, husband—she will begin to save her soul.

All human life, from the magnificent and cosmically profound life of Jesus Christ to the insignificant and really trivial life of Temple Drake Stevens, exists for Faulkner in an attitude of outrage, either quiet or bellowing, toward the mysteries which surround it and the doom which awaits it. Faulkner's claim that human creativity is a way of "saying no to death" places rebellion at the center of the spirit's quest for immortality. The human spirit is engaged in an eternal rebellion against the crippling "foreknowledge of death" which hangs over all human endeavor, threatening life with insignificance. And yet, for the spirit to succeed in its negation it must create permanent structures. It must canonize, build, establish; it must create the very machinery of its subjugation and oppression. After all, history, literary history anyway, has "canonized" the defender and maker of the apocrypha, transforming Faulkner's apocrypha into an established *oeurve* with all the weighty oppressiveness of that concept. Perhaps this is why in the years following the Nobel Prize, Faulkner spoke so insistently on the human capacity to "revolt and change," and why his fiction in the 1950s takes a radical shift towards a celebration of rebellion.

Faulkner was often no less insistent in his public pronouncements concerning local issues. In 1953, after establishing in the Pine

Manor Address the human right and capability to "revolt and change," Faulkner placed the starting point of any human struggle in the local community. "Because it begins at home," he explained. He went on to define what he meant by "home." "Home is not merely four walls—a house, a yard on a particular street, with a number on the gate. It can be a rented room or apartment—any four walls which can house a marriage or a career or both the marriage and the career at once. But it must be all the rooms or apartments, all the houses on that street and all the streets in that association of streets until they become a whole, an integer, of people who have the same aspirations and hopes and duties." A home is movable, Faulkner continued, "providing and demanding only that we are willing to accept the new problems and duties and aspirations" of the new community, replacing "the old ones which we left behind us" with "the hopes and aspirations of the people already there, who had established that place as an integer worthy of being served." In return, the people "already there" must be "willing to accept our hopes and aspirations in return for their duties and problems."[13] Hence, the community is characterized by a tension between the "hopes and aspirations" of individuals moving through their lives and careers, and the "hopes and aspirations" of the community itself, which predate the arrival or development of individual aspiration. Any individual, of course, depending upon the circumstances of the moment, can either be a mover or a person "already there" in the community.

In the latter half of the Pine Manor Address, Faulkner moves away from his initial, cosmological discussion of the "unfinished universe" and toward a local, regionalistic conception of human responsibility. "Let us think first of, work first toward, saving the integer, association, collection which we call home." Here Faulkner signals his shift from the epic scope of *A Fable* toward the localist scope of *The Town*, the novel he would publish next. "In fact, we must break ourselves of thinking in the terms foisted on us by the split-offs of the old dark spirit's ambition and ruthlessness: the empty clanging terms of 'nation' and 'fatherland' or 'race' or 'color' or 'creed.' We need look no further than home, we need only work for what we want and deserve here."[14] In the 1950s, even "home" was not safe for Faulkner from the divisions brought upon by "the empty clanging terms" of ideology. In the face of mass politization— in Faulkner's eyes, the intrusion of national political ideology into local affairs—Faulkner urged personal and local autonomy in his public statements and in his fiction.

The "empty clanging terms of 'nation' and 'fatherland' " echo the epitaphs of Man's spirit after its suffocation by the warmakers at the end of *A Fable:* "They shall not pass. My country right or wrong. Here is a spot which is forever England." At Pine Manor, Faulkner gave local application or interpretation to the "epitaphs" of the human spirit, including the volatile American notions of "race," "color," and "creed." These ideologically divisive characterizations of humanity, Faulkner suggests, impede human interaction at every level of society. Overcoming them at home provides more than enough room for human improvement, he told his daughter's graduating class, more than enough evidence of ideological influences on human relations. In statements regarding his own most divisive local problem, racism and race relations, Faulkner reveals not only an antagonism for the interference of national abstractions on the local issue but also the tension in the community between fulfilling its need to revolt and change, and holding to its traditional social practices. While his insistence that the race issue be understood locally was unrealistic, his appreciation of the fundamental community schism over the matter was more insightful than critics have suggested.[15] "We have much tragic trouble in Mississippi about Negroes," Faulkner wrote in 1955, following the Supreme Court's decision in *Brown vs. Board of Education.* "I am doing what I can. . . . But human beings are terrible. One must believe well in man to endure him, wait out his folly and savagery and inhumanity."[16]

In his involvement in the civil rights movement in the 1950s, however, Faulkner's actions never quite matched the fervor of his words. In fact, he was inconsistent, hesitant, and at times racist in his "doing what I can" about civil rights in the South. His behavior, nevertheless, fits a general pattern. In 1948, when he threw a party at Rowan Oak for the cast of the film *Intruder in the Dust,* he capitulated to local pressure and did not include on the invitation list the black man playing Lucas Beauchamp. In 1954, after writing the radical prefatory statement to explain *A Fable,* he did not insist on its use after his editor suppressed it. And throughout the 1950s, Faulkner would often back down from confrontational situations rather than force his views on his community. Faulkner, no matter what his strengths as a writer, was no community leader and was arguably a poor example, in hindsight, of the behavior of an intellectual in a social crisis. His apocrypha provides by itself a powerful example of radical opposition to orthodox understandings of history and social reality. He wrote eloquently about rebellion and succeeded in creating a literature that defines the human spirit as rebellious, but writing was the extent of his own rebellion, the summation of his own spirit. He lived his life not as a social activist but in a way designed to protect his ability to write. As a political actor, Faulkner was profoundly ineffectual.

When Faulkner wrote to University of Alabama officials in 1956 regarding Autherine Lucy's attempt to enroll there in violation of its white-only admissions policy, he stressed local control of the issue. "Segregation is going, whether we like it or not," he commented. "The only choice we now have is how, by what means."[17] In other words, either the community would change by its own volition and thus maintain its autonomy, or it would be compelled to abandon its tradition by force. If pressured to change, community autonomy would be abdicated to external authorities, a far worse thing to lose than a segregated school system. Once lost, as Faulkner demonstrated in the Courthouse essay, creative control over community institutions is not easily regained.

Faulkner recognized that grandiose national statements about "equality" and "integration" would be translated, locally, into threatening messages of "change your ways" and "what you stand for is wrong." Within the context of the community's schism between permanence and change, tradition will be defended in the face of external assaults, and alteration will be possible only when originating internally. Of segregation, Faulkner continued in his letter to the University of Alabama, "I vote we ourselves choose to abolish it" in order to maintain control over the affairs and social practices of the community. "That is the simple expediency of the matter, apart from the morality of it."[18] Through his recognition of human resistance to external control—the protection of its right to define and create its universe and then to defend that creation—Faulkner spoke for flexibility above all virtues. When he urged Negroes in the South to "go slow" in their drive for equal treatment, "I meant," he said, " 'Be flexible.' " This did not mean that "the individual Negro" was "to abandon or lower one jot his hope and will for equality," Faulkner explained, but that the "leaders and organizations" at the vanguard of the new civil rights movement must "always be flexible and adaptable to circumstance and locality in their methods of gaining it."[19] As abhorrent as racial inequities were in the South in his lifetime, Faulkner placed a greater emphasis and a greater value on the maintenance of local and individual control over social and economic order in the community. Although he clearly felt that racist practices were wrong and that racism was an evil, he also asserted that national compulsion in the affairs of "the home" was equally dangerous to human independence. It was another instance of the "lords and proprietors" of democracy gearing up, as in wartime, to compel the masses into acting and believing in accordance with the values of the overlords. The fact that the overlords were right in this particular issue only complicated the matter.

Faulkner's insistence on local control and initiative in rectifying racial inequities in the South frustrated both Northern liberals and Southern defenders of "states' rights." Liberals saw Faulkner as too moderate; conservatives saw him as too soft on the race issue. His "politics" was, in fact, of a piece with his fundamental belief in the primacy of individual proprietorship in the affairs of human lives and of his "long view" of the human struggle. On a rhetorical level, he told a high school graduating class in 1951 that it was "not man in the mass who can and will save Man. It is Man himself. . . . Man, the individual, men and women, who will refuse always to be tricked or frightened or bribed into surrendering."[20] A threat greater than local racial injustice faced the human race, Faulkner believed. It was a threat from which America's original settlers took flight but which had begun to re-emerge even in this country. "This was the American Dream," Faulkner wrote in his 1955 essay "On Privacy": "a sanctuary on the earth for the individual man: a condition in which he could be free not only of the old established closed-corporation hierarchies of arbitrary power which had oppressed him as a mass, but free of that mass into which the hierarchies of church and state had compressed and held him individually thralled and individually impotent." But the Dream is over, Faulkner continued, lost to Americans while they were inattentive. "We dozed, slept, and it abandoned us." Now we hear only "a cacaphony of terror and conciliation and compromise babbling only the mouthsounds; the loud and empty words which we have emasculated of all meaning whatever—freedom, democracy, patriotism."[21]

Throughout Faulkner's statements on racial issues in the 1950s is a pathetic sense of personal detachment owing to his reliance upon abstract characterizations of the problem. He seemed incapable of seeing the actual world before him with anywhere near the same degree of specificity and physicality with which he saw his own apocryphal universe. We can see the *principles* influencing Faulkner's statement to the University of Alabama, to Negro leaders in the South, and to the high school graduating class, but debating principles is the privilege of the powerful and the comfortable, while political action is the imperative of the dispossessed. This is made perfectly clear in *A Fable*. Telling Negro leaders to "be flexible and adaptable" does little to announce, in a time of crisis and confrontation, which side he was on. And finally, the fact that the "overlords" *were* right in the case of civil rights only added to the urgency with which the local community, including recognized spokespersons like William Faulkner, had to insist upon a clean house to save its autonomy. Faulkner's introduction of philosophical abstractions and vague principles into a clearly defined struggle for legal, social, and economic justice only serves to emphasize his personal aversion to confrontation. If the civil rights movement would just go away, in other words, William Faulkner would be free to keep writing without being interrupted for his opinion on things. In the 1950s, Faulkner might have done better to answer all questions about racial matters and the efficacy of social rebellion by referring interlocutors to his fiction.

Faulkner's eloquence with abstractions, however, served him well in other forums. As Nobel Laureate during the Cold War, Faulkner spoke often about such abstract issues as individualism and human freedom. At the University of Virginia, Faulkner told students in a prepared address that he had devoted his life to denying "the mythology that one single individual man is nothing, and can have weight and substance only when organized into the anonymity of a group where he will have surrendered his individual soul for a number."[22] After the Second World War, Faulkner became increasingly vocal in his challenges to the docility he saw in modern individuals, giving particular attention to the easy retreat into group identity or ideology. The health of the community depends, in Faulkner's view, not on allegiance so much as upon the vitality of independent members. Freedom is not a belief, he wrote in 1956, but an activity, a practice.[23]

In his many pronouncements on the theme of human responsibility, for example, Faulkner repeated the characterization of freedom as a burden, not a natural right. It was standard Cold War ideology, the rallying cry of a united literary front, and Faulkner delivered variations on it throughout the decade. "Not just the right," he said in 1951, "but the duty of man to be responsible if he wishes to remain free."[24] Occasionally, however, Faulkner's apocrypha would undercut his Cold War partisanship. To protect their freedom, Faulkner claimed at Virginia, citizens need to see their roles as independent actors in the community. As such, citizens are responsible for their own beliefs and opinions, and should not be reliant on established definitions or "official" interpretations or representations of reality. Racism itself, as Faulkner understood it, is not due to inherent antagonisms among peoples but to the artificial antagonisms created by abstract cultural representations and perpetuated by historical mythologies. "It is possible that the white race and the Negro race can never really like and trust each other," he said in 1958. "This is for the reason that the white man can never really know the Negro, because the white man has forced the Negro to be always a Negro rather than another human being in their dealings."[25] In the context of such novels as *Light in August* and *Intruder in the Dust,* this statement would seem to contradict Faulkner's public statements about the virtues (or even the possibility) of independent individualism. No one seems to have asked him to clarify this at Virginia, and Faulkner, true to form, never insisted upon it.

Faulkner often expressed an antagonism for the prejudgmental attitudes and stereotypes which so often characterize community behavior. He told students at Virginia that one ought to "watch people, to have—to never judge people. To watch people, what they do, without intolerance."[26] When individuals interact on personal rather than on racial or ideological levels, Faulkner implies, the seemingly irresolvable, abstract tensions often melt away before the sympathies of the flesh. Once again, however, Faulkner's pronouncements are pathetically weak, and they ignore the political realities around him. His statements may be inspirational, but inspiration must be translated into a program of action in order to be fulfilled. Furthermore, Faulkner's stand on "individualism" has a darker underside of which he seems to have been unaware. It allows an easy retreat into smug self-satisfaction when, in the midst of racial conflict, and oppression, the individualist says, "Not me!" Individualism, the orthodoxy of the American Cold War, did serve the survivor-writer. It provided the man who had outlasted the radical decade of the 1930s and the red-baiting decade of the postwar era a way to (nearly?) survive the civil rights era—and to continue creating his highly politicized apocrypha. In any case, there seems little connection between the quality or content of Faulkner's art and that of his political life. It may also be in the nature of the apocryphal writer to see a failure in his relationship to the actual world, a personal incompletion which, in itself, feeds the apocrypha. In the final analysis, there is a great deal of significance in Faulkner's statement that he was not a "literary man," given the meaning of that word in the postwar era and given what the literary men were doing to canonize his work. There is as well a great deal to his insistence upon maintaining his role as a farmer and a Mississippi mule breeder. The man who raised mules against common wisdom (it was not very profitable) may be the Faulkner who truly did not find the actual world a comfortable or nurturing place, but a realm of over-whelming failure and profound incompletion.

Faulkner's involvement in political matters in the 1950s clearly shows a man inexperienced in the language and discourse of public debate. He found himself explaining his own language, for example, as often as he found himself offering his views on racial politics. Nonetheless, the 1950s saw Faulkner moving more and more to-ward a position in which he believed it was his place to speak out on public issues and to defend his community against what he consid-ered misunderstanding and misguided criticism. Similarly, he would return to his apocryphal community, finally finishing the *Snopes* project which he had begun long before anyone cared about his political opinions. Politics and community existence, however, form the core of Faulkner's *Snopes* trilogy, issues which he had for most of his career put aside in favor of more pressing aesthetic concerns. While stumbling and falling in a web of political actualities of the 1950s, Faulkner was busy sublimating those actualities to the politi-cal concerns of his apocryphal county.

◆ Country Boy/Mule Farmer

Faulkner was telling tall tales and writing about the Snopes clan from his earliest years as a storyteller. In the early 1920s, according to a local Oxford woman, Faulkner's friend and mentor Phil Stone "cajoled, browbeat, and swore at" Faulkner in order to get him to "write down the stories which he could tell aloud so well."[27] Among these stories were undoubtedly the tall tales about the Snopes clan. Faulkner's early ideas about "art," however, kept him from taking seriously such local color material and, in his poetry and in his first attempts at fiction, this material was suppressed. Nonetheless, it was not Phil Stone alone who tried to convince Faulkner that what he knew best he could relate aesthetically. When Faulkner recalled

Sherwood Anderson in an essay written in 1953, he remembered Anderson's early advice to him during their acquaintance in New Orleans in the 1920s. "I have learned that, to be a writer, one has first got to be what he is, what he was born," Faulkner wrote, echoing the lessons and recalling the advice of Anderson.

> You have to have somewhere to start from: then you can begin to learn," he told me. "It dont matter where it was, just so you can remember it and aint ashamed of it. Because one place to start from is just as important as any other. You're a country boy, all you know is that little patch up there in Mississippi where you started from. But that's all right too. It's America too; pull it out, as little and unknown as it is, and the whole thing will collapse, like when you pull a prize brick out of a wall.[28]

Faulkner's recollection of Anderson's advice fits well, of course, into his general move "back home" in the mid-1950s. He also liked the keystone image which Anderson apparently suggested to him in the 1920s and appropriated it in an interview with Cynthia Grenier in 1955. When Grenier asked him how he felt about his books "being read and discussed all over the world," Faulkner responded: "I like the idea of the world I created being a kind of keystone in the universe. Feel that if I ever took it away the universe around the keystone would crumble away."[29]

Although Faulkner took the combined advice of Stone and Anderson and "came home" for his fictional settings at the end of the 1920s, setting *Sartoris* and *The Sound and the Fury* in Mississippi, the Snopes clan would not figure centrally in any novel until *The Hamlet* in 1940. Despite this, he continually thought and wrote about Snopes and the community over which the clan would eventually dominate throughout his career. Critics have often pointed to the fact that the trilogy is largely dependent on re-written short story material and have taken this dependence as evidence of Faulkner's declining literary powers.[30] It seems more likely that critics who prefer the intensity of the early Faulkner novels see as a falling off in creative power what is actually a shift in narrative strategy, subject matter, and literary purpose. *Absalom, Absalom!*, for example, contains material from one story that had been published in *Doctor Martino and Other Stories* (1934) and is actually based upon another story that Faulkner had been unable to publish.[31] Access to Faulkner's papers has led critics to more such connections, making it wholly plausible now to say that Faulkner considered any short story he wrote as potential raw material for more seriously aesthetic treatment in a novel. Although it would be some twenty years between the time Faulkner first began to tell stories about Snopes and the publication of the trilogy's first volume, he did publish "raw material" about the clan and the community throughout his career. Rather than let the material sit under the bed until he was ready to write seriously about Snopes, Faulkner, with a steady eye toward publication and a commitment to making a living by writing, sold the stories as they were completed to whatever magazine would buy them.[32]

After finishing *The Wild Palms* in 1938, Faulkner began to consider getting started on his trilogy about Snopes. In a letter written in December 1938, he gave R. K. Haas an outline of his intended plan for the three novels. Volume one was to be called "The Peasants" and was to tell the story of "Flem Snopes' beginning in the country, as he gradually consumes a small village until there is nothing left in it for him to eat." The volume would end with Flem getting "a foothold in Jefferson, to which he moves with his wife, leaving his successor kinsmen to carry on in the country." Faulkner intended to call volume two "Rus in Urbe" and in it deal with Flem's rise in the town by using any means, including trading "on his wife's infidelity, modest blackmail of her lover" until he becomes "secure in the presidency of a bank." In the final volume, "Ilium Falling," Faulkner would tell about "the gradual eating-up of Jefferson by Snopes, who corrupt local government with crooked politics, buy up all the colonial homes and tear them down and chop up the lots into subdivisions." "This," he told Haas, "is the plot, if any."[33] Following the precedent he had established with the chapter titles in *The Unvanquished,* the original titles of the second and third Snopes volumes were ironic, if esoteric comments on their contents. The essential "plot" sketch, however, remained generally constant as the books were written. It is important to remember, then, that *Snopes* was intended from its inception as material for serious literary treatment—as a *trilogy*. On at least one occasion after the three volumes were completed Faulkner spoke of "someday" printing "the three volumes as a simultaneous trilogy, same binding, imprint, etc; and sell the old prints as antiques."[34]

Critics who have analyzed the *Snopes* trilogy have worked hard to show that in *Snopes*, Faulkner was doing what he had always done in his fiction, with the qualification that he was not doing it as well. Most critical analyses of *Snopes*, however, have had more to say about

Faulkner *in general* than about the trilogy *in particular.* Very few critics are able to muster the same level of enthusiasm often brought to Faulkner's earlier novels. Elizabeth Kerr, placing "Snopes" in a central position in Faulkner's "absurd world," points to "those who provide value and meaning" in the face of meaninglessness, "as Ratliff and Gavin do for the absurd world of the Snopeses."[35] James Watson has called the trilogy "Faulkner's most extended and comprehensive statement of the nature of man and the outcome of his struggle." Watson sees the trilogy as unified in theme and structure "by the sustention of dramatic tension between morality and amorality, motion and stasis" typified in the study of Flem. "The unrelieved amorality of Flem and the opulence and complexity of the moral universe that his machinations uncover clearly show," according to Watson, "the measure of Faulkner's achievement."[36] The generalized, aesthetic, and philosophically moralistic nature of these comments are more typical than not of analyses of the trilogy. Even Warren Beck's insightful early work resorts, at times, to what is an abstract analysis of Faulkner in general in his discussion of *Snopes.* "Faulkner rises to a genuine realism which not only documents events and searches motives but celebrates the saving mystery of man's innate urge to postulate values and react in terms of those evaluations," according to Beck, "in resistance to devaluation and in successive, and often ironic corrections of his own eccentricities."[37] The same statement, accurate as it is, can be applied to *Absalom, Absalom!,* for example, without changing a word and without distinguishing between Faulkner's literary concerns in either project.

What too many critical analyses have done with the Snopes material is to show how the "old Faulkner" of the 1930s and 1940s is still alive and well in the trilogy as a whole. While there is no question that continuities are present in the trilogy as they are in the whole of Faulkner's output, it is not necessary, and perhaps it is counterproductive to critical analysis, to demonstrate or try to prove that the trilogy is as vital or brilliant as anything else Faulkner ever did in his maturity. For example, when Elizabeth Rankin describes "the central characters" of Snopes' environment as sharing "a common disillusion with life," she is grafting a common view of Faulkner's early work onto the trilogy in an attempt, perhaps, to make it more "urgent." "They sense that life is meaningless," she says of the traders in the "Spotted Horses" episode, "that honor, justice, and dignity are lost concepts; and that they have been deserted in this meaningless universe by a god who is either indifferent or hostile to their plights. It is the basic existential dilemma," Rankin concludes, "unarticulated and not fully understood here in the backwater hamlet, but still very real and very urgent."[38] Again, while this analysis is an adept and, I think, valid assessment of Faulkner's people as a whole, it could be quoted verbatim in a discussion as *As I Lay Dying* or, by dropping the reference to the "backwater hamlet," to *The Sound and the Fury* and a number of other works and parts of works. Similarly, Woodrow Stroble gives an *As I Lay Dying cum Absalom, Absalom!* interpretation of Flem Snopes or of Ratliff's efforts to understand Flem. "Ratliff's reliability is compromised by virtue of the competing viewpoints of his fellow narrators Charles Mallison and Gavin Stevens," Stroble points out. "Ratliff's reconstruction and forseeing of events are impressive feats, but the reader is constantly reminded—by the shifting narrative perspectives—that human testimony is inherently fallible."[39]

Everything quoted here is unquestionably true about the trilogy or about parts of it. It has an epistemological concern for narration and fabulation; it has a spiritual concern for the apparent abandonment of humanity by God; and it has as well a strong and consistent concern for human beings as sensual, sexually driven creatures. Yet despite this wholism, and perhaps partially due to it, there is something *very different* about the Snopes books. Something seems different about *The Hamlet* as it sits bibliographically nestled between *The Wild Palms* (1939) and *Go Down, Moses* (1942), and something is unquestionably different about *The Town* and *The Mansion*.[40] What distinguishes the trilogy from the rest of Faulkner's output is, I think, its intensely personal nature. In the Snopes trilogy, as suggested above, Faulkner has come "home." He is a "country boy" again, seeing life in all its complexity—sexual, intellectual, spiritual—but mainly talking about people, including himself, in various guises and capacities. Faulkner put off writing in novel form the local color perspective on his "little patch up there in Mississippi" until he had proven himself the master of great fiction. He delayed completing the project until he had a firm grasp on his apocryphal vision and on its implications to himself and to his community. The result was a *Snopes* trilogy that greatly exceeded its original design and scope, encompassing the whole of the Yoknapatawpha apocrypha in principle and content. If *A Fable* establishes the universal parameters and cosmological significance of Faulkner's vision, *Snopes* illustrates its local, community relevance and demonstrates its political vitality. In the apocrypha, *Snopes* is the attenuation of the human spirit's rebellion into its vulgar, fleshy form. Before proceeding to

individual analyses of the three volumes, then, I would like to
articulate the way in which that attenuation is realized in the trilogy
and define the localistic form taken by the apocryphal human spirit
down in Yoknapatawpha. It is a tale of survival, told by the mule
breeder who has learned something profoundly important from his
mules.

◆ The Nay-Saying "Sons of Bitches": Snopes and Faulkner

If Faulkner admired the Snopes clan, it was for their refusal to allow
anyone to treat them like the dirt they sprang from. Always saying
no to abuse by their social and economic "superiors," Snopes—
S'Nopes—are characterized by their rascality and resistance. Because
the landowners who traditionally control and even oppress their
class expect passivity, the Snopes' will to rise in the community takes
the bourgeoisie by surprise. As a clan they are skillful manipulators,
able to turn what seems to be class disadvantage into surprising
triumphs and apparent buffoonery into a vehicle for personal gain.
As Montgomery Ward Snopes says in *The Mansion,* since the world
expects Snopes to be "a clan, a race, maybe even a species, of pure
sons of bitches," then *"we'll just show them . . . every Snopes will make it
his private and personal aim to have the whole world recognize him as
THE son of a bitch's son of a bitch"* (87). Faulkner may have laughed at
the Snopes clan and their ridiculous given names, their lack of
sophistication, their mulish stubbornness, but he held a great respect
for their spirit. At Virginia in 1957, for example, he stated simply
that a Snopes recognizes that "he will have to cope with his environment or his environment will destroy him."[41] Snopeses, of course,
are known to do considerably more than just "cope."

Chapter five of this study analyzes the *Snopes* trilogy as a coherent
whole, dealing with each novel successively. Before getting to that,
however, I would first like to establish parallels or points of affinity
between Flem and Faulkner that indicate the author's growing identification with the Snopes clan over the course of writing the trilogy.
The point is not simply that Flem is constructed from Faulkner's
psyche, for that is to belabor the obvious. Instead, the point is that
the trilogy and Snopes, and Flem Snopes above all, occupy a much
more central, vital, and autonomous place in Faulkner's apocrypha
than has been critically established. In many ways, Flem is the
apocryphal Faulkner.

There is a lot of William Faulkner the "country boy" in Snopes,
particularly in Flem Snopes, the Snopes' masterpiece. The identification is muted in *The Hamlet* of 1940, but when Faulkner returned to

the trilogy in the 1950s, he saw and made the identification more explicit. In 1956, Faulkner told Jean Stein that a writer "is completely amoral in that he will rob, borrow, beg or steal from anybody and everybody to get the work done."[42] By substituting the writing for the getting rich, Faulkner's vision of the writer's amorality sounds a lot like his view of Flem in 1957. "Snopes' design was pretty base," Faulkner explained, "he just wanted to get rich, he didn't care how."[43] In the Jean Stein interview, Faulkner continued on the subject of the writer's ruthlessness. "The writer's only responsibility is to his art. He will be completely ruthless if he is a good one. He has a dream. It anguishes him so much he must get rid of it. He has no peace until then. Everything goes by the board: honor, pride, decency, security, happiness, all, to get the book written. If a writer has to rob his mother, he will not hesitate."[44]

Faulkner was as driven to master his community, that of literary artists, as was Flem to master the community of Jefferson. Both men, at roughly parallel points in their careers, begin to crave "respectability": Faulkner in the university, Flem in his mansion. In 1957, Faulkner agreed that he had admired Flem "until he was bitten by the bug to be respectable, and then he let me down." Flem, Faulkner said, had found out "almost too late that he'd have to have respectability" to truly be a master. In fact, "he didn't want it until he found out he had to have it."[45] Hence, while Faulkner was charting Flem's disappointing bid for membership in the middle class, Faulkner himself was reversing a lifelong avowal to stay clear of the literary establishment. In 1932, he wrote of the oppressive "jail corridor of literary talk" in which "I seem to lose all perspective and do things like a coon in a tree."[46] In 1957, perhaps because he had found out that he "had to have" respectability, Faulkner was the writer-in-residence at the University of Virginia, answering the tedious and repetitive questions about things he had written twenty and thirty years before. In 1948, he told Hamilton Basso of *The New Yorker* that he was "working tooth and nail at my ambition to be the last private individual on earth,"[47] but seven years later he was on the payroll of the State Department en route to Japan. Blotner claims that the anxiety Faulkner felt over his new public role, his "respectability," was sufficient to lead to an increase in the frequency and intensity of his lifelong escape route, intoxication.[48] Faulkner eventually became resigned to his role as Laureate and even seemed to enjoy it, but he could never forget the distance he had travelled from the days when he was challenging the established practices of literature and making a name for himself as Hollywood's "problem child."[49]

By the 1950s, Faulkner, like Flem, had realized that he would have to have respectability if he were to receive the recognition and literary influence he had always craved. Recognition and respectability resulted from what Faulkner had established and were evidence of his permanence. Faulkner knew, however, and made clear in *Requiem for a Nun* that permanence threatens creativity with complacency and inertia. To survive as an artist, then, Faulkner would need to disdain the very success and recognition his creative powers earned him. This is at the core of what made Faulkner so ambivalent about his literary status in the 1950s. He had been ruthless in his ambition to make an apocrypha—ruthless in his life and ruthless in his art. As a result, he was canonized and made respectable. Flem may well have come to symbolize in Faulkner's imagination a "dark twin." For Flem, amoral conniving and slick maneuvering resulted in his winning a seat at the pinnacle of the capitalist order, as the community assimilates those who prove victorious and who successfully exploit it. For Faulkner, a lifetime of apocryphal writing had resulted in the canonization of a mythmaker, and librarians, like the "mouse-colored" one in "Appendix: Compson," now spent their lives trying to keep *Sanctuary* and *The Wild Palms* "out of the hands of the high school juniors and seniors who could reach them down" from where they were hidden (413).

It has been suggested that a "synthesis" of Flem Snopes' character "is either impossible or meaningless: no amount of generalization . . . will produce a reliable portrait of the man." According to Joseph Arpad, Flem's existence is "primarily" known as legend, and his real nature is "outside the narrative, unavailable for analysis."[50] James Watson, in his study of the trilogy, claims that Flem is "the ominous figure" at the center of the work. "Lacking those primary human responses that Faulkner considered so essential to moral existence, Watson states, "Flem is a character so resistant to moral definition as to be literally inhuman."[51] Flem's true character seems to be as difficult to pin down as is Faulkner's own biographical "true" self. One reason is that Faulkner gave to Flem Snopes all the adaptability and plasticity of character which Faulkner himself possessed and practiced. Although it may be impossible to know exactly what Flem thinks about—Faulkner never gives him a narrative of his own—it is possible to know quite a bit about Flem by examining what he says and does in the context of the continuum of his place and time as Faulkner presents it to us. Flem may be an enigma, but the enigma is firmly "rooted like a tree"[52] in the textual landscape of the trilogy.

Flem's father Ab was a class-conscious and class-antagonistic gypsy sharecropper. When Jody Varner tells him in *The Hamlet* that he will be required to use Varners' store while he works on Varners' property, Ab voices his futile protest. "I see," he states firmly. "Furnished in six-bit dollars" (8). According to Ratliff, Ab Snopes is a "soured" man (27, 29). During the Civil War, Ratliff says, recalling the events of *The Unvanquished*, Ab's horse-trading business was interfered with by "political convictions," something of which Ab wants no part (29). Later, when Pat Stamper took advantage of Ab's local community by outtrading its members, Ab attempted to get the better of Stamper to avenge the community's humiliation. He lost, of course, but the effort was made alone, according to Ratliff, "not for profit but for honor" (36). The accumulation of losses has "soured" Ab, but what has disappointed him more than any series of events is the simple recognition that despite his personal efforts to better himself, he is somehow destined to remain, in the refrain of *The Mansion,* a "poor son of a bitch."

With the economic and political system stacked against Ab, he turns to criminal activity as a source of power and respect. His reputation as a "barn burner" who has deviously escaped prosecution follows him into Frenchman's Bend and compels his boss, Jody Varner, to treat him with the kind of respect only reserved for men of Varner's own class, never for such social inferiors as Ab Snopes. While Ab and his family are moving into their new home as sharecroppers on Varner's property, "the barren yard littered with the rubbish—the ashes, the shards of pottery and tin cans—of its last tenants" (19), Jody Varner is learning about his newest employee from Ratliff. Ab last worked for De Spain, Ratliff explains, and lived in a shack which "aint fitten for hawgs" to inhabit (13). At least, this is what Ab reportedly said when he viewed De Spain's tenant housing. In his frustration, Ab soiled De Spain's mansion rug "on deliberate purpose" by rubbing the manure from his boots on the landowner's carpet (15). After the ensuing legal struggle, De Spain's barn mysteriously burns to the ground and the next morning Ab "cancels" his contract with De Spain. Alarmed by this information, Varner visits Ab and tries to get a sense of the man's intentions. "I figure I'll stay," Ab tells him. "The house aint fitten for hogs. But I reckon I can make out with it" (20). Jody Varner's fear of Ab Snopes

("I dont dare say leave here. . . . I dont even dare to have him arrested for barn-burning for fear he'll set my barn a-fire" [20]) leads him to treat Ab entirely differently from the way in which he would normally treat a tenant. "We'll get along," he assures Ab. "Anything that comes up, all you got to do is come down to the store." Jody's initial reaction to Ab's history is, of course, to try to use it against him. He tells his father that he plans to have Ab make the Varner crop and then have him arrested for burning down De Spain's barn. Not until he learns from Ratliff that Ab is no fool, that he is too smart to be caught or to have left evidence, does Jody begin to deal with Ab from a position of fear and grudging respect, and not condescension.

From his father, then, Flem learns that in their economic dealings, men do not respect nor treat other men fairly unless they have some reason to fear them. "I hear your father has had a little trouble once or twice with landlords," Jody says to Flem. "Maybe they never treated him right" (22). Truly his father's son, Flem capitalizes on Ab's reputation in order to lift himself out of his sharecropper class. Jody recognizes the Snopeses as an "independent" clan—not "dependent," presumably, as he considers sharecroppers in general— and therefore decides to make their and his interests the same (27). This includes fair treatment of Ab and the strategic placement of Flem in his store. To be a "Snopes" is to refuse class typification and identification as "fate," to refuse subordinate status based on class position, and to say no (or nope) to class stigma and class-based economic determinism in general. Yet Faulkner is not building an Horatio Alger paradigm here. Significantly, the Ab-Snopes is driven to and quite naturally turns to criminal activity (crimes against property) in order to redress his social and economic handicaps. And in a capitalist economy, crimes against property are as serious as murder. "Durn little club foot murderer" is what Jody thinks to himself about the barn burner Ab Snopes (20). Flem's initial ascent in Frenchman's Bend is based not upon self-reliance or some belief in the capitalist system but upon the intimidation of a landlord and the threat of violence. In this sense, Flem is a localized, entirely earthly descendant of the corporal in *A Fable*. Both men say no to their oppression, and both translate their negations—the peasant's nope and the cosmic Nope—into programs of rebellion. Critically, however, it is only by threats of violence and insurrection that the two rebels gain the attention of their oppressors.

The "independence" of the Snopes clan sets the farmers, traders, and landowners of Frenchman's Bend on edge in *The Hamlet*. Ratliff, the sewing machine agent, sells a sewing machine to Mink Snopes in a scheme to divide the Snopes clan and beat Flam in trade, but he fails due to a lack of nerve. "I quit too soon," he thinks to himself (88). The attempt turns Ratliff into Flem's enemy nonetheless, and Flem eventually gets even with Ratliff in the salted mine trick that concludes the volume. Even then Ratliff engages in illegal and dishonest means (trespassing on Flem's property) to gain an advantage over Flem. Flem simply outfoxes him at his own game. Knowing the practices of the community and knowing how members of the community think, Flem merely has to spend a few nights "hunting" for money and then "salting" the property in order to lure someone into attempting to cheat him.

Flem is, above all, an observer. Learning the value of a close tongue, Flem's curtailed verbal style is in direct contradistinction to the verbosity of Ratliff and later, in Jefferson, of Gavin Stevens. Flem literally interprets the phrase "private enterprise" and allows no one access to his mind. "The first man Flem would tell his' business to would be the last man that was left after the last man died," according to one incredulous Frenchman's Bend peasant in *The Hamlet*. "Flem Snopes dont even tell himself what he is up to" (279–80). Instead of telling other men his business, Flem does all he can to ascertain and internalize theirs. When Henry Armstid abuses his wife in public, verbally and physically accosting her in the "Spotted Horses" episode, the other men of the community will not look. "Only Flem was still watching," Faulkner narrates, "standing in his little island of isolation" (295). Flem, as Watson has pointed out, becomes a master at learning the local practices of the community and "parrots" its forms of behavior. His is not, however, "an alien nature," as Watson would have it.[53] Rather, he is the product of his community, a self-made man who masters the arts of his community through continuous observation and quiet determination. Unlike Ratliff, for example, who can narrate the events of others and manage to get by in his small business, Flem narrates nothing and quickly rises out of his father's economic and social class. Ab got "soured," but Flem got ambitious.

What makes Flem particularly odious to his fellows is his refusal to place artificial boundaries around his business practices or to allow any "personal" weaknesses or obligations to interfere with his economic climb. "Flem would trim Eck or any other of his kin as quick as he would us," claims one man, referring to Flem's seeming immunity to familial dependencies (280). What makes it even worse is the absence, on Flem's part, of a natural sexual drive that might impede or complicate his socio-economic determination. Unlike other men, for example, who might be personally or even socially compromised by an illegitimate child, Flem actually uses the existence of an unwed pregnant woman to further his ends. Eula's pregnancy is, to Flem, just one more mistake made by other men on which he can capitalize. In this case, the "mistake" is the Varners' need to make Eula socially legitimate. Like Jody Varner's identification with his property and Ratliff's weakness for easy money, the Varners' sensitivity to their daughter's social status is used by Flem for his own gain.

Flem knows Frenchman's Bend so well that he readily manipulates it. With no weaknesses and apparently no pleasures desired, Flem is a grotesque portrait of the kind of "self-denial" said to be necessary for success. Only in Flem's case, there is nothing to be denied: when he chews, he chews air. Apparently Flem has no demanding sensations of taste, just as he has no demanding loins. The hatred visited upon him by others, then, is more accurately directed upon themselves. Unlike Flem, most of *The Hamlet*'s peasants are, to some extent, slaves to their appetites, or rather they see their cravings as a form of slavery. The extent to which Flem can rise in the community, Faulkner suggests, is the extent to which social and economic success is measured by one's denial of physical cravings, or the alienation of the man from his body. Because Flem "feels" nothing, Faulkner implies, he is the perfect candidate from among the peasants of Frenchman's Bend to go to Jefferson in search of fortune. Flem is truly an "independent" man, as Jody suspected, and he is independent even of his own body. If Faulkner felt himself overly sensitive to life's sensualities, the sadnesses as well as the ecstacies, he could have created no more polar opposite, no darker twin than Flem Snopes.

In Jefferson, Flem comes into his own. Giving off no image of himself but simply reflecting and enlarging the images and values of the community, Flem is able to manipulate and capitalize his way up the social and economic ladder of the community. "You couldn't see behind Mr. Snopes' eyes because they were not really looking at you at all," observed Charles Mallison in *The Town*. Flem's eyes were more like mirrors, "like a pond of stagnant water is not really looking at you" but merely reflecting your image (166). In this sense, Flem is like the Author, reflecting in his texts what he sees around him.

Actually, Flem is more like the text, a product of the author's sense of his place and time. Faulkner said many times that he wrote only what he saw around him, the good and the bad, striving only to tell the "truth." As he told Malcolm Cowley, "I listen to the voices, and when I put down what the voices say, it's right. Sometimes I don't like what they say, but I don't change it."[54] Flem and Faulkner were both in this sense survivors, adapting to their changing circumstances, always observing, listening, hearing the "voices" around them and within them. Each would do anything to achieve his aim in life—to get rich, to get the books written—and each had his eye on an institution. "The last thing he would ever do is hurt that bank," Ratliff explains. "Because any bank . . . stands for money, and the last thing he would do is insult or degrade money" (142). Faulkner, of course, aimed his sights on literature. "I have no time to wonder who is reading me," he told Jean Stein in 1956. "Mine is the standard which has to be met, which is when the work makes me feel the way I do when I read *La Tentation de Saint Antoine* or the Old Testament."[55]

Just as Faulkner maintained a sense of his own ephemerality (he told Stein that "if I had not existed, someone else would have written me"[56]) in the face of the power of his image as Author, he gave Flem a sense of his own self that few of Flem's observers could share. When Flem goes to buy furniture for his mansion in *The Town,* the salesman first appeals to his pride and suggests that he buy articles that look "expensive." Flem refuses. Next, the salesman appeals to his vanity, suggesting the "successful" look. Again, Flem says no. Then the salesman appeals to hypocrisy by suggesting an antique look, conjuring images of a distinguished Snopes ancestry. This time, according to Eula, Flem speaks up, giving one of his longest orations in the trilogy. "I had a grandfather because everybody had," he tells the furniture salesman. "I dont know who he was but I know that whoever he was he never owned enough furniture for a room, let alone a house. Besides," Flem concludes, "I dont aim to fool anybody. Only a fool would try to fool smart people, and anybody that needs to fool fools is already one" (222). The furniture he does buy is of a mass-produced "original" design, and Gavin Stevens recognizes it from the magazine ads. *"This is neither a Copy nor a Reproduction,"* as the ad might read. *"It is our own Model scaled to your individual Requirements"* (221). Flem has no more of a "statement" to make by his home furnishings and personal lifestyle than he has "uses" for his riches. As a capitalist, Flem is an "artist." The getting is important; the money itself, like the work of art, has no intrinsic "use" or purpose. It is up to others—in the case of the work of art, it is up to the critics—to interpret (or spend) the results of the artist's hard work. As explained earlier, Faulkner never contradicted a thoughtful interpretation of his work. Flem Snopes, the small town capitalist, has a character that is consistent with Faulkner's view of the artist. He merely reflects and represents his place and time. He pursues his own career (listening to the "voices") and others react to his creations. "The artist is of no importance," Faulkner continued in his interview with Jean Stein. "Only what he creates is important, since there is nothing new to be said."[57]

What Flem represents in his lifetime, what he has created, is an "image" of a man which reflects all that the community dislikes about itself, or more accurately, all that the community denies it even possesses. The episode in *The Town* concerning Montgomery Ward's peep show dramatizes how little difference there is between "Flemism,"[58] as Edmond L. Volpe has called Flem's behavior, and the extreme behavior of Jefferson officials. Most of the time, Jefferson citizens do not act like Flem, but when circumstances compel extreme action, Flem's amorality becomes an acceptable option. When Gavin and Ratliff learn about the peep show, Gavin asserts, "You simply cant do that in Jefferson" (124). Yet because Montgomery Ward's offense is more against the community's self-image than it is criminal, Gavin, the county attorney, must resort to arresting Montgomery Ward on a technicality. By arresting and jailing the man on an obsolete and never-enforced charge of operating a motor vehicle in town, Gavin is able to "legally" impound Montgomery Ward's property and effectively enforce the town's morality. The fact that the arrest is arbitrary, not to mention in violation of Montgomery Ward's constitutional rights, does not faze Gavin nor any of the other local law enforcement officials.

When Flem appears in Gavin's office with the plan to "plant" illegal whiskey on Montgomery Ward's property, thus giving Gavin something more serious to charge him with than obscenity or driving, Gavin is wholly receptive. He is also deluded. "You're like me," he tells Flem. "You dont give a damn about truth either. What you're interested in is justice." Given Gavin's behavior in the Montgomery Ward affair, the words "truth" and "justice" are absolutely meaningless, and his claim to either one of them is completely spurious. Flem, on the other hand, knows exactly what he is doing and why. "I'm interested in Jefferson," he counters. "We got to live here"

(176). The tactics and purposes of Gavin and Flem are exactly the same here. Both men want Montgomery Ward's peep show out of Jefferson because it is contrary to the image they share of their town, and both will engage in extralegal maneuvering to expel it. The only difference is in their respective views of their selves in the process.[59]

Gavin, as an upstanding member of the community, has internalized the town's interests so that when he acts, he believes he upholds the general will. If the will of the community is hypocritical, Gavin will fulfill even that with sincerity. Flem, on the other hand, while mastering the arts of community success, does not necessarily believe in any of it. He merely studies and observes the town's behavior in business and, increasingly, in civic affairs. To Flem, "respectability" and "civic virtue" (177) have nothing to do with truth and justice. Rather, they are additional possessions to acquire and consume, and they are necessary to complete his representation and reflection of the community. When their interests demand it, Faulkner suggests in this episode, community members have it within their capacity to act the same way as Flem Snopes does. The only difference, as Gavin Stevens demonstrates in *The Town*, is that they will not recognize their behavior for what it is; indeed, they may even justify it in terms of "truth" and "justice." When Flem counters Gavin's delusions with his simple statement of community (and self-) interest, he challenges the county attorney to face what he really represents.

The confrontation of Flem and Gavin concerning Montgomery Ward is a kind of symbolic confrontation of art and community. If Flem may be seen as an "artist," as I have suggested, then his function before Gavin is to compel Stevens to examine himself, or at least to confront what the artist is attempting to communicate. In chapter seventeen of *The Town*, Stevens gives an interpretation of Flem that further draws the parallels between Flem's character and Faulkner's view of himself. According to Gavin, Flem "realized that he himself had nothing and would never have more than nothing unless he wrested it from his environment and time, and the only weapon he would ever have to do it with would be money" (263). By once again substituting "words" for "money," Gavin could be describing Faulkner. The parallels continue in Gavin's statement, including the images of a lifetime of "sacrifice" in the name of his calling, an incapacity to find fulfillment in love, and acting in the role of father to another man's child. According to Gavin, Flem always had to work too hard for his achievements, knowing at the same time that as long as life lasted he could never for one second relax his vigilance, not just to add to it but simply to keep, hang on to, what he already had, had so far accumulated. Amassing it by terrible and picayune nickel by nickel, having learned too soon . . . that he would never have any other single method of gaining it save simple and ruthless antlike industry since (and this was the first time he had ever experienced humility) he knew now that he not only had not the education with which to cope with those who did have education, whom he must outguess and outfigure and despoil, but that he never would have that education now, since his was the fate to have first the need for the money before he had opportunity to acquire the means to get it (264–65).

This is a very odd statement for Gavin to make about Flem, particularly the final comments about education. It is not, however, a surprising self-assessment for Faulkner to make in 1956. Faulkner's lack of formal education, while it never seems to have hindered his ability to create (he had an early "need for" that), did leave him ill-prepared to move about in literary circles. Never mastering the language of the university, Faulkner often preferred to project the image of "country farmer" at the University of Virginia or that of the simple, untutored verbal craftsman. Part of his reluctance in his public role in the 1950s might very well have been due to the kinds of anxieties Gavin attributes to Flem. According to Gavin, Flem "had no evidence yet that he could cope with and fend off that enemy which the word Education represented to him, yet had neither qualm nor doubt that he was going to try" (264). Faulkner was "going to try" also. In the same year that *The Town* was published, Faulkner became writer-in-residence at the University of Virginia. While there, he had worked out a reconciliation with "Education." In one of his first recorded classroom conferences there, Faulkner distinguishes between "writing men" and "literary men." "I think that to be a literary man infers a certain amount of— well, even formal education, and there are some writers that never had formal education. Of course, you can be literary without the formal education, but I've got to talk in terms of what I know about Faulkner, now, you see, and Sherwood Anderson—that we were not literary men in the sense that Edmund Wilson is a literary man or Malcolm Cowley, for instance."[60] Instead of trying to "fool anybody" at the university, fools or otherwise, Faulkner presented himself as a kind of literary anachronism, a writer out of the era of Sherwood Anderson rather than that of Malcolm Cowley. When faced with the types of questions that might require knowledge of formal education, Faulkner would beg off with what might be called aggressive humility. "Well, as an old veteran sixth grader," he began in response to a question about English composition, "that question is out of my province, because I never got to freshman English."[61]

Faulkner, as others have pointed out, was never comfortable with his institutional role as Laureate and was never at ease with his canonization. Indeed, a canonical apocrypha is as profoundly oppositional as a respectable Snopes. Gavin's meditation on Flem Snopes is the first (and the only) extended presentation of Flem as a suffering human being, as a candidate for human pity. It is interesting, then, that during the writing of *The Town*, Faulkner began to experience feelings of extreme self-pity, particularly in the form of doubts about whether he would be able to maintain his career. In January 1956, for example, he wrote to Harold Ober about getting "some advice about what to so with the money I have" in order to make it last for him. "I will probably live longer than I will write and earn."[62] Fears that he would outlive his creative drive or outlive his ability to "outguess and outfigure and despoil" the educated ones of the literary community were especially burdensome. With nothing to write, Faulkner would have nothing to live for. As early as 1938 he had foreseen the same fate for Flem Snopes. "By this time Flem has eaten up Jefferson too," Faulkner projected for the third volume of the trilogy. "There is nothing else he can gain, and worse than this, nothing else he wants."[63]

In *The Mansion*, Flem's ambition has brought him to the limits of the success possible in his community: he has nowhere else to climb. As a banker, Flem has "made it" in Jefferson and, according to Faulkner, "the rest of his career in Jefferson was doomed to respectability" (57). What begins to afflict Flem in *The Mansion*, in the eyes of his observers, is something that might be called the anxiety of establishment. Given his insignificant origins and his lack of training, Flem always considered himself an outsider. In Mink's mind, Flem was "the one Snopes of them all who had risen, broken free, had either been born with or had learned, taught himself, the knack or the luck to cope with, hold his own, handle the They or Them which he, Mink, apparently did not have the knack or the luck to do" (38). Even Ratliff, perhaps the man most jealous of Flem in Jefferson, acknowledges that Flem had to work hard for his money and his social status, "had to earn both of them, snatch and tear and scrabble both of them outen the hard enduring resisting rock you might say"

(153). Now, however, in the last year of Flem's life (it is 1946 in *The Mansion;* this is the same year *The Portable Faulkner* was initially published and recognition of Faulkner's "achievement" began to coalesce in literary circles), he has climbed to the top of the community's success ladder, where he sits in silence. According to Charles Mallison, Flem "had begun life as a nihilist and then softened into a mere anarchist and now was not only a conservative but a tory too: a pillar, rock-fixed, of things as they are" (222). When Flem dies, he dies willingly, offering no resistance to Mink's intentions. "Maybe he was just bored," Ratliff says. "The pore son of a bitch" (430).

Flem's murder occurs as a result of the ultimate "Snopes-ish" trick of the entire trilogy, when Gavin more or less acquiesces in Linda's plan to get Mink released from prison. His attempts to block Mink's intentions, anyway, are feeble. Noel Polk has pointed out that critical acceptance of Flem's murder as right and just is a major misunderstanding of the trilogy. Flem's life story, Polk argues, is "being played out every day in every city in America" as social and economic fortunes rise and fall. No matter how personally odious any given successful capitalist may be, Polk asks, "how many of them deserve to die by an assassin's bullet?"[64] Flem's death and the machinations of Gavin and Linda behind his murder further dramatize, I would suggest, that Flem's whole character, his whole life story, has never been anything more than the product of his place and time. Flem may not have a singular, "personal" character, but he has an authentic public existence. His tactics and behavior throughout the trilogy have reflected, in a purified, or purist form the existing tactics and models of behavior made available to him by the community. No matter how devious or secretive Flem may appear to be, he never did anything that did not have some kind of public precedent, or would or could be challenged publically by his fellows. When his scheme with the water company's brass backfires in the "Centaur in Brass" episode, he pays for the damages out of his own pocket. The way in which he is killed merely demonstrates that as much as Flem reflected community standards or morality (including occasional amorality or dishonesty, when called for), the community itself is still the *source* of those standards and mores. What Gavin and Linda do in *The Mansion* is simply to expand the definition of the community and the parameters of how we might act to accomplish our ends. Had Flem survived, doubtless he would have become a conspiratorial assassin as well.

At the end of the trilogy and at the end of his life, Flem sits in his antebellum mansion doing nothing. "Not reading, just sitting there with his feet propped and his hat on," according to Faulkner, "his jaw moving faintly and steadily as if he were chewing" (413). The anxiety of establishment, of having reached the top and become "a pillar, rock-fixed, of things as they are" leaves him without a purpose. He "had no auspices," Faulkner says at Flem's death. He belonged to no "fraternal, civic, nor military" organizations but only to "finance; not the economy—cotton or cattle or anything else . . . but belonged simply to Money" (419).

There is a point, of course, where the parallels between Faulkner's sense of himself and his portrait of Flem become ponderous. Flem is no allegorical self, even if the parallels are compelling. When Faulkner killed off Flem at the end of *The Mansion,* he may also have extinguished himself as a potential object of self-pity, paving the way for a renewed assertion of the apocrypha. His next book, *The Reivers,* despite its nostalgic atmosphere, reads like a fresh approach to fiction for Faulkner after the extended and deliberate pace of the trilogy. Nonetheless, there is one quality worthy of respect in Flem, which Flem himself may have forgotten by the end of his life, but which Faulkner did not. "That was humility," Ratliff says in *The Mansion,* a quality Flem carried with him from his peasant origins. It was "the only kind of humility that's worth a hoot: the humility to know there's a heap of things you dont know yet but if you jest got the patience to be humble and watchful long enough, especially keeping one eye on your back trail, you will" (157). When Flem reached a point where there was nothing left for him to consume in Jefferson, nothing worth the watching and the learning in order to master, it was time, in Faulkner's imagination, to let him die. As for Faulkner, he would continue writing. "I am a veteran member of a living literature," he wrote to Random House editor Albert Erskine during the editing of *The Mansion*. "So if what I write in 1958 aint better than what I wrote in 1938, I should have stopped writing twenty years ago; or, since 'being alive' equals 'motion,' I should be 20 years in the grave."[65]

"Snopes," and the main product of "Snopes" is their "Flem," means the personification of community values and behavior in the negative. Snopes—S'Nopes—means the turning of the community's values and behavior against the community itself, in the way that a mirror reverses the images it reflects. A Snopes, however, does not simply reflect in a passive manner; rather, a Snopes is a reflection in motion, a rebellion, a peasant's nope. All Snopeses are continually moving, from one job in the community to another, from one capacity to another, from hamlet to town and city. At the end of *The Town*, this movement is parodied when Snopeses are actually *mailed* to one another in "The Waifs" episode. In *The Mansion*, Gavin finds the attempt to stop Snopes motion "hopeless. Even when you get rid of one Snopes, there's already one behind you even before you can turn around" (349). Snopeses, rascals they may be, want life and crave movement; they refuse to be "stopped" or determined by community controls. Of all his clan, Flem is the one Snopes who has figured out how to direct his motion upward, translating motion into progress and achievement. Flem only appears to be phlegmatic; actually, he is quite active. "In my synonymity," Faulkner wrote concerning *The Mansion*, " 'living' equals 'motion, change, constant alteration,' equals 'evolution,' which in my optimistic synonymity equals 'improvement.' "[66] The "constant alteration" of Faulkner's apocrypha and the fluid relationship of his apocryphal world to the actual world is what the trilogy as a whole represents. Flem is an *apocryphal* Faulkner, a challenge to the man Faulkner may have thought he was as he devoted his life to re-creating his world. In all, as the next chapter will argue, *Snopes* is Faulkner's apocryphal summation, his private testament of rebellion and triumph in Yoknapatawpha.

1. "Address to the Graduating Class, Pine Manor Junior College, June 8, 1953," in *Essays, Speeches and Public Letters*, p. 135.
2. This principle is discussed at length in Mikhail Bakhtin, *Rabelais and His World*, translated by Helene Iswolsky (Cambridge: M.I.T. Press, 1968). See especially the Introduction and Chapters 5 and 6.
3. Slatoff, *Quest for Failure*, p. 146.
4. Coughlin, *The Private World of William Faulkner*, p. 140.
5. See, for example, Joseph Blotner's "Introduction" to the *Mississippi Poems* half of *Helen: A Courtship and Mississippi Poems*, p. 137. Blotner quotes Faulkner: "I believe that any writer wants first to be a poet. When he finds that he cant write first-rate poetry . . . then he tries short stories, which is the next severe medium. When that fails, he goes to the novel." In an interview at the University of Mississippi in 1947, "Faulkner said that primarily he was a poet and not a prose writer; that he began writing verse when he was seventeen; and that he quit writing poetry at twenty-three because he could not write so well as Shakespeare and Shelley had written and because he found his best medium to be fiction." See *William Faulkner of Oxford*, p. 133.
6. *Lion in the Garden*, p. 81.
7. *Ibid.*, p. 93.
8. *Essays, Speeches and Public Letters*, p. 138.
9. See "An Introduction to *The Sound and the Fury*," in Richard Brodhead, ed., *Faulkner: New Perspectives* (Englewood Cliffs, NJ: Prentice Hall, 1983), p. 24.

10. Robert Penn Warren has characterized Faulkner as "an apolitical writer" in his introduction to Warren, ed., *Faulkner: A Collection of Critical Essays*, p. 17; Richard King, "Memory and Tradition," in Doreen Fowler and Ann J. Abadie, eds., *Faulkner and the Southern Renaissance* (Jackson: University Press of Mississippi, 1982), pp. 155, 156, notes that "for all the richness of Faulkner's world, it is one which presents no political 'space' within which collective, public action can be taken seriously." In considering *A Fable*, King maintains his position that "Faulkner fails to create convincing images of political consideration or action in his fiction." Andre Bleikasten, "For/Against an Ideological Reading of Faulkner's Novels," in Gresset and Samway, S. J., eds., *Faulkner and Idealism*, p. 30, on the other hand, has taken Faulkner critics to task on just this issue. He notes "the conspicuous absence, in Faulkner criticism, of any sustained and serious consideration of the ideological aspects of his fiction." What critics do, Bleikasten observes, is "to censure all questions about ideology—which tells us something, at least, about the ideology of the critics." Although Joseph Blotner reports that, according to Lillian Hellman, Faulkner was "very anti-radical," it is true that when Vincent Sheean asked Faulkner for a contribution to a relief fund for Spanish Loyalists in 1939, Faulkner sent him the manuscript of *Absalom, Absalom!* See *Faulkner: A Biography*, pp. 741 and 1030. Yashir Kemal, a Turkish novelist, once told Paul Theroux on the Orient Express that "the greatest Marxist writer was William Faulkner" in his opinion. Quoted in Elizabeth Kerr, *William Faulkner's Gothic Domain* (Port Washington, NY: Kennikat Press, 1979), p. 246. George C. Bedell, *Kierkegaard and Faulkner: Modalities of Existence* (Baton Rouge: Louisiana State University Press, 1972), pp. 72–73, has grappled with Faulkner's politics and concluded that "he had no 'System' to which his fictional output could be subjected" because Faulkner's politics were always "subverted by his accuracy in the perception and recording of the social scene in which his characters were placed." Finally, Margaret Walker Alexander, "Faulkner and Race," In Evan Harrington and Ann J. Abadie, eds., *The Maker and the Myth* (Jackson: University Press of Mississippi, 1978), p. 108, has surveyed previous political assessments of Faulkner, finding "critics who first judged him as a Communist, a Socialist realist, or a naturalist such as Granville Hicks and, even later, by the New Critics from the Ivy League who began to read everything in terms of the Christian myth of redemption. . . . Faulkner has been treated as a stoic humanist, Christian, and segregationist—the three are not necessarily compatible." Alexander, however, sees Faulkner as "a symbolist treating characters as symbols and types, preferring to deal with the standards of life as human rather than divine or bestial, hating always the nonhuman, the mechanical, or mechanistic, and believing always in the human spirit, the human being, the human heart. Faulkner should be read as one reads the Bible—not literally but figuratively."

11. Noel Polk, *Faulkner's Requiem for a Nun: A Critical Study* (Bloomington: Indiana University Press, 1981), p. 9, was among the first to recognize Temple's "courageous attempt to accept the responsibility for her actions and to live with the consequences." Polk also points out the absurdity of considering Nancy Mannigoe a saint (139).

12. Quoted in Pagels, *The Gnostic Gospels*, p. 35.

13. *Essays, Speeches and Public Letters*, pp. 140–41.

14. *Ibid.*, pp. 141–42.

15. Blotner, *Faulkner: A Biography*, p. 1687, sees Faulkner growing more conservative on the race issue in the later 1950s, a conservatism Blotner attributes to his not being "very optimistic about integration" as the decade progressed.

16. *Selected Letters*, pp. 381–82.

17. *Ibid.*, p. 395.

18. *Ibid.*

19. *Essays, Speeches and Public Letters*, pp. 108–109.

20. *Ibid.*, p. 123.

21. *Ibid.*, pp. 62, 65–66.
22. *Ibid.*, p. 162. Also printed in *Faulkner in the University*, p. 242.
23. See "On Fear," in *Essays, Speeches and Public Letters*, p. 106: "We must be free not because we claim freedom, but because we practise it."
24. "Address to the Delta Council," *ibid.*, p. 129; in a speech to Delta State Teachers College in May 1952, Faulkner spoke of "the duty of a man, the individual . . . to be responsible for the consequences of his own acts, to pay his own score, owing nothing to any man." See *Faulkner: A Biography*, p. 1416. Similarly, in 1955 in Manila, Faulkner insisted upon "a responsibility that goes with the privilege of saying what one thinks." See *Lion in the Garden*, p. 206.
25. *Essays, Speeches and Public Letters*, p. 155.
26. *Faulkner in the University*, p. 192.
27. The words are those of Edith Brown Douds, a neighbor, in *William Faulkner of Oxford*, p. 50. All three volumes of the trilogy are dedicated to Phil Stone. According to Stone, he was the only person in Faulkner's home town "with whom Faulkner could discuss his literary plans and hopes and his technical trials and aspirations and you may be sure I kept his feet upon the ground. . . . Day after day for years," Stone reports, "he had drilled into him the obvious truths that the world owed no man anything; that true greatness was in creating great things and not in pretending them; that the only road to literary success was by sure, patient, hard intelligent work. . . . Most of all was drilled into him through that great weapon ridicule," Stone concludes, "the idea of avoiding contemporary literary cliques with their febrile, twittering barrenness, the idea of literature growing from its own natural soil, and the dread of the easy and bottomless pit of surface cleverness." *Ibid.*, p. 7 (Stone's words were written in 1934). It seems impossible to measure the extent of Stone's influence on Faulkner, although by the content of Stone's own testimony here it appears that he knew Faulkner better than many critics do even today. Some critics have attempted to downplay Stone's importance as Faulkner's mentor. According to David Minter, *William Faulkner: His Life and Work*, pp. 26–27, for example, "Phil developed a faulty sense of what his younger friend was doing. Later he believed there was almost nothing he had not taught William: all the literature, philosophy, and history, everything from commas . . . to moral philosophy." For another view of Stone's influence on Faulkner, See H. Edward Richardson, *William Faulkner: The Journey to Self-Discovery* (Columbia: University of Missouri Press, 1969), pp. 24–25 and 166–67. Richardson attributes Faulkner's abandoning formal education to "a plan arrived at partially through the influence of his older friend Phil Stone" and attributes to Stone Faulkner's decision to write for himself and not for publishers, the decision which, Richardson implies, led to the composition of *The Sound and the Fury* in the late 1920s.
28. "A note on Sherwood Anderson," in *Essays, Speeches and Public Letters*, p. 8.
29. *Lion in the Garden*, p. 223.
30. See, for example, Gold, *William Faulkner: A Study in Humanism*, p. 5: "*The Town* and *The Mansion* seem to have come from an artist who was torn between a compulsion to sermonize and a wish to recapture the vigor of the imaginative early work." Judith Bryant Wittenberg, *Faulkner: The Transfiguration of Biography* (Lincoln: University of Nebraska Press, 1979), p. 182, is much more direct and indicting: "As time went on, Faulkner would increasingly turn back to early 'source works' like 'Father Abraham' for inspiration, and he conceived almost no fiction that was fully 'new' after the early 1930s. This is testimony to the rich suggestiveness of Faulkner's early fiction, but it also makes a poignant comment on his growing inability to find new ideas." While it is not entirely clear what Wittenberg means by "find new ideas," it does not mean, I think, that Faulkner's narrative strategies remained static. Wittenberg refers to Faulkner's subject matter and seems to interpret a lifelong devotion to a literary project as stagnation.
31. The published story is "Wash," in *Doctor Martino and Other Stories* (New

York: Smith and Haas, 1934); the unpublished story is now available. See "Evangeline" in *Uncollected Stories of William Faulkner,* edited by Joseph Blotner (New York: Random House, 1979).

32. And so, *The Hamlet* contains revised versions of "Fool About a Horse," *Scribners* (August 1936), "The Hound," *Doctor Martino* (1934), "Spotted Horses," *Scribners* (June 1931), and "Lizards in Jamshyd's Courtyard," *Saturday Evening Post* (February 27, 1932); also, the content of "Barn Burning," *Harpers* (June 1939) is referred to, as is "Afternoon of a Cow," *Furioso* (Summer 1947), which was written at least as early as 1937 and read to friends (see Blotner, ed., *Uncollected Stories,* notes, p. 702). *The Town* contains revised versions of "Centaur in Brass" and "Mule in the Yard" both published in *Collected Stories* (1950) and contains the story, "The Waifs," published shortly before the novel itself was released in the *Saturday Evening Post* (May 4, 1957). *The Mansion* contains revised versions of "By the People," *Mademoiselle* (October 1955) and "Hog Pawn," an unpublished story (see Blotner, ed., *Uncollected Stories*); it also contains "Mink Snopes," *Esquire* (December 1959), which was published separately *after* the novel was released. For complete information on Faulkner's short stories and their bibliographies, see James B. Meriwether, "The Short Fiction of William Faulkner: A Bibliography," in Joseph Katz, ed., *Proof: The Yearbook of American Bibliographical and Textual Studies,* volume 1 (Columbia: University of South Carolina Press, 1971); see also the notes to *Uncollected Stories.*

33. *Selected Letters,* p. 107. In January 1939, Faulkner foresaw the trilogy as a one-thousand-page volume called, simply, *Snopes. Ibid.,* p. 109.

34. *Ibid.,* p. 424.

35. Kerr, *William Faulkner's Gothic Domain,* p. 245.

36. James Gray Watson, *The Snopes Dilemma: Faulkner's Trilogy* (Coral Gables, FL: University of Miami Press, 1970), p. 229.

37. Warren Beck, *Man in Motion: Faulkner's Trilogy* (Madison: University of Wisconsin Press, 1961), p. 185; see also pp. 5, 61, 76, 168 for Beck's epistemological view of the trilogy. Beck refers to the repetition of events as evidence of "Faulkner's own willingness to take a second look for a possible refinement and enlargement of awareness" (p. 5); "the guild of Faulkner's spectator-interlocutors" with their "imaginative penetration of reality" gets particular play in *The Town* (p. 61); Beck characterizes the trilogy as a "dramatization of inquiry and appraisal" (p. 76) and states that "Ratliff and others are poetizers of the fable, transmuting the historical into the imaginative, enhancing it for the delineation of theme, vivifying it by sympathy, focusing upon it by the refractions of irony" (p. 168). As interesting and instructive as Beck's observations are, they do not indicate to what end Beck believes Faulkner employs this strategy. The question is no longer *how* Faulkner does it, but *why* Faulkner does it.

38. Elizabeth D. Rankin, "Chasing Spotted Horses: The Quest for Human Dignity in Faulkner's *Snopes* Trilogy," in Glenn O. Carey, ed., *Faulkner: The Unappeased Imagination: A Collection of Critical Essays* (Troy, NY: Whitson Publishing Co., 1980), p. 140.

39. Woodrow Stroble, "Flem Snopes: A Crazed Mirror," in Carey, ed., *Faulkner: The Unappeased Imagination,* p. 198.

40. On the shift in narrative purpose from *The Hamlet* to the next two volumes of the trilogy, Stroble, *ibid.,* p. 196, claims that in the first volume, "right and wrong are clearly defined values. . . . Then, in the next two volumes, right and wrong shade into less well-defined hues; ambiguity, doubt, and paradox govern events."

41. *Faulkner in the University,* p. 283.

42. *Lion in the Garden,* p. 239.

43. *Faulkner in the University,* p. 97.

44. *Lion in the Garden,* p. 239.

45. *Faulkner in the University,* pp. 33, 98. See also Cleanth Brooks, *William*

Faulkner: Toward Yoknapatawpha and Beyond (New Haven, CT: Yale University Press, 1978), p. 219, where Brooks concludes, "Faulkner apparently always had an admiration for the autonomous and high-hearted spirit, and a loathing for the person who was herd-minded. . . . Even Flem Snopes may just possibly elicit a kind of grudging respect until in the end he capitulates to respectability; that, for Faulkner, is the truly unpardonable sin."

46. *Selected Letters,* p. 56.

47. *Ibid.,* p. 276.

48. *Faulkner: A Biography,* p. 1541.

49. The phrase is Stephen Longstreet's, who was referring to Faulkner's tendency to turn in *too much* material to producers. For example, he would hand in fifty to sixty pages a day when he was assigned to *To Have and Have Not,* far too much for them to read and far too complex for them to use. See Longstreet, "William Faulkner in California," p. 29. See also Bruce Kawin, *Faulkner's MGM Screenplays* (Knoxville: University of Tennessee Press, 1982), p. xxv, for an account of Faulkner's initial blackballing in Hollywood.

50. Joseph J. Arpad, "William Faulkner's Legendary Novels: The Snopes Trilogy," in Leland H. Cox, ed. *William Faulkner: Critical Collection: A Guide to Critical Statements by Faulkner and Evaluative Essays on His Works* (Detroit: Gale Research Co., 1982), p. 326.

51. Watson, *The Snopes Dilemma,* p. 95.

52. See Poem XLIV of *A Green Bough* in Faulkner, *The Marble Faun and A Green Bough* (New York: Random House, 1965), p. 67. The poem is also known as "My Epitaph."

53. Watson, *The Snopes Dilemma,* p. 114.

54. *The Faulkner-Cowley File,* from Malcolm Cowley's notebook, "Faulkner's Visit," October 26, 1948, p. 114.

55. *Lion in the Garden,* p. 243.

56. *Ibid.,* p. 238.

57. *Ibid.*

58. Edmond L. Volpe, *A Reader's Guide to William Faulkner* (New York: Noonday Press, 1964), p. 309.

59. Faulkner makes this point a second time in *The Town* in the "Mule in the Yard" episode. Flem buys off I. O. Snopes and runs him out of town. Gavin Stevens is hired as a "witness," but what he witnesses is I. O. and Hait confessing to the bilking of the railroad company and to Mr. Hait's suicide on the tracks. These criminal acts are ignored by County Attorney Stevens in the name of his idea of justice. Ratliff, observing Flem and Gavin in action, rightly comments, "Because as soon as you set down to laugh at it, you find it aint funny at all" (257).

60. *Faulkner in the University,* p. 23.

61. *Ibid.,* p. 33.

62. *Selected Letters,* p. 392. Pity, of course, is something Faulkner did not want. After Eula tells Gavin of Flem's impotence, she warns him, "You've got to be careful or you'll have to pity him. You'll have to. He couldn't bear that, and it's no use to hurt people if you dont get anything for it" (331).

63. *Selected Letters,* p. 108.

64. Noel Polk, "Idealism in *The Mansion,*" in Gresset and Samway, eds., *Faulkner and Idealism,* p. 117.

65. *Selected Letters,* p. 429.

66. *Ibid.*

5. The Summation of the Apocrypha
Snopes

The *Snopes* trilogy is Faulkner's apocryphal, narrative trinity: it is a meditation on the sensual, intellectual, and spiritual dimensions of the apocryphal vision. As the one fictional project that occupied Faulkner's attention and sustained his creative interests throughout his career, *Snopes,* in its final form, can be understood as a definitive representation of what Faulkner meant by "apocryphal county." Critics, taking their cue from Cowley and others, have misconstrued the trilogy as a "chronological picture" of the Yoknapatawpha Snopes clan—and as chronology, it is deeply disappointing. It may be more significant than coincidental that Faulkner encountered Malcolm Cowley in between the first and second books of the *Snopes* trilogy. For while *The Hamlet* may suggest to the reader a "chronological picture," *The Town* dispenses with that narrative strategy and engages the reader in an entirely different kind of drama. If we take Faulkner's lead and strike out the "chronology" presumption, the importance of the trilogy as a trinitarian meditation finally emerges. As trinity, the trilogy represents the flesh, the mind, and the spirit as the tripartite building blocks or texts of the human experience. In the apocrypha, the trilogy offers a three-dimensional study of human rebellion against the death of the body, the intellect, and the soul.

The Hamlet is a deeply sensual work that displays and examines a full range of human passions and appetites. It shows a richly sensual peasantry, a world both characterized by the interactions of males and females but also rocked by the distinctions between the sexes. *The Town* is consciously intellectual, presenting epistemological and ideological meditations on *Snopes*. Its three narrators devote their mental energies to understanding and thereby controlling their small world. *The Mansion,* finally, is a restatement of Faulkner's spirituality brought "home" from *A Fable.* It depends heavily upon materials from the previous volumes, and it reflects the "content" of the body and the mind as it achieves its own, independent summation. The *Snopes* trilogy, as Faulkner says in the prefatory note to *The Mansion,* was alive in his imagination throughout his career as a fictionalist. It began with the tall stories he told friends about "Snopeses" in the 1920s and continued piecemeal in short stories and in novels until the completion of the trilogy in 1959. The final product, the assembled trinitarian apocrypha, thus represents the assembly of Faulkner's aesthetics into a single, coherent, and wholistic form. With the trilogy, Faulkner's apocryphal vision reaches its apotheosis.

I In Defense of the Body: *The Hamlet* (1940)

Faulkner had "the Snopes book" in mind as early as 1932 when he predicted it would take "about 2 years" to write it. When he signed contracts with Random House in July 1933, he apparently intended it as his next project and worked on the manuscript over the summer. In October, he put the idea aside for the *Requiem for a Nun* project, although he continued to send Snopes stories to magazines. In January 1934, he told Harrison Smith that he could not finish *Requiem for a Nun* "in good time" because "the Snopes stuff" would not "lie quiet." By February, however, he delayed both projects to begin work on the manuscript of *Absalom, Absalom!*[1] It was probably too early in Faulkner's career for "the Snopes stuff" to emerge from his imagination satisfactorily. *Absalom, Absalom!* would occupy his attention and would itself lead to other projects for the next two years. *Requiem for a Nun* would have to wait nearly twenty years.

In December 1938, Faulkner was back to work on the Snopes material. Now, however, he envisioned "three books, whether big enough to be three separate volumes I dont know yet, though I think it will." He was, he told Robert K. Haas, "half through" with the first volume,[2] but the novel presented problems unlike those he had experienced with previous novels. He seems to have been a little unsure of the material at first. In March 1939, he sent Haas a large portion of the manuscript and solicited his opinion of it. "Let me know what you think of the novel I am sending in," he wrote, "when you have time to read it." In April, he sent Haas some corrections—page inserts—to "tighten it up." His additions were meant to give the book "density, make the people stand up." His faith in the project had rebounded since March, and he said he was pleased with the revisions he had made. At the bottom of the typescript he added, in pen, "I am the best in America, by God."[3] The manuscript was completed in October 1939, when Faulkner also decided on the titles of the three volumes as they now stand. Although continuing to hammer out magazine stories for money, he made revisions on the manuscript at least through December.[4] *The Hamlet* was published on April 1, 1940.

The composition of *The Hamlet* spans the seven-year period between the completion of *Light in August* in 1932 and the publication of *The Wild Palms* in 1939. It reflects the carnality of those two books as well, yet with none of the extreme violence of the early work and none of the grievous frustration of the later one. Critics have generally recognized the passion of *The Hamlet* although analysis of the novel tends, understandably so, toward preoccupation with Snopes. Cleanth Brooks has discussed the "examples of human love" in the novel, including that of the Varners, the Eula-Labove-McCarron-Flem episode, Ike and the cow, and the Armstids.[5] James Watson, on the other hand, sees a "betrayal of human passion" in the novel, illustrated by the marriage of the sexually inspiring Eula to the passionless Flem.[6] It is clear, however, that in the novel the realm of the male and of the female are clearly distinguished. Although the two intersect sexually and passionately, they are demarcated socially. "Like Ab Snopes," Sally Page explains, "most of the men in *The Hamlet* welcome the chance to escape the routine pattern of labor whenever events offer them an opportunity to exploit their desire for physical and economic adventure." The women, on the other hand, "devote themselves to the regular, unexciting and laborious pattern of family sustenance." This division of social activity is best illustrated in the "Spotted Horses" episode, when Mrs. Littlejohn's domestic chores continue throughout the men's catastrophic trading.[7]

The structure of *The Hamlet* encourages a look at the division of society into male and female spheres. The first book, "Flem," examines masculinity and presents a distorted figure of a being who is active socially and economically but inactive personally and sexually. Flem has almost no need for women, and in his dealings with men he is detached and passionless. He sustains nothing but himself. His marriage to Eula, which is a grotesque denial of human passion, is made in the name of social and economic gain rather than love or even procreation. The marriage is part of the package deal by which Flem gets his foothold in Jefferson; in Faulkner's imagination, the package is the way the passionless rise to power. The second book, "Eula," presents an equally grotesque portrait of the female, who is socially and economically inactive and, despite herself, a dynamic personal and sexual entity. The female is as alienated from her public body—her significance to men—as the male is removed from the sensual, sustaining world of women. Eula has no need for men, and in her responses to her own body she is passionless and detached. Her marriage may be a disdainful repudiation of her fertility, but then again it is the men around her who control her public life and attach public importance to her immense sensuality.

The third book, "The Long Summer," looks at love and presents a series of ghastly examples of human passion. Significantly, and ironically of course, Flem and Eula are on their "honeymoon" during the long summer of human lust, loss, and manslaughter. Ike and his cow represent mindless, asocial, anarchic passion; Houston and Lucy symbolize passion resisted—by the man—and finally lost; Mink and Houston stand for homosensual cruelty as murder emerges as love's Other. By the end of "The Long Summer," human passion has swept through Frenchman's Bend and left in its wake a dead cow, a dead wife, and a dead landowner. The final book, "The Peasants," is a grotesque characterization of society, where trading and competition exist not for the good of the community, not even for personal gain, but for individual amusement and diversion. Flem takes the game seriously, however, and ups the stakes. The novel's denouemont is Flem's (and Eula's) apotheosis: the erotically dead triumphantly move to the city, trading the lusty world of stallions and heifers for the world of banks and middle-class craving, where a different kind of lust drives men and women.

◆ Heterosensuality: Men and Women in the Bend

"I'll declare," Mrs. Littlejohn says over Henry Armstid's beaten body in the "Spotted Horses" episode. "You men" (305). Public life, the so-called real world of human social and economic interaction, is a very male place in *The Hamlet*. Gary Lee Stonum characterizes the novel as taking a hard and critical look at "the myth of male society," which "is not simply a pretty fiction designated to cover up a greedily acquisitive society." The "myth" is comprised of "social and cultural forms," according to Stonum, which are supposed to "establish human values" but more likely represent "either cloaks for exploitation and brutality or empty fictions that carry no value or force in themselves."[8] Whatever we call male society—myth, cloak, or fiction—it is a very real and oppressive thing to the life of the human body as Faulkner presents it. When Mrs. Tull's husband is seriously injured by one of the wild ponies in "The Peasants," her outrage, Faulkner states, was "directed not at any Snopes or at any other man in particular but at all men, all males, and of which Tull himself was not at all the victim but the subject" (323). Mrs. Tull and the other wives of the Bend, including Mrs. Littlejohn, who is a kind of "public wife," recognize the Snopeses as prototypically male. In *The Town,* where figuring out Snopes becomes an ideological project, Gavin decides that "all Snopes are male" and that "Snopesishness" is carried from male to male genetically, terminating in the female (136). In *The Hamlet,* the breeding ground for Snopeses, social and economic intercourse is the exclusive haven of men.

Although women are excluded from public business in *The Hamlet,* they are far from immune to masculine prerogative. A definite problem arises, for example, when we try to attach an identity to Eula Varner. Faulkner remembered her, in 1957, as being "larger than life," too big, he said, for any human environment to hold.[9] Her overwhelming physical presence is prohibitive, in fact. It stands between her and her identity, precluding even her own knowledge of herself. The reason, of course, is that her body does not belong to her, and she knows it. Her brother Jody, for instance, considers her a part of the Varner property holdings. He will make her wear a camouflaging corset "and exactly as he would have felt the back of a new horse for old saddle sores, grimly explore with his hard heavy hand to see if she had the corset on or not" (133). Jody is attempting to protect Eula from the threat of seduction or even rape—in any case, guard against the destruction of Varner property. Labove, the schoolteacher, sees her as a kind of eternal female. The town boys compete for Eula, considering her a prize to go to the winner in their homosensual struggle. Flem, of course, sees Eula as a vehicle, part of the world's resources with which to trade and prosper. In the face of this masculine bombardment, Eula, at the onset of adolescence and puberty, is wholly alienated from her body. She develops into a young woman of two separate lives, Faulkner explains. "There was one Eula who supplied blood and nourishment to the buttocks and legs and breasts; there was the other Eula Varner who merely inhabited them, who went where they went because it was less trouble to do so, who was comfortable there but in their doings she intended to have no part, as you are in a house which you did not design but where the furniture is all settled and the rent paid up" (100). Eula's alienation is a conscious defense against the public significance of her body—a significance in which "she intended to have no part."

As Temple Drake experienced in *Sanctuary,* sexuality is the better part of destiny for Eula Varner in *The Hamlet.* Eula does not have to do anything (in fact, as Faulkner makes clear, she prefers not to move at all) to fulfill her social role as woman. As she tries to remain still, sitting "at her place in a kind of sullen bemusement," her "rife young female flesh" will provide the social world around her with all it needs to know about her. Those "definite breasts even at thirteen and eyes like cloudy hothouse grapes" and that "full damp mouth always slightly open" (10) place Eula in a status of furious movement against which all her resistance is futile. Despite her insistence upon neutrality, Eula is sensually doomed, but like Temple, she is also defiant. Her apparent laziness is not, as Faulkner says, like her father's "constant bustling cheerful idleness" but is "an actual force impregnable and even ruthless." It is as if by recognizing at an early age that she would have no say in her destiny, Eula makes an attempt to reverse, or at least freeze the course of her development.

She makes a stand, initially, to remain in her infant's perambulator until "she was graduated from it by force. Then," Faulkner adds, "she began to sit in chairs" (95). As she gets older she is compelled into movement by others—by her mother, her brother, the Negro manservant—but it is clear throughout Faulkner's depiction of her childhood that Eula wants no part of the moving world around her. When she plays maternally with her dolls in the toy perambulator, she attempts to protect her make-believe offspring from the fate that awaits her. "She would place all the dolls in it and sit in a chair beside it," Faulkner narrates. What the adults first think is indifference to the toy (because she does not *move* the perambulator around) and later decide is laziness is actually a form of defiance. Eula is destined, by the significance of her body to the rest of the community, to a particular kind of life. If that is so, she seems to state by her stasis, then let the community do all that is required to make her destiny. As for Eula herself, passive resistance (she practices a kind of sexual sit-in) is an available and effective mode of rebellion. In *The Town,* her resistance to community sexual mores and expectations, and her battle against sexual determinism are played out in her affair with De Spain. Eula's suicide marks the triumph of the community to dictate what is publicly acceptable in heterosocial relations. Even though Eula is a doomed woman in *The Hamlet,* her real tragedy lies in the fact that she seems to have always known it, even as a child.

Eula's rebellion against the community's expectations of her is demonstrated by her attempts to protect her body from violation. She refuses "to be pawed at" by the adolescent boys in the sexual experimentations of youth, acting against the suggestiveness of her young body by "preserving even within that aura of license and invitation in which she seemed to breathe and walk—or sit rather—a ruthless chastity" (128). Her insistence on physical autonomy is a "ruthless" act in its denial of masculine prerogative and community insistence. Yet Eula is not vicious; she simply wants to be left alone. The community, however, will not allow her this option. As fecund woman, as the local sexual prize, Eula is too valuable to the community to be granted personal autonomy. She will be forced, if necessary, into her sexual fate no matter what she does. Recognizing this oppression as her social reality, Eula gives up on participation, and on involvement in general, early in life. Labove, who elevates the eleven-year-old Eula to the status "of the very goddesses in his Homer and Thucydides" (113), realizes in his lust what she is about. When she sees him kneeling at her vacant seat in the schoolhouse, "he knew at once that she was neither frightened nor laughing at him," but "that she simply did not care" (120). This rebellious indifference (its form is actually indebted to the passive resistance of the slave) characterizes Eula throughout *The Hamlet.* When she returns to Frenchman's Bend as Mrs. Flem Snopes, her face passes her father's store without so much as a glance. "It passed in profile, calm, oblivious, incurious. It was not a tragic face: it was just damned" (265). It is the same face Faulkner envisioned on Temple Drake at the end of *Sanctuary* and on Caddy Compson at the end of his description of her in the "Appendix: Compson": the cold, serene, "damned" face of a woman brutalized and beaten, but also symbolic of rebellion and resistance. When Eula leaves the hamlet for Jefferson, her face is "calm and beautiful and by its expression carven or even corpse like," but she is not looking at the bystanders around her, "and maybe," Faulkner concludes, "not at anything they knew" (363).

Sexuality and sexual behavior is closely controlled by the community, and the fate of Eula Varner is only a small piece in a larger, enforced heterosocial design in *The Hamlet*. The primary symbol of the community's control over the sexual activity of its members is V. K. Ratliff, the itinerant sewing machine salesman and source of community information—or gossip. It is Ratliff who thinks of Flem and Eula with "outrage at the waste, the useless squandering" (159) of Eula's sensuality. Although Ratliff is a kind of self-appointed moral gadfly in *The Hamlet* (he thinks, for example, that the peasants ought to do something about the growing power of Snopes in the Bend; Tull, on the other hand, says "it aint right, but it aint none of our business" [71]), he also has the most actively immoral imagination of all the characters in the novel. He fantasizes about Lump Snopes, the storekeeper in Flem's absence, procuring sexual favors from the poor and ignorant peasant girls in return for his nickel-and-dime products (163–64). He has this fantasy as he walks toward the shed to investigate the peep show that is attracting the men of the Bend to Lump's barn.

Although all the men voyeuristically enjoy the sight of Ike's passion for the cow, Ratliff is sickened by it. Public displays of passion are as repugnant to Ratliff as they are to Flem. When Ratliff looks through the crack in the planks at Ike and the cow, "it was as though it were himself inside that stall with the cow, himself looking out of the blustered tongueless face at the row of faces watching him who had been given the wordless passions but not the specious words" (196). Whereas the voyeurs all, to the extent they enjoy the show, identify with Ike's lust (they are not identifying with the cow), only Ratliff attaches *shame* to the display of "wordless passion." Of Ike's entire active body, Ratliff identifies with the idiot's face. Ratliff, the quintessentially public man, shrinks from the intrusion of passion into the community's social and public affairs, and can read only humiliation in Ike's innocent desires. Perhaps the real reason Ratliff is so obsessed with Flem Snopes, then, is because the two men are, in their sensual lives, quite similiar. Yet where Flem uses his passionless nature to rise to the top of the community, Ratliff remains a Protestant moral watchdog of the common people.

Mrs. Littlejohn, who sees nothing wrong with Ike's love for the cow, has Ratliff's number. "So that's it," she says of his antagonism towards Ike's pruriency. "It aint that it is that itches you. It's that somebody named Snopes, or that particular Snopes, is making something out of it and you dont know what it is." Here Mrs. Littlejohn narrows in on Ratliff. "Or is it because folks come and watch?" she says. "It's all right for it to be, but folks mustn't know, see it" (198). All of what Mrs. Littlejohn says is true. Ratliff cannot stand to see Lump Snopes using Ike's passion for personal gain, just as he was outraged by Flem's use of Eula for personal gain, and he cannot stand a public display of human sexuality. Whatever sexuality is to Ratliff, it is clear that it cannot be integrated into the public realm where men interact politically and socially. Sexuality and sexual passion are such rarities in the marketplace that they can be exploited by men like Lump Snopes, men who capitalize on the kind of Ratliffian morality which grips the community. When sexuality enters the marketplace, according to Ratliff, it must be suppressed as something evil, something not to be acknowledged or looked upon. Ratliff's vision is, of course, a perversion of human nature, which is as sexual as it is social, and actually reflects the kind of pornographic economy practiced by Lump Snopes. Flem Snopes best exemplifies Ratliff's vision of what a public man ought to be, although Ratliff would never admit it. It is wholly appropriate, therefore, that Flem should outwit Ratliff in the land swindle that catapults him to Jefferson.

In the same way and with the same narrative strategy by which Faulkner paints the grotesque exaggeration of the male in Flem and the female in Eula, he presents a deformed vision of asocial sexuality in Ike and the cow. The narrative demonstrates the means by which the community, or someone acting in the name of the community's morals, corrects sexual deviancy. Ratliff introduces the community to the sin of pride in order to suppress Ike's display of unashamed lust. "I aint cussing you folks," he tells the voyeurs. "I'm cussing all of us" (197). Ratliff takes his public shame to I. O. Snopes and appeals to his pride. I. O. bites. "A man cant have his good name drug in the alleys," he says to the man who has done more dragging of the Snopes name than anyone. (Although there are no "alleys" in the countryside, it is a civic virtue that Ratliff enforces here.) "The Snopes name has done held its head up too long in this country to have no such reproaches against it like stock diddling" (201). By appealing to the pride of the individuals responsible for Ike, Ratliff teaches them to be ashamed of their sexuality and to suppress their bodily cravings in the name of public respectability. (Significantly, it is "respectability" which Ratliff knows Flem is after in *The Town*. He knows it because he is its guardian in *The Hamlet*.)

When the peasants kill the cow and feed it to Ike, they have murdered—and silenced forever—the yearnings of eros within them all. When the traders barter their unabashed sexuality for community respectability, they have demonstrated what their champion, Flem Snopes, personifies: there is no place for passion, for eros, or for women in the affairs of men in public. When Ratliff tells Bookwright that he could do more to check the rise of Snopes but he refuses to ("I never made them Snopes and I never made the folks that cant wait to bare their backsides to them. I could do more, but I wont. I wont, I tell you" [321]) he is speaking hypocritically, if vulgarly, of his own standards. Ratliff, more than anyone in the Bend, has acted to turn Snopeses from country farmers to potential community leaders. He teaches them the all-important first lesson of a suppressed love of the body.

◆ Homosensuality: Men and Men in the Bend

As the hold of the capitalist agricultural system becomes more apparent in Frenchman's Bend, the bifurcation of life into public and private realms emerges with greater distinction. The old leaders of the Bend's society, typified by Will Varner, knew no such demarcation. Will Varner is described by Faulkner as "shrewd, secret, and merry, of a Rabelasian turn of mind, and very probably still lusty (he had fathered sixteen children . . .) as the spring of his hair which even at sixty was still more red than grey, would indicate" (5). When the likes of Will Varner controlled the countryside, sexuality and public life were inseparable, Faulkner suggests, or at least men did not suppress their sexual natures. Unlike his son Jody, Will Varner is not alarmed or paranoid over Eula's voluptuousness, nor does he necessarily consider her "property." According to Faulkner, Will does not believe in "female chastity" as an entity or as a male possession. Although he does carry on sexual liaisons with the wives of his tenant farmers on occasion (140), it is not at all apparent that he does so for personal gain or in return for economic favors, at least Faulkner does not say he does. Rather than being an instrument of his economic power, Will Varner's sexuality is "Rabelasian" in nature, not bourgeois.

His son Jody, on the other hand, is sexually inactive, "the apotheosis of the masculine Singular" (7). He and the new generation of businessmen-farmers reflect the middle-class bifurcation of human life into public and private realms. They present the community with cold, imperturbable exteriors, keeping their passions in check. Of I. O. Snopes, for example, Faulkner can point out that "there was considerable more force and motion to his private life, his sex life anyway, than would appear on the surface of his public one" (66). These upwardly mobile farmers and traders learn the bourgeois standards of sensual identity and public behavior, that is, of civility. If they do crave sexual activity publicly, they direct their bodies into the city's whorehouses, where "scorched scars of merchandised lust" (212) are produced by their standards of respectability.

In the public realm of *The Hamlet* where men interact with other men, social and economic intercourse is carried on with a minimum of sensuality. Homosensuality is a cold thing in the marketplace as men buy, sell, and trade without concern for the sensual well-being of one another. If anything, homosensual *cruelty*, not caretaking, typifies the marketplace. The capitalist-agricultural community of Frenchman's Bend is a place "where breath inhaled and suspired and men established the foundations of their existences on the currency of coin" (199) and not on the well-being of their bodies. It is the assumption that the economy exists for its own benefit and perpetuation, and not in the name of general human welfare, which allows men like Ab Snopes to live in dwellings that "aint fitten for hogs" and to act cruelly toward one another in the name of business. In *The Hamlet,* the most striking demonstration of homosensual cruelty is found in the story of Mink Snopes.

Mink's antagonism toward his pathetic indigence is aimed primarily at Flem, who, he believes, is rising in economic and social position for himself only, while he leaves his poorer relatives, such as his cousin Mink, to fend for themselves. Flem is a good capitalist, disregarding obligations that might impede his ascent, and Mink is an angry, dispossessed, capitalist "failure." It is not entirely true, however, that Flem abandoned Mink. The land Mink farms unsuccessfully once belonged to Houston until Will Varner, on Flem's instigation, foreclosed on the land and rented it, in turn, to Mink. To Mink, the farm symbolizes not a chance to better himself but the dead-end of his economic and social destiny. According to Faulkner, his house, "the desolate and foodless cabin . . . symbolised the impasse his life had reached" (231). Compared to the economic advantages with which Houston, for instance, began his marriage, Mink's circumstances are actually criminal. Faulkner describes

> the paintless two-room cabin with an open hallway between and a lean-
> to kitchen, which was not his, on which he paid rent but not taxes,

paying almost as much in rent in one year as the house had cost to build; not old, yet the roof of which already leaked and the weather-stripping had already begun to rot away from the wall planks and which was just like the one he had been born in which had not belonged to his father either, and just like the one he would die in if he died indoors (219).

Mink is indigent, but he is an American poor man and believes in the American ideology of personal responsibility for individual gain or loss in the marketplace. His anger, then, is not directed toward the tenant-farmer system which oppresses him but toward individual men whom he deems "responsible" for his pathetic condition. Houston, in Mink's mind, symbolizes an entire lifetime of economic oppression and class-destined indigence and humiliation. When he kills Houston it is to settle a *personal* humiliation—*"This is what happens to men who impound Mink Snopes' cattle"* (218)—and not to address a class issue or make a political statement. Despite Mink's false consciousness, his crime against Houston (or rather, against society) is, whether Mink knows it or not, a political action. Because he is politically and economically impotent, the only power Mink has over other men is criminally based: murder, theft, violence in general. When Ratliff says that Mink is "a different kind of Snopes like a cotton-mouth is a different kind of snake" (91), he is being politically naive. Mink's threat to the community is no different from Flems in principle, only in practice. Unlike Flem, who transforms hostility into a program of community dominance, Mink's anger is translated into criminal activity. Both men wish to strike out against the community, and if Mink is a cotton-mouth, then Flem must certainly be a water moccasin—two names for one snake. Flem, however, cannot be locked up for his activities; he must be assimilated into a community that is based on exploitation of itself by its members. Mink, on the other hand, is dealt with summarily. Having no advantages on which to capitalize, he turns to criminal activity and removes himself from society. Once a snake reveals itself in public, it must be put away. Mink acts the way the socially and economically dispossessed in America are expected to act: submissive, obedient, and unfortunately, occasionally criminal.

The homosensual community is characterized by the violence of men against men in *The Hamlet*. Because the body is regarded as but one more human possession, a piece of private property, men exploit one another's bodies (and those of their dependents) in *The Hamlet* as they exploit property in general. Arthur Kinney has characterized the novel as "an anatomy of possessiveness. Frenchman's Bend is obsessed with who owns what, with who gains and who loses what."[10] Everything is potential material for exploitation in the economy of Frenchman's Bend: horses, shanties, sons and daughters, men and women. The social and economic system actually promotes and encourages men to deny their sensual existences in the name of their private economic ambitions and their public images. The human community in *The Hamlet* displays a frightening tendency toward the atrophy of sensuality in the name of an artificial and life-denying system of "respectability." A human community founded not upon the life and welfare of the human body but upon "the currency of coin" is no human thing at all but some form of perverse incarceration of the flesh. In *The Hamlet*, the only ways in which a man can express antagonism or hostility toward the system of his dispossession is by turning the tables and exploiting other men. One way is to do what Flem does, that is, master the tactics of success and consistently "beat" other men in the marketplace, while he considers himself responsible for no one's welfare but his own. Another way is to destroy property by burning barns or by killing other men in the name of personal dignity.[11] Flem's method of revenge on the community is the most threatening because it is legal and is actually encouraged by the American rags-to-riches mythology.[12] Ab's arsonist method is not legal, but he was never caught and his threat was localized. Mink's tactics lie on the darker side of Flem's; he is "criminal" in his method of revenge even though his motivational hatred is no different from that of his cousin. Because Mink breaks the rules of homosensual intercourse, he is put into prison.

Flem does not abandon Mink to prison because he is cruel, however, but because Mink represents all that Flem must suppress in himself and all that he has learned to incarcerate somewhere in his soul. Flem realized early in his life and then put away forever the outward signs of the anger, the antagonism, the hatred for a community that compels men to live like hogs if they are poor and, to carry the image, like pigs if they are rich. When he faced Jody Varner at the beginning of the novel and traded his father's notoriety for a place in the Varners' store, Flem might have spent his anger then by abusing Varner or by walking away. Instead, Flem consumes Varner economically in *The Hamlet*. By seeing Mink go to prison, Flem reaffirms the suppression of the type of revenge which he knows is not tolerated. Both Mink and Flem respond to cruelty with cruelty: Mink's is personal and sensual and criminal; Flem's is public and systematic and ambitious. In the human community Faulkner creates in *The Hamlet*, all forms of human sensual passion are silenced by the very standards and forms on which the community is based. The men kill the cow (the object of "wordless passion") and trade on the spotted ponies, objects of blind and arbitrary destruction. The human community in *The Hamlet* (the same "community" that banished Caddy Compson) has attenuated the human capacity for love and passion in public, making it a frighteningly cold and ruthless place.

II In Defense of the Mind: *The Town* (1956)

When *A Fable* was published in 1954, Faulkner was just beginning an active schedule of public duties and performances. He returned from a trip to Europe (working with Howard Hawks some of the time) in April and left on a State Department mission to South America in August. He was equally active in personal matters. His daughter Jill was married in August, and over the course of 1954, starting in Europe and continuing later in the year in New York, Faulkner became involved with Jean Stein. He continued his full public schedule in 1955, getting more deeply involved in the integration controversy in his home region before leaving for Japan in July. He published a series of essays in these years as well. The semi-autobiographical "Mississippi" was published in *Holiday* in April 1954; *Harpers* published the essays "On Privacy (The American Dream: What Happened to It?)" in July 1955 and "On Fear: Deep South in Labor: Mississippi" in June 1956. *Life* included "A Letter North" in March 1956, and *Ebony* printed his "If I Were a Negro" in September of that year. In addition, Faulkner wrote numerous letters to various newspapers in these years and delivered public speeches to such audiences as The Southern Historical Association, the Athens Academy, the Academy of Arts and Letters, and organizations affiliated with the University of Virginia.[13]

   The pace of Faulkner's life in the years immediately following the publication of *A Fable* was unprecedented in his career. Although his schedule left little time for fiction, he did collect a group of hunting stories and write the new connecting material that would become *Big Woods*, published in October 1955. He had told a friend the previous June that he had a number of projects planned but was afraid "I wont live long enough to do all I have in mind even if I live to be 100." The publication of *Big Woods* seemed to impress upon him the need to get back to his life's work, the apocrypha, and not channel all his time and powers into public affairs. "I know I want to live long enough to write all I need to write about my imaginary county and country," he wrote in October, "so I must not waste what I have left."[14] *A Fable* had led Faulkner fictionally and personally around the world and into public affairs. Two years later it was time to come home and get back to work, specifically to return to the trilogy and complete the unassembled structure of the apocrypha.

Faulkner completed the manuscript of *The Town* during the height of civil rights tensions in his community. He was simultaneously involved in both writing *The Town* and participating in the local controversy. Indeed, among the notes for and genealogies of Snopes, and on the versos of many typescript pages of *The Town* are numerous drafts of letters to various individuals and newspapers concerning not only Negroes but Communism and other social problems and issues.[15] It seems, then, that the idea of "town" and community issues in general were intersecting in 1955 and 1956 in Faulkner's actual and apocryphal worlds, but *The Town* has nothing to do with integration and very little to do with actual political issues of the times. It does present the *idea* of a political community apocryphally, but not as a setting for social realism. In other words, *The Town* is a sublimation of actual Mississippi politics into an apocryphal form that is more concerned with the structures of political interaction than with specific political issues. "Doing a little work on the next Snopes book," Faulkner wrote in 1955. "Have not taken fire in the old way yet, so it goes slow, but unless I am burned out, I will heat up soon and get right on with it. Miss. such an unhappy state to live in now, that I need something like a book to get lost in."[16] Far from being an apolitical book, however, *The Town* is a perfect example of apocryphal sublimation from one "state" to another. It is politically apocryphal; the issues and events are far removed from the "official" historical record, but the principal problems of the political community persist and are addressed in the narrative. Unlike *Intruder in the Dust* (1948), which dealt directly with racial issues, *The Town* is more concerned with the way in which community issues are understood and acted upon by citizens. If the novel represents a retreat from the local (and national) controversy, it is a retreat from the issues of the historical moment and a return, for Faulkner, to the apocryphal Yoknapatawpha town and to what he might have called the revolving problems and conflicts of political existence.

During the composition of *The Town*, Faulkner corresponded frequently with Jean Stein, sending her portions of the manuscript for her reactions and generally writing the novel "for" her in the way he had written earlier novels for other women. "I feel pretty good over your reaction to the new Snopes stuff," he wrote Stein in January 1956. "I still feel, as I did last year, that perhaps I have written myself out and all that remains now is the empty craftsmanship—no fire, force, passion, anymore in the words and sentences." These fears on Faulkner's part had occurred before in his life and could usually be assuaged by a young woman showing interest in his work. (Writing, aside from everything else, was always a form of seduction for Faulkner.) "But as long as it pleases you," he told Stein, "I will have to go on; I want to believe I am wrong you see."[17] Faulkner continued to write in the winter and spring of 1956, but the task was never easy. He suffered recurring doubts over the quality of his work. "I still cant tell," he wrote Saxe Commins in July, "it may be trash except for certain parts, though I think not. I still think it is funny, and at times very moving; two women characters I am proud of."[18] According to Blotner, the entire project of *The Town* was, for Faulkner, a reluctant task, one book he perhaps did not want to write at all.[19] Nonetheless, when he finished the volume in August he was quite pleased with it. The writing had gotten easier in the summer ("going splendidly," he reported, "too easy") and upon completing the novel claimed, "Will break the heart. Thought it was just funny but was wrong."[20] Whatever the relief of completion meant to Faulkner, it is clear that the writing of *The Town* was a painful experience. He approached the book as a kind of "duty" perhaps as something he had to do to get on with his work. It was, after all, only volume two of a trilogy, and completing it only meant another demand awaiting his attention. On the other hand, something was still driving Faulkner to create. There was still the sense, in his mind, that he was not quite finished putting together the Faulkner "keystone." "Each time I begin to hope I am written out and can quit," he wrote in August 1956, "I discover I am not at all cured and the sickness will probably kill me."[21]

Part of Faulkner's problem in composing *The Town* may well have been due to external pressures, specifically, the pressure of the limelight, as Joseph Gold has suggested. With the public eagerly awaiting the Laureate's next work, Faulkner may have found it increasingly difficult to write purely for himself and his own fictional purposes.[22] Of all the Snopes volumes, criticism of *The Town* has been the least enthusiastic. Cleanth Brooks has even suggested that the reader might skip it and move directly from *The Hamlet* to *The Mansion* and "lose nothing very essential."[23] Despite Faulkner's reluctance in the writing of it, and despite Brooks' considering it superfluous, *The Town,* as this analysis will demonstrate, has an indispensable place in the middle of the trilogy. The anxiety of establishment may well have ached at Faulkner during the composition of the novel. He found himself, a man self-conceived as an outsider standing apart from the literary circles of the day, thrust into the official establishment of American letters. Faulkner had always written for himself, as he said, listening to the "voices" within him and meeting his own standards of aesthetic value. In 1956, however, he may have felt, as Gavin says of Flem in *The Town,* "the humility of not knowing, of never having the chance to learn the rules and methods of the deadly game in which he gauged his life" (266).

In 1956, the "country boy" was the American Laureate of world literature. What he wrote and published was, as Gold says, eagerly awaited and would probably be read by more people as it came off the presses than any previous Faulkner first editions. What the public expected was a masterpiece of literature to make up, in part, for what it had missed when those early masterpieces were published. What Faulkner had before him was simply the second volume of a trilogy he had envisioned in 1938 that concerned people he had begun to think and write about in the 1920s. The limelight was on "Faulkner," but the country boy was still hammering away at the apocrypha to which he had devoted his life. Like Flem, Faulkner had had "to start from scratch (scratch? scratch was a euphemism indeed for where he started from)" (283), and in 1956 he was still "scratching," still writing and taking his apocryphal vision to Yoknapatawpha.

◆ Public Epistemology; or, The Politics of Knowledge

The Town is largely concerned with how things are known, how knowledge is communicated, and how human beings might change their environment intellectually and politically. Its epistemological thrust is toward what might be called the politics of knowledge. The emphasis is not so much on "how things are known" as it is on how known things are communicated and used. Although the novel may not necessarily be didactic, it is *about* didacticism. More succinctly, *The Town* does not ask, How do we know? but, How do we learn and change? The shift in emphasis is due to the fact that from a communal standpoint, what the individual experiences as private understanding and self-knowledge manifests itself in the public realm as political development and social change. The struggle of the individual to comprehend his world is not absent from *The Town;* it is simply left implicit. Charles Mallison, for example, at one point cries out in frustration in words that echo Faulkner's earlier fictions of the human mind. "You cant talk to anybody, not even others your age because they too are rushing on out into space where you cant touch anybody, you dont dare try, you are too busy just hanging on; and you know that all the others out there are just as afraid of asking as you are, nobody to ask, nothing to do but make noise, the louder the better, then at least the other scared ones wont know how scared you are" (304).

Criticism of *The Town,* unfortunately, has seen the second volume of the trilogy as intended to build progressively upon the events of the first volume. *The Town* is not, however, primarily a linear continuation of *The Hamlet,* even though it does dutifully trace a number of temporal developments pertinent to the plot of *Snopes.* Rather, *The Town* is better understood as an intellectual commentary on the overall subject matter of the trilogy and on the meaning of the trilogy *as a whole.* To apply a Faulknerian parallel, the events of *The Town* stand in relation to the volume's meaning in the same way that the story of Sutpen stands in relation to the meaning of *Absalom, Absalom!* The events of *The Town* are interesting and important only as they inform the dialogue of the fiction itself. Failing to recognize this fictional strategy, critics have, for example, either stressed the thematic moral "message" of *The Town,*[24] the tragic fate of Eula[25] (which is merely a footnote to her clearly stated destiny in *The Hamlet*), or the relative benevolence or arrogance of Gavin Stevens.[26]

The various narrators of *The Town* attempt to come to terms with Snopeses, who are, as we know from *The Hamlet,* reflections of themselves and of their own community. "So when I say 'we' and 'we thought,' " Mallison makes clear on the first page of *The Town,* "what I mean is Jefferson and what Jefferson thought" (3). At stake in *The Town* is public knowledge: the community's image as felt, or thought, by its representative citizens, or narrators. This is why nothing seems to happen in the novel and why Brooks, as mentioned above, would just as soon do without it. It has none of the colorful realism of peasant life in *The Hamlet,*[27] and none of the spiritual drama of *The Mansion*. Rather, it is a meditation—a long midrash or an interlude between volume one and volume three of *Snopes*—in which Faulkner once again makes his point "that fiction," as Hyatt Waggoner has argued, "is neither a lie nor document but a kind of knowledge which has no substitute and to which there is no imaginative shortcut."[28]

Ratliff and Gavin, according to Mallison, "were both interested in people—or so Uncle Gavin said. Because what I always thought they were mainly interested in was curiosity" (4). In this statement Mallison makes two crucial points about *The Town*, one consciously stated, the other unconsciously demonstrated. First, to be "interested in people" is a prerequisite to community knowledge. Gavin and Ratliff are intense observers and social gadabouts; they enjoy trading their findings and opinions with each other and have a sincere, if at times misguided, sense of the community's welfare. They are, above all, "political" men, alive in the marketplace of public interaction. Second, when Mallison corrects Gavin's self-image with one of his own opinions, saying that Gavin's interest is not in people so much as simply in what he knows or can find out about people, he demonstrates the emphasis on dialogue in *The Town*. Mallison weighs Gavin's testimony against his own observation of Gavin and Ratliff, and produces an independent assessment. To say that Gavin is "mainly interested in . . . curiosity" is to say that he is an intellectual, but not necessarily that he is a good man.

The point of the relation between dialogue and public knowledge is exhibited repeatedly throughout the novel, such as when the details of successive narrations consciously diverge, or when a narrator's version of events from *The Hamlet* are seen to serve motives ulterior to simple recapitulation. Gavin and Ratliff, for example, disagree over how Flem will orchestrate his meeting with the Varners and over what he will say to them concerning Eula and De Spain. Ratliff's account also deviates from Gavin's version of how Flem received Varner's support in his effort to become bank president, bolstering his argument with facts and common sense, as he says, in place of Gavin's sense of or insistence upon drama (290–300). Even the version of the origin of Snopes in Frenchman's Bend which Ratliff delivers at the beginning of *The Town* is misinformed. Ratliff adds an aura of mystery and human doubt to a story which he knows as well as anyone in the county. For example, he calls Ab "an old man who seemed to be [Flem's] father" (why "seemed to be"?) and claims that Flem found something secret on the Varners' property. "Whatever it was Uncle Billy and Jody had buried out there and thought was safe" (5). This something that Flem found, Ratliff explains, enabled him steadily to take over Frenchman's Bend. Ratliff's mystery (his own sense of drama) is uncalled for factually. He knows *exactly* how Flem established his foothold in Frenchman's Bend because Ratliff is the man who frightened Jody with the barn-burning story in the first place and compelled Jody to give Flem a job in his store. The only explanation for Ratliff's coyness at the beginning of *The Town* is that, as Mallison said, he is interested more in curiosity than in people, and his main purpose in telling the story is to intrigue and incite Gavin's own love of curiosity. Taking the lead from Ratliff, "Snopes" will become an abstraction to Gavin, akin to the way in which Southern whites, as Faulkner once said, thought about "Negroes." Snopeses will remain a curiosity in *The Town* because, as Mallison notes, these men are not interested in people, but in curiosities.

What makes Snopeses such marvels, and what makes Snopeslore so entertaining, is that Gavin, for one, does not even consider them individual human beings. According to Gavin, "they none of them seemed to bear any specific kinship to one another; they were just Snopeses, like colonies of rats or termites are just rats and termites" (41). This sounds suspiciously similar to Gavin's comments about local Negroes at the end of *Go Down, Moses,* where he observes, "They were like that. You could know two of them for years, bearing different names. Then suddenly by chance you learn that they are brothers or sisters" (372). Gavin and the other Snopes-watchers recruited by Ratliff are unable to see very far beyond the prejudicial barrier they have erected between themselves and this alien clan, a barrier they are taught to place there by the way Ratliff introduces Snopeslore to Jefferson. "Snopes" is, in *The Town,* a kind of emblem of human bigotry, attracting a combination of responses and reactions that are indicative of intolerance and are reserved for "other" kinds of people. Gavin, for example, thinks of Snopeses as some sort of organization similar to the Masons, "forever sworn to show a common front to life" and also to conspire and operate secretively (36). Mallison echoes this prototypically xenophobic sentiment by defining Snopes as "a condition composed of success by means of a single rule and regulation and sacred oath of never to tell anyone" (107). When the widowed Linda Snopes Kohl returns to Jefferson, the anti-Semitic and anti-Communist graffiti that is scrawled outside the young woman's home acts to confirm the function of "Snopes" as an apocryphal amalgamation of bigotries, a kind of magnet for human ignorance.

The individual Snopeses encountered in *The Town* are far from the mass-produced alien race which Gavin envisions. Wallstreet Panic is a hard-working small businessman who builds an expanding grocery trade in the county; Montgomery Ward is a more rebellious entrepreneur, but nevertheless a "real" person. Yet Gavin never sees any Snopes except as a moral derivative of Flem, holding a Flem-like threat to the established hierarchy of Jefferson. At one point he compares Snopeses to a herd of tigers, preferring, he says, to have them penned up "where we could at least watch them" instead of having them "roaming and strolling loose all over every where in the entire country." Although he says he accepts their presence in town as a fact now, he is not happy about it. "So it's for us to cope, to resist," Gavin says, "us to endure, and (if we can) survive" (102). This melodramatic parody of Faulknerian principles in this context smacks not of community spirit but of an incipient fascism. Keep an eye on Snopeses, Gavin insists. Lock up the Snopeses.

Gavin Stevens, according to his nephew, began to talk about Snopeses all the time, "like something wound up that couldn't even run down, let alone stop" (45). He acquired the obsession from Ratliff "and he even got interested in it, like a game, a contest or even a battle, a war," according to Charles Mallison, believing "that Snopeses had to be watched continually like an invasion of snakes or wildcats and that Uncle Gavin and Ratliff were doing it or trying to do it because no one else in Jefferson seemed to recognize the danger" (106). Yet Snopeses are just one of Gavin's objects of study. He is primarily a student of human complexity and complication. "He's a lawyer," Ratliff explains, "and to a lawyer, if it aint complicated it dont matter whether it works or not because if it aint complicated up enough it aint right and so even if it works, you dont believe it" (296). As a lawyer, Gavin deals in a legal system by which human behavior is regulated. Again, as Mallison said, not people but curiosity interests Gavin, not behavior but the laws of behavior. This is why Gavin is at once such an intelligent man and yet so stupid sometimes. He often mapped out the forest perfectly without being aware that he had been drawing trees. For example, all the while Ratliff is trying to make Gavin recognize that what Flem is after is respectability, Gavin fully understands the concept but is unable to apply it to a human being. "That was it: the very words *reputation* and *good name*," he tells himself of Linda Snopes, "merely to say them, speak them aloud . . . would irrevocably soil and besmirch them . . . leaving them not just vulnerable but already doomed" (202). Gavin knows exactly how "respectability" operates and how one acquires and loses it, but he is unable to recognize a man in pursuit of it.

Gavin exists in a world of hypotheses and premises about human life. His formulation of human love and heterosexual union, for instance, rings strikingly true. "Something worthy to match not just today's innocent and terrified and terrifying passion," Gavin muses, echoing Faulkner's 1925 essay on marriage,[29] "but tomorrow's strength and capacity for serenity and growth and accomplishment and the realisation of hope and at last the contentment of one mutual peace and one mutual combined old age" (288–89). Yet Gavin's own romantic life is far from reflective of these sentiments. I simply cannot imagine Gavin Stevens experiencing an "innocent and terrified and terrifying passion," for as true as the words might be, he cannot breathe "living breath" into them or experience their meaning physically. As such, Gavin remains sensually handicapped in *The Town*. When Gavin looks out over Jefferson and "all Yoknapatawpha," seeing the countryside in one panoramic authorial vision, he thinks not of land or people but of words. "Then, as though on signal, the fireflies—lightning bugs in the Mississippi child's vernacular—myriad and frenetic, random and frantic, pulsing; not questing, not quiring, but choiring as if they were tiny incessant appeaseless voices, cries, words. And you stand suzrain and solitary above the whole sum of your life beneath that incessant ephemeral spangling" (315). The human community in Faulkner's apocrypha is comprised of "incessant appeaseless voices" all flicking like fireflies, all attempting by their "myriad and frenetic, random and frantic, pulsing" to find meaning in their private lives. Yet as Gavin seems to recognize, the words themselves are the meaning. "The whole sum of your life" amounts to what is created by "that incessant spangling" of words. The interaction of these words leads to the formulation of public knowledge in *The Town;* the politics of knowledge is the comingling of the incessant voices. Words, in the apocryphal community Faulkner presents, are powerful things—definitions, assumptions, understandings—with political consequences.

The community knows itself by the words it uses to describe itself and its components; in other words, by its ideology. In *The Town*, the community is characterized by a continual ideological activity in which narrators attempt to discern what can be known authoritatively (about Snopeses, primarily) and to project that authority publicly. Snopeses, however, threaten to expose the ideology as a contrived and duplicitous thing, something that serves and protects such entrenched powers as Gavin and Ratliff. The ongoing discussion in *The Town* about "facts and truth" illustrates this problem. Gavin claims that "poets are almost always wrong about facts. That's because they are not really interested in facts: only in truth: which is why the truth they speak is so true that even those who hate poets by simple natural instinct are exalted and terrified by it" (88). Sorting out "facts" to find "truth" is a major preoccupation of the three narrators in *The Town*. The facts often get in the way of what in a political sense needs to be true or ideologically consistent, and this usually results in a suppression of the facts. Gavin's lie to Linda about her real father or Flem's planting whiskey in Montgomery Ward's shop are instances where facts need to be ignored or manufactured to protect ideological concerns. To Flem, of course, facts are simply additional material to exploit for his own purposes, as seen in the monument he erects to his wife's memory. Rarely in *The Town* are facts accepted if they compel a change in belief. If facts and ideology conflict, it is far more efficient to dispense with or alter factual information than to engage in ideological reorientation. In this sense a poet, or a maker of an apocrypha, is not interested in facts but in the "truth" of ideological existence.

In his attempt to educate Gavin regarding Flem's desire for respectability, Ratliff demonstrates—and explains—the difficulty that education or intelligence has in changing ideology. Ratliff makes Faulkner's case against didacticism and in favor of aesthetic persuasion. Gavin knows what Ratliff is up to even if he cannot understand what Ratliff is trying to tell him. "Between the voice and the face there were always two Ratliffs," Gavin observes, "the second one offering you a fair and open chance to divine what the first one really meant by what it was saying, providing you were smart enough" (150). In one example of Ratliff's teaching method, he tries to get Gavin to think for himself what it is that Flem wants. The dialogue has been isolated to make the illustration more evident.

RATLIFF: "What's the one thing in Jefferson that Flem aint got yet? The one thing he might want?"
GAVIN: "To be president of [the bank] himself. . . . No! . . . It cant be! It must not be! . . . Nonsense."

RATLIFF: "Why nonsense?"
GAVIN: "Because . . . he's got to use his wife too." [Gavin doesn't believe
Flem can get Eula to help him.] "Dont you agree? . . . How can he hope
for that?"
RATLIFF: "That would jest be when he finally runs out of the
bushes. . . . Out to where we can see him. Into the clearing. What's that
clearing?"
GAVIN: "Clearing?"
RATLIFF: "That he was working toward? . . . That druv him to burrow
through the bushes to get out of them?"
GAVIN: "Rapacity. . . . Greed. Money. What else does he need? What?
What else has ever driven him?" (151–52)

At this juncture, Ratliff lessens the tension of the discussion and just
looks at Gavin. "Because he missed it," Ratliff says of his obtuse
student. "He missed it completely" (153).

Gavin has a fixed idea of Snopes that impedes the further development of his understanding of Flem's behavior and goals. He
cannot get past his image of Snopes (and of all Snopeses) as
rapacious, greedy, and self-serving. He is actually similar in his
mental intransigence to the narrators in *Absalom, Absalom!* Just as
Rosa could not get past her demon-vision of Sutpen, and Quentin
could not get past the Henry-Judith-Bon triangle, Gavin cannot
"see" Flem's true character through the cloud of his preoccupations.
The reason, of course, is that what he cannot see in Flem is what
obsesses himself as well: the quest for (or in Gavin's case, the attempt
to maintain) respectability and a "good name" in the community. It
is Gavin, remember, who takes it upon himself to close down
Montgomery Ward's peep show. It is also Gavin who intercedes at
the Cotillon Ball to put an end to Eula's flagrant show of sexuality,
"that splendid unshame" in her dance with De Spain. Mallison
recognizes that "Mrs. Snopes was dancing that way, letting Mr. de
Spain get her into dancing that way in public, simply because she
was alive and not ashamed of it like . . . Mr. de Spain and Uncle
Gavin had been ashamed" (75). Gavin becomes involved in the name
of respectability, to stop "unshame" and enforce "chastity and virtue
in women" (76). He is in fact enforcing his own presupposed image
of women, of the community, and of his own role in the community.
The extent to which Gavin cannot comprehend what Flem really
wants from Jefferson thus reaches as far as his lack of awareness of his
own ideological base. If Gavin knew what he stood for, in other
words, he might be able to see another man in pursuit of the same

quality. Flem knows precisely what he wants in Jefferson, and he knows that Gavin possesses it. Gavin, however, is unaware that he already has the thing for his master.

Ratliff, then, cannot "tell" Gavin what it is he misses because Gavin would not see it. He tells Gavin's nephew Charles Mallison why: "Because he wouldn't believe me. This here is the kind of thing you—a man has got to know his—himself. He has got to learn it out of his own hard dread and skeer. Because what somebody else jest tells you, you jest half believe, unless it was something you already wanted to hear. . . . But something you dont want to hear is something you had done already made up your mind against . . ." (258). Ratliff knows that by telling Gavin what he "missed" about Flem, he would be calling Gavin a hypocrite. Worse than that, however, he would be telling Gavin that he and Flem are not so very different, something Gavin is not prepared to accept. Whereas Gavin was born into and has spent a lifetime defending "respectable" behavior, Flem has had to work his way up to a position where he, too, has a right to exert the public power implicit in that defense.

The three narrators in *The Town* who represent "the tiny incessant appeaseless voices" that make up Faulkner's apocryphal community symbolize the eternal human effort to understand its environment, its place and time, and itself. They are three very different narrators. Charles Mallison is a kind of social historian; he explains, records, and documents action. Gavin Stevens is more of a philosopher; he constructs theories, hypotheses, and formulates definitions. V. K. Ratliff is a sort of teacher; he questions and inquires, criticizes and instructs. They are also actors in the drama of the community, however, and their own actions and behavior are among the phenomena they seek to understand. The continued interactions between narrators and actors, narrators and selves, and narrators and other narrators comprise what drama there is in *The Town*. This is a very "political" work in the sense that men and women are always talking to each other, always challenging one another's opinions, always looking into one another's motives and consciences. In the second book of Faulkner's apocryphal summation, ideology and public action inform community politics, and political crises occur when the two are at odds with each other.

The themes of human passion that dominate *The Hamlet* are present in the drama of *The Town:* sensual life continues in Jefferson, Gavin lusts for Eula, and husbands and wives continue to struggle and love in what Noel Polk has called "the most domestic of all" of

Faulkner's novels.[30] The narrative emphasis in *The Town*, however, is not on domesticity but on the politics of knowledge and understanding, specifically on the human capacity to change its mind. The novel opens with a highly charged, although comic episode in which Flem Snopes attempts to capitalize on a rivalry between two black men, Tom Tom and Tomey's Turl, in order to steal brass fittings from the city. The two men nonetheless overcome their division and band together to outmaneuver Flem, delivering him one of his few defeats in the trilogy. Instead of fighting between themselves, Turl and Tom Tom "just sat in the moonlight . . . and talked," and "in mutual and complete federation" decided than their quarrel is not with each other but with Flem Snopes (27–28).

This opening episode sets the tone of the novel. Flem must pay out of his own pocket for the stolen brass. What he is "paying for" is the knowledge that he cannot manipulate something he does not understand (something others have paid for in their dealings with Flem). That the two black men with their antebellum names are successful against the indomitable Flem indicates a primary flaw in his or in the community's ideology. An entrenched ideology can only explain and manipulate phenomena it knows. Faced with an unknown or unprecedented situation, the ideology must either revolve and change, or else "pay up" and save itself. Flem does not learn from his defeat and is astonished ("We?") by the common stand the two men take against him. He will be astonished again in *The Mansion*, when the abandoned Mink returns to kill him with the same principle in mind. The water tank with the useless brass in it is no "monument" to his achievement but rather a "footprint" marking his steady rise in power. It is assured at this point that wherever he will go, he will get there unchanged and resistant to change. Flem does not alter his thinking when his method or his ideology fails him. He simply pays damages and moves on.

While on its surface *The Town* seems to sidestep the political issues of Faulkner's place and time, it actually cuts to the core of the nature of political controversy. As an ideology itself, Faulkner's apocrypha challenges ideological orthodoxy. Minds are not easy things to change in *The Town*, and the most intransigent and entrenched mind in the community (aside from Flem's) belongs to its most educated and informed member, Gavin Stevens. For Gavin to accept an apocryphal understanding of his self and place and time would mean an acceptance of the essentially provisional nature of all knowledge, truth, and social organization. Such provisionalism would strike Gavin as contradictory, and a contradiction would strike him as a falsehood, or at least a weakness. Ratliff seems to know this about Gavin, and so finds him obtuse. The absence of apocryphal understanding in the community means that revolutions in social existence (and here Faulkner may have been thinking about the civil rights movement), born of contradiction and indebted to provisionalism, will be resisted by human beings more comfortable with consistency and order than with re-creation and change.

III In Defense of the Spirit: *The Mansion* (1959)

Faulkner finished writing *The Town* in August 1956. By December, he had begun work on *The Mansion*. He wrote to a friend at that time that he was having "what is probably the last flare, burning of my talent" and was "now working on the third volume" of the trilogy. *The Mansion*, he said, "will finish it, and maybe then my talent will have burnt out, and I can break the pencil and throw away the paper and rest, for I feel very tired."[31] Finishing the trilogy would complete the assembly of his life's work, bringing him to "the moment: dark: sleep" when the edifice was standing, the monument done. Faulkner was able to put aside the third volume of the trilogy early in 1957, however, when he became writer-in-residence at the University of Virginia. He also took leave of his writing by travelling to Greece for two weeks in March on behalf of the State Department and then returned to finish the semester at Virginia. His pace of composition on *The Mansion* was slow at first and by April 1958 reported to be "about ⅓ through the last volume of my Snopes trilogy." He also expressed fears that "I shall not have time to finish the work I want to do" during his work on the manuscript. In May, he declined to join a group of writers planning to travel to Russia on another State Department mission, commenting that "I am 60 now and have possibly done all the good work I am capable of, was intended to do."[32] Over the summer and fall of 1958, Faulkner began serious work on *The Mansion*, telling Random House he was on the "back stretch" of the effort in September; and in January, he reported "finishing the first draft" of the manuscript.[33] In February 1959, he sent Albert Erskine of Random House the completed first section, "Mink," and explained that two more sections would follow. Later that month he sent the completed "Linda" and in March submitted "Flem" to finish the manuscript.[34] In late 1958 and early

1959, Faulkner was writing with the old "flare" and "burning" that had characterized his earlier compositions, saying little about his work in progress and working steadily. According to Joseph Blotner, Faulkner approached *The Mansion* with some reluctance but with an eagerness to get the job done. "The way he felt now," in 1959, according to Blotner, "it would be his last major work. He could finish the saga, discharge his obligation to [Phil] Stone, and then break the pencil."[35]

Faulkner, however, was far from finished with *The Mansion* when he completed the manuscript. Outnumbered by and perhaps too hesitant to challenge the critics and editors who, like Blotner, considered the trilogy a mythic "saga," Faulkner found himself overwhelmed by editorial attempts to make the details and events of his trilogy "consistent" in all three volumes. Although Blotner claims that "Faulkner seemed to appreciate the meticulous editorial scrutiny his work now received,"[36] his correspondence with Random House during the winter and spring of 1959 does not indicate appreciation. In fact, the concern editors and academics had for literal consistency actually appears to have greatly annoyed the author, making the task of preparing *The Mansion* for publication an onerous one. He told Albert Erskine that "since I believe that fact had nothing to do with truth, I wouldn't even bother to change HAMLET" to make it conform with *The Mansion*. He then refers to his use of "The Hound" in the trilogy, in which he changed the original name of the main character from "Cotton" to "Mink Snopes," indicating that it was not until he wrote *The Mansion* that he discovered that "The Hound" was actually a part of the Snopes trilogy. That inconsistency, Faulkner added sarcastically, "hasn't outraged too many academic gumshoes," sending no one back to change "The Hound." And so, Faulkner continued, he felt at liberty to make "factual" alterations in his current work when necessary to get at the truth of the story.[37] By May 1959, after a winter of correspondence concerning "discrepancies" in the three volumes, Faulkner had decided to write a foreword explaining his theory of change and alteration—something which until then had been left implicit in the trilogy's structure—in order to "steal all the thunder beforehand" and head off, perhaps even "despoil" the "academical gumshoes."

It thus seems that Faulkner never saw the purpose in having so much "editorial scrutiny" over his work, but he kept his objections at a subtle level, perhaps not wanting to challenge directly those with education. "I dont know what you need Meriwether for, so I cant advise," he told Erskine upon learning that James Meriwether had been brought in to help edit *The Mansion*. "All I know is two: one to read the mss. and galley, that's you, and the other to tell what's wrong, that's me, and see he does all right. . . . Meriwether can work with us if you like," Faulkner then conceded. "That is, you know I'm no prima donna. I will let anyone do the work who will." Faulkner insisted, however, upon editorial control over his most recent work. *The Mansion,* he said, should be the "definitive" volume, and the first two volumes "can be edited in subsequent editions to conform, presumably far enough in the future when Faulkner would not be there to witness. "Unless of course," he added, "the discrepancy is paradoxical and outrageous."[38] As to the nit-picking of the "academical gumshoes," Faulkner was certainly opposed. To comb through the trilogy with fine-toothed editorial scrutiny would actually violate a premise of the apocrypha itself, that the "truth" of the human experience is more vital than ephemeral facts, which are certain to change with successive narrators and viewpoints. "We should know what and where [any discrepancies] are, even if we dont use, correct them," Faulkner told Erskine. "What I am trying to say is, the essential truth of those people and their doings is the thing; the facts are not important." The distance between Faulkner and his editors on this point indicates the distance between them on the meaning of the apocryphal trilogy in general, and of the implications of *The Town* in particular. Yet as with his encounter with Malcolm Cowley the decade before, or with Saxe Commins concerning the prefatory note to *A Fable,* Faulkner did not press his case too insistently. Nevertheless, it must have been distressing for Faulkner to defend repeatedly "inconsistency," as the editors defined it, while attempting to challenge the application of what he might have called "factism" and intransigent meaning to his fiction. He was often nearly incoherent in his arguments. "If we know the discrepancy," he told Erskine, "maybe, if to change the present to fix the past injures the present, we will not come right out and state the contravention, we will try to, you might say, de-clutch past it somehow."[39]

Faulkner was interested in knowing what the discrepancies amounted to in the trilogy; however, the knowledge of an inconsistency did not necessarily mean that editorial corrections were in order. Some discrepancies, in other words, were "true" discrepancies. The trilogy is not a saga; it is not a social history nor a fictional documentation, although it does contain elements of social history and documentation. It is, rather, three distinct, apocryphal depictions of human life over time. In the preface to *The Mansion*, Faulkner describes the book as not just "the final chapter of" the Snopes trilogy but also "the summation of" that work. Although he calls the work a "chronicle," it is one with a "thirty-four-year progress." In other words, it is a chronicle not so much of the fictional Snopes clan (which has, actually, a fifty-year span in Yoknapatawpha) but of the time between "1925," when the work was "conceived and begun" when Faulkner was telling stories about the Snopes clan to Phil Stone and others, and 1959, when *The Mansion* was published. The Snopes trilogy records the evolution of Faulkner's study and meditation "about the human heart and its dilemma," he states in the preface, and not simply the infestation of Yoknapatawpha by Snopeses. In *The Hamlet,* Faulkner concentrated on the sensual struggles of human beings; in *The Town,* he looked at the intellectual and political implications of human knowledge; in *The Mansion*, "the summation," he turns to a consideration of the human spirit. In all, the trilogy represents the final assembly of Faulkner's apocrypha: an "unofficial" rendering of time and place, an unorthodox and often contradictory chronicle, a grand statement of alternative. It is *A Fable* on a local scale, with "local color" and local, apocryphal concerns. The third book, *The Mansion*, is the summation of the local apocrypha.

◆ Poor Sons of Bitches

As "the summation of" the trilogy, *The Mansion* is, in a sense, a reprise to *The Hamlet* and *The Town*. Structurally, it is an amalgam of both volumes. *The Mansion* is divided into three books, as is *The Hamlet,* but it is narrated not only by an omniscient narrator but also, in several chapters, by individual narrators, thus echoing the structure of *The Town*. In addition, *The Mansion* retells many of the events and stories that originate in the first two volumes, contributing to their implication and significance. This is particularly apparent in the case of Mink Snopes, in which the rebellious, dispossessed farmer's story is given a central place in the structure and meaning of the novel. As a foil to Flem, Mink emerges in *The Mansion* in thematic contradistinction to his successful cousin. Flem is a repugnant success, a man who represents capitalist, or individualist tendencies toward producing selfish amorality. He rises, because of those tendencies, to a position of wealth and power in society. Mink, on the other hand, is a capitalist, or individualist criminal, a man who resents the tendencies that produce Flem and acts to counter them. Mink descends, because of his resentment, to the status of a cold-blooded, premeditated murderer. Neither man, however, is wholly good or evil, and both are driven, as we know from *The Hamlet*, by the same set of antagonisms. *The Mansion*, then, plays out the Mink/ Flem duality set up implicitly in the first volume of the trilogy. At the same time, it re-examines the "curiosities" of *The Town*. Before proceding to an analysis of the Mink Snopes story which opens and closes *The Mansion*, it is important first to understand the middle of the text (which corresponds to the mid-section of the trilogy), the defusing of anti-Snopes bigotry.

In *The Mansion*, Gavin and Ratliff continue to represent bourgeois society's reaction to the assault on propriety, decorum, and orthodox social structure by Snopes. As he was in *The Town*, Gavin is portrayed in *The Mansion* as more interested in the politics of knowledge than he is in people. Faulkner narrates:

> His [Charles Mallison's] Uncle Gavin always said that he was not really interested in truth nor even justice: that all he wanted was just to know, to find out, whether the answer was any of his business or not; and that all means to that end were valid, provided he left neither hostile witnesses nor incriminating evidence. Charles didn't believe him; some of his methods were not only too hard, they took too long; and there are some things you simply do not do even to find out. But he Uncle Gavin said that Charles was wrong: that curiosity is another of the mistresses whose slaves decline no sacrifice (343).

Here Faulkner oversees a dialogue between uncle and nephew concerning the politics of information and the uses of public knowledge. Gavin insists that he will hold complete control over his methods and over the uses to which he puts his knowledge. In the Meadowfill episode, for example, Gavin finds out that legally Meadowfill owns more land than even he thinks, giving Meadowfill an even stronger case against Orestes Snopes. Gavin decides extralegally, however, not to tell Meadowfill. By withholding this information, Gavin knows, it will be easier to convince Meadowfill to be reasonable and move away, allowing the modern development of the land to continue (334). Gavin's tactics in *The Mansion* continue to be indistinguishable from what he calls, out of the other side of his mouth, Snopesishness.

Ratliff also emerges in *The Mansion* as a resourceful man capable of turning a dirty trick. According to Faulkner, Ratliff has mastered the arts of political knowledge by simple observation and a lifetime of attention to public affairs. "To be unschooled, untravelled, and to an extent unread," Faulkner says, "Ratliff had a terrifying capacity for knowledge or local information or acquaintanceship to match the need of any local crisis" (381). Ratliff puts his expertise to work in the "By the People" episode in order to teach Clarence Snopes a lesson and to discredit his senatorial hopes. Ratliff's method—soiling Snopes' pants leg with switches from the dog thicket, the "dog post office" (316)—is something he comes up with based on his knowledge of local canine customs and behavior, which he brings to Jefferson from his Rabelasian background in Frenchman's Bend. Had Ratliff been schooled and read he might have known his prank had literary precedent in *Gargantua and Pantagruel.* "How Panurge Played a Trick on the Parisian Lady Which Was Not At All to Her Advantage" tells the story of a similar humiliation. By sprinkling the gown and sleeves of an upper-class woman with the ground-up pieces of that part of a "hot sheep dog bitch . . . which the Greek necromancers know," Panurge gets the dogs of the town to do to the Parisian Lady what Ratliff compelled the Jefferson dogs to do to Snopes.[40] Ratliff's Rabelasian stunt and Gavin's extralegal suppression of information, which follows immediately in the text, establish these two characters as political men. They act not due to purely selfish means (in the sense of incurring solely personal aggrandizement) but according to their personal visions of the good of the community.

Gavin and Ratliff demonstrate the political uses of knowledge and insight into human affairs. In *The Mansion,* both men make efforts to put to use what they know despite a growing sense that time is running out on them. Ratliff claims that only "when you are young enough, you can believe. When you are young enough and brave enough at the same time, you can hate intolerance and believe in hope and, if you are sho enough brave, act on it. . . . I wish it was me" (161). What Ratliff hates even more than "intolerance," of course, is the idea of the primacy or political power of Snopes, any Snopes. In any case, Ratliff is not about to retire from public activities, as his disposal of Clarence Snopes illustrates. When Gavin congratulates himself and Ratliff for having "carried on the good work of getting things into the shape they're in now," he adds that as far as maintaining the fight, "it's too late for us now. We cant now; maybe we're just afraid to stick our necks out again," he says. "Call it just tired, too tired to be afraid any longer of losing" (307). Later in the novel Faulkner clarifies what Gavin means by "tired." "He meant of course the effort: not just the capacity to concentrate but to believe in it; he was too old now," Faulkner concludes, "and the real tragedy of age is that no anguish is any longer grievous enough to demand, justify, any sacrifice" (392). And perhaps it is just as well. As Charles Mallison's objections to his uncle's methods indicate, the times have changed, and Gavin Stevens' personal brand of political hegemony is repugnant to the coming generation.

Gavin's ideas continue to interfere with his ability to act in *The Mansion* and continue to blind him to the actual human circumstances of given situations. For all his talk about being too old or too tired to act, Gavin remains socially and politically active in *The Mansion*, right to the end of the novel. What his rhetoric of ageing masks is a growing self-knowledge of real social impotence. Gavin comes to realize in *The Mansion* that despite his philosophic or moralistic purposes, he is actually incapable of doing very much at all to stop what he calls "evil." "Just to hate evil is not enough," he tells Ratliff. "You—somebody—has got to do something about it" (307). Ratliff interprets this purposefully (his use of the dog post office follows it) but Gavin is expressing a depressing sense of moral irrelevance in the community. He is learning, late in his life, that for all his hypothesizing on good and evil and on justice and injustice, and for all his devious actions on behalf of the community's welfare, there are, he will soon learn conclusively, no purely good or purely evil actions. In *The Mansion*, Faulkner makes explicit what had remained in *The Town*, a structural implication. The way in which the human community is understood—the stories and the events, the individual members and narrators—is neither good nor evil but merely useful. In the purposes of the community, Faulkner suggests, and in the values it defends and upholds, lie its ultimate worth and its ultimate definition.

The test of Gavin's ability to act comes in his handling of the Mink Snopes pardon. When Gavin sends the money to bribe Mink into abandoning his intention to kill Flem, Gavin operates under the assumption that Mink is, definitively, a Gavinian "Snopes." To Gavin, this means that Mink will take the money because Snopeses, like rats and termites, have no principled existences. (Gavin's logic here is the same Flem applied to Turl and Tom Tom at the beginning of *The Town*: the logic of bigotry.) The plan compels Mink to decide between selling out (taking the bribe money) and returning to prison. The plan nicely insulates Gavin from direct participation, and with the arrogant confidence that characterizes this theoretician, he never suspects that Mink might outwit him. When he learns the plan has failed, he condemns himself as a coward, but also defends himself as a humanitarian. He wanted, after all, Mink to be let out of prison and Flem to be protected from an assassin. Yet his conscience, "a quantity, an entity," Faulkner says, "with which he had spent a great deal of his life" in dialogue, deflates his distinction between cowardice and humanitarianism. *"You are not even an original,"* the conscience tells him, *"that word is customarily used as a euphemism for it"* (378–79). Just as he had argued in the unpublished preface to *A Fable* that pacifism is ineffectual to end war, Faulkner suggests here that "humanitarian" tactics are ineffectual to combat human evil. In *The Town* and *The Mansion,* Gavin has acted with less than legal means (the arrest of Montgomery Ward Snopes, for example) when necessary. It is just that he always justified his actions as "humanitarian," or claimed to act in the name of truth or justice. Gavin has never seen himself and his partisan, public role nakedly, without the cloakings of ideological "respectability." He has yet to realize, in other words, that he is not a saint but a political actor in a political struggle, and that his opponents are not demons but fellow human beings. In dealing with Mink, he again made the mistake of thinking a Snopes was a different "kind" of human being than a Stevens.

When Gavin warns Flem about Mink's release from prison and of the failure of his plan—thus telling Flem, in essence, of his attempts to save Flem's life—he delivers to Flem, according to Ratliff, what he had been after all along. How much more "respectable" can a man be than to have the county prosecutor put up two hundred fifty dollars of his own money to save his life? When Gavin tries to warn Flem of the danger he is in, Flem offers the only words of appreciation or gratitude he has ever uttered in the trilogy. His "much obliged" to Gavin is an expression of triumph as much as it is one of thanks. Gavin has welcomed Flem as a legitimate member of the community. After Flem is dead and Gavin accepts complicity in his murder, he indicates signs of abandoning his reliance on moral standards of behavior and abstract notions of truth and justice by which to judge people, including himself. Actually, he is expressing at the end of *The Mansion* the realization that the way in which Gavin Stevens has always acted is not "moral" but practical and political. "So maybe there's even a moral in it," Ratliff suggests of Flem's death, "if you jest know where to look." Gavin disagrees. "There aren't any morals," he claims. "People just do the best they can" (429). Here, finally, Gavin has acquired an insight into his own behavior and into the political realities of the human community. His next exchange with Ratliff will take the two of them even further.

"The poor sons of bitches" is a signal throughout *The Mansion* for a sense of shared oppression or a common foe. Miss Reba refers to the common suffering of her class in her refrain, "All of us. Every one of us. The poor son of a bitches" (83). Montgomery Ward Snopes, of course, realizing that to be born a Snopes is to be born prejudged as a son of a bitch, vows that every Snopes will be *"THE son of a bitch's son of a bitch"* (87). Even the Reverend Goodyhay uses the phrase of solidarity in his prayers at the end of his church service. "Save us Christ," he prays, "the poor sons of bitches" (271, 281). People who "just do the best they can" in the face of events they cannot control, Gavin affirms, are all "poor sons of bitches." In the daily economic and political struggles of the community, the dispossessed, unlike Gavin and Ratliff perhaps, have little use for philosophic or moralistic preaching but have to "do the best they can" with—and sometimes against—what they have. Ratliff includes Flem in this observation of the human experience. "Maybe he was just bored too," Ratliff says, aligning Flem and Eula, for the first time, in his imagination. "The pore son of a bitch" (430).

Gavin's attempt to save Flem's life and Ratliff's affirmation of Flem's basic humanity mark the progression made by these two men from prejudicial and dehumanizing opinions about "Snopeses" to an intelligent acceptance of them as human beings. Together they have realized that Flem, like any other son of a bitch in the community, has always simply done the best he could, given his place and time, and his ambition. Their "Snopes alarm" and their hatred and fear of Flem and his clan have been based on pure ignorance that "Snopeses" are really no different from any other human beings, including themselves, even though they may be restive and dissatisfied instead of complacent or resigned to their social and economic fate. All of the Snopes-watching of Gavin and Ratliff finally pays off for them in the trilogy in the form of knowledge about human reactions to "other" human beings. Their journey, their "chronicle" in the Snopes trilogy, has been the narrative of the unmasking of human bigotry.

◆ A Peasant's Rebellion

Ratliff says early in *The Town* that "Mink Snopes was mean. He was the only out-and-out mean Snopes we ever experienced." Unlike the other Snopeses, who might be shrewd or manipulative or even foolish, Mink, according to Ratliff, was "just mean without no profit consideration or hope atall" (79). In *The Mansion,* where Faulkner returns to Mink's story, he makes it clear that while Mink may initially appear "mean" to the likes of Ratliff, his meanness is actually the appearance, or the naked face of rebellion. Mink, Faulkner narrates, "had said No not just to all the hard savage years of his hard and barren life, but to Death too" (290). In *The Mansion,* Mink communicates in his thoughts and in his deeds the consciousness of the dispossessed proletarian farmer. On his way to Jefferson from Parchman prison, Mink thinks back on all the events of his life, "connected, involved in some crisis of the constant outrage and injustice he was always having to drop everything to cope with, handle, with no proper tools and equipment for it, not even the time to spare from the unremitting work it took to feed himself and his family" (405). His life has been characterized by "the constant outrage and injustice" brought upon by a social and economic system that demands from his class "unremitting work" simply to provide sustenance for immediate families. Ratliff, with the perspective of the municipal middle class, is blind to the real source of Mink's "meanness." Indeed, according to Charles Mallison, even most of the working class in Jefferson were unconscious of their permanent disinherited status. Mallison explains that this lack of awareness was "a condition in which the Jefferson proletariat declined not only to know it was the proletariat but even to be content as the middle class, being convinced instead that it was merely in a temporary interim state toward owning in its turn Mr. Snopes's bank or Wallstreet Snopes's wholesale grocery chain or (who knows?) on the way to the governor's mansion in Jackson or even to the White House in Washington" (213–14). The way this ideology seems to work, Mallison suggests, is that the fortunate ascendency of a few individuals acts to dispel the political or economic anxieties of the masses of men and women in the community. It is precisely this "system" against which Mink Snopes rails and murders in personal defiance, for this ideology has produced his rebellion.

Criticism of Mink Snopes has generally seen him as a villain "obsessed with self-righteous pride"[41] or as an example of the human will to survive and serve itself, an instance of "dogged determinism and absolute commitment to himself."[42] Such views seem more reflective of an Ratliffian attitude—that Mink is mean and evil—than investigative of the sources of Mink's antagonism. It is clear from *The Hamlet,* as discussed above, that Mink and Flem share the same origins and come from the same place and time, and yet Flem's "meanness" is manifested in social ascendency and Mink's "meanness" manifests itself in murder—twice. Aside from challenging the bogy of environmental determinism, Faulkner is suggesting that unjust social and economic circumstances do produce antagonisms in people, which naturally lead to violent attacks on the system itself. Whereas much, even most, of the proletariat in apocryphal Yoknapatawpha county remains passively deluded into imagining itself as the middle class, as Mallison said, there are examples, in Mink and Flem, of individuals who do become conscious of their oppression. Out of the hatred of the community which is produced by the consciousness of dispossession emerge two kinds of people in Faulkner's trilogy: criminals and entrepreneurs.

"People of his kind," Faulkner says of Mink, "had never owned even temporarily the land which they believe they had rented. . . . It was the land itself which owned them" (91). Not owning the means of his own livelihood produces in the proletarian farmer a hatred for the earth. According to Faulkner, it was "the ground, the dirt which any and every tenant farmer and sharecropper knew to be his sworn for and mortal enemy—the hard implacable land which wore out his youth and his tools and his body itself" (90). Mink is smart enough not to direct too great a wrath at the land but not quite smart enough to direct it at the sharecropping system. Rather, his anger is aimed at an individual symbol of his oppression, the rich farmer Houston. Mink's antagonism toward Houston is based on and fueled by the knowledge that the landowner's barn "was warmer and tighter against the weather than the cabin he lived in" and that his livestock were "to be fed by the hired Negro who wore warmer clothing than any he and his family possessed" (11). Inhibiting Mink's consciousness of the system that oppresses him is his envy of an individual man's economic position and the racism he shares with all classes of white men. Because Mink is an American individualist—"cursing above all the individual man through or because of whose wealth such a condition could obtain" (12)—his class antagonisms are manifested in criminal action against individuals. Faulkner makes it clear, for example, that what looked like "revenge and vengeance" in Mink's murder of Houston "he himself believed to be simple justice and inalienable rights" (12).

Although Mink is treated as a murderer and sent to a prison that holds criminals, he is, by his own definition of what he did, more of a political prisoner. If his class antagonism motivates an attack upon the system, or upon a representative of that system which oppresses him, no matter what he actually does, he acts politically. Even his original "crime" of allowing his cow to feed in Houston's pasture was politically and economically motivated. As a man who is wholly subjugated to property, including the very "property" he farms but cannot own, anything Mink does to challenge or attack the source of his dispossession is likely to be adjudged, by a system that protects property, as "criminal." Mink, however, considers himself a lawful man. "I just wanted to know the Law," he tells Varner in the midst of his troubles with Houston. "And if that's the Law, I reckon there aint nothing for a law-abiding feller like me to do but jest put up with it. Because if folks dont put up with the Law," Mink concludes, "what's the sense of all the trouble and expense of having it?" (29). He remains "a law-abiding feller" until it becomes clear to him that even by obeying the law and being a good citizen he is still subject to Houston's dominance. When he kills Houston, he does so because Houston does not have the law as his master, but as his ally. "I killed you because of that-ere extry one-dollar pound fee" (39), Mink claims, because of the way Houston was able to use his mastery of the law to humiliate Mink. Since Mink owns nothing, not even knowledge of the laws that govern the community, and controls nothing by which to meet Houston as an equal, he turns to criminal activity.

Beneath Mink's individualist response to injustice is a glimmer of what really drives Houston to oppress him. "Likely Will Varner couldn't do nothing else" but support Houston, Mink believes, "being a rich man too and all you rich folks got to stick together or else maybe someday the ones that aint rich might take a notion to raise up and take it away from you" (39). Mink's attitudes and actions—the seeming gulf between his "honorable" tenets and his murderous activities—have confused critics of *The Mansion* into debating his "true" character. Even the lawyer at his trial thinks he is insane and wants to send him to Jackson instead of Parchman. Mink's attitudes and actions have their basis in a deep-seated but barely articulated class antagonism, one so foreign to his lawyer— and so seldom recognized in Faulkner—as to be interpreted as evidence of Mink's insanity rather than as an organic product of his dispossession.

There is one thing that Mink owns, of course, and that is his time. It is the only thing the state can deprive him of in return for the crime he committed. He is fully conscious of this, however, and

Faulkner presents him in prison "cursing his own condition that the only justice available to him must be this prolonged and passive one" (12). Mink has always "spent his time" in return for his survival, which is one reason why, as Faulkner says, his rebellion is not simply against "his hard and barren life" but against "Death too," which will come no matter how he uses his time. When he owes Houston the pound fee for boarding and feeding his cow over the winter, the propertyless Mink must pay it back in his "spare" time from his own labor on his rented farm. He does so at the expense of sleeping at night. Yet in this one possession of time Mink holds all the pride of ownership of a rich man, pleased with his complete control over the spending of it "because patience was his pride too," Faulkner explains. Patience was the one weapon he had in his struggle against what he saw as the blind forces that oppress him. "Never to be reconciled," the defiant Mink maintains, "since by this means he could beat Them; They might be stronger for a moment but nobody, no man, no nothing could wait longer than he could wait when nothing else but waiting would do, would work, would serve him" (22). Mink's patience in prison and his refusal to forget the "simple justice" which demands that he kill Flem means that all the time he serves will not lessen the outrage and anger he holds for Flem, the second object of his oppression. When Mink kills Flem, he articulates the other side of his class antagonism: hatred for his own class for not banding together in the face of the Houstons and Varners of the world. Flem had been defeated once in *The Town*, when Turl and Tom Tom combined to outmanuever him. Mink Snopes may be Faulkner's way of saying that Flem had not finished "paying" for ignoring their example.

There is a certain pathos in Mink's murder of Flem. I do not think it is due to Flem's finally getting his comeuppance for "violations of blood kinship . . . [and] his exploitation of all human principles,"[43] nor do I think there is any relative justice involved in Mink's action.[44] Rather, the pathos is more in the simple confrontation of the two old men, each prepared to die and neither about to struggle against it, two cousins who have waited a long time for this moment and have accepted its meaning. Flem has become as successful as is humanly possible in his community; Mink has fallen to the nadir of human degradation in his premeditated—for thirty-eight years—murder. Both men come from the same dirt-farmer origins, and both harbor unmatched and therefore shared antagonism for the community that meant to fate them to lives of inconsequential service to the wills and property holdings of others. He didn't need to say, "Look at me, Flem." His cousin was already doing that, his head turned over his shoulder. Otherwise he hadn't moved, only the jaws ceased chewing in midmotion then he moved, leaned slightly forward in the chair and he had just begun to lower his propped feet from the ledge, the chair beginning to swivel around, when Mink from about five feet away stopped and raised the toad-shaped iron-rust-colored weapon in both hands and cocked and steadied it (415).

The weapon fails to fire at first, but Flem sits and watches Mink patiently, "his feet now flat on the floor and the chair almost swiveled to face him" until Mink finally, after a second try, gets the pistol to fire and kills Flem. In his silent immobility, Flem acquiesces in his murder as if to say to Mink, you're right.

At the end of *The Mansion*, Flem symbolizes the emptiness that individualist success amounts to, and the extreme danger one invites in saying no, or nope, to the cosmos or to the community. Rebellion, as Faulkner has demonstrated in *A Fable* and in *Snopes* (and in Caddy of "Appendix: Compson"), is costly, and his rebels pay dearly for their stands against oppressive pre-determination and against authority. Although Flem's class antagonism has driven a lifelong ambition to succeed and to escape the fate of his father, he has, as Joseph Gold has said, "really gained nothing when he has gained everything."[45] The loneliness and emptiness at the apex of the individualist ethos is twinned in *The Mansion* by Mink's degradation, or the loneliness and emptiness at society's nadir. Both men lash out against their place and time, and reach the polar extremes of their social potentials. When they come together in murder, Flem sees in Mink's eyes the negation of himself and his life, that is, death itself. Mink kills Flem by the same individualist logic by which he convinced himself that Houston had to be killed. Flem represents to Mink the betrayal of Mink Snopes by a member of his own class. Whereas Houston individually symbolized the general oppression Mink experienced from above, Flem individually represented the general betrayal he experienced from his equals.

Back at the beginning of *The Hamlet*, Ratliff observed that Flem was equally exploiting both ends of the social structure—"working the top and the bottom," as Ratliff put it (71)—in order to gain power in the Bend and fulfill his ambitions. In his lifetime, Mink has done the same, killing Houston at the top, and Flem, who in Mink's eyes will always be his equal, at the bottom. Once he has worked "the top and the bottom" of his class antagonisms, Mink, like Flem, achieves his "success" and is ready to die. When Mink dies, he believes he has finally found justice. In death, Mink knows that all human beings are "mixed and jumbled up comfortable and easy so wouldn't nobody even know or even care who was which any more, himself among them," Faulkner concludes, "equal to any, good as any, brave as any, being inextricable from, anonymous with all of them" (435).

The journey that Flem and Mink make in the trilogy is a chronicle of human ambition based not upon a desire to band together and to direct a community but founded instead upon a hatred and an antagonism for the community. The antagonism of these two men is based, furthermore, on the cruelty that characterized their time and place and their condition: the cruelty of the homosensual community of *The Hamlet*, the cruelty of the prejudgmental world of *The Town*. Neither man, born of sharecroppers in the Mississippi countryside, was expected to rise in the community or to participate in the operation of its structures of authority. When they step outside the boundaries of what is expected of men of their class, they are considered either criminal or ruthless. What Faulkner suggests by the story of Mink and Flem is that criminality and ruthless ambition will continue in a society that rewards exploitation of itself and subordinates legitimate rebellions and evidence of injustices to the rights of property and ownership. By implying, moreover, that criminality and ambition—murder and personal aggrandizement, destruction and entrepreneurship—are dual manifestations of the same motivating forces, Faulkner implicates the darker side of the individualist ethos in a deadly system based upon hatred and personal satisfactions. What is sacrificed in the trilogy is the integrity of the community itself. Tom Tom and Turl's triumph over Flem in *The Town* is a singular exception, but theirs is a separate, dissenting community of racial outcasts. Nonetheless, the exception they represent resonates throughout the trilogy, which is primarily characterized by individualist failings. Until the community inspires ambitions based upon commonality and not self-interest, Faulkner demonstrates, and until it inspires hatred for injustice and not for the victims of its injustices, the community will continue to produce, as it does in the *Snopes* trilogy, Minks and Flems.

For Faulkner, the answer to the problems of the human community do not lie in the "community" but in the "humans" who compose it. Faulkner is no institutionalist, no social elitist, no believer in party politics or political panacea of any kind. "Anybody that thinks all he's got to do is sit on his stern and have salvation come down on him like a cloudburst or something, doesn't belong here," asserts Reverend Goodyhay's activist, apocryphally-inspired sermon. "You got to get up on your feet and hunt it down. . . . And if you cant find it," Goodyhay concludes, "then by God make it. Make a salvation" (229). Salvation will not come to the human community in some religious or ideological system or program, in Faulkner's view, and the individual will not be "saved" by believing in the right faith or ideology and awaiting the cloudburst—or the revolution. Charles Mallison learns the same thing from Ratliff's check on Clarence Snopes. "So what you need is to learn how to trust in God without depending on Him," Mallison says. "In fact, we need to fix things so He can depend on us for a while. Then he wont need to waste Himself being everywhere at once" (321). The will to "make a salvation" is similar to the will to make an apocrypha. To lend to human experiences the kind of authority reserved for orthodoxy is to question the validity of any authority immune to death and re-creation.

"Individualism" was a political byword in the Cold War, the era in which Faulkner completed the trilogy. In the context of postwar international tension, individualism was meant to mean something opposed to communism, and so implicitly meant capitalism and Americanism. In the *Snopes* trilogy, however, Faulkner defines individualism as neither good nor evil but simply as the stuff of experience—capitalist or communist, singular or banded together. Faulkner defines the individual in the triology as having a tripartite existence. Sensuality, political activism, and rebelliousness emerge from the trilogy as composing Faulkner's *apocryphal* individual, wholly distinct from orthodox understandings of individualism, with its self-interested, private, and ambitious connotations. Individual ambition is both productive and destructive in *The Mansion;* collective resistence is wholly effective in *The Town;* personal resistance fails in *The Hamlet*. It is difficult to apply the ideological categorizations of the 1950s to *Snopes* because, as apocrypha, the trilogy is opposed to the structure of such categorization. In other words, the *Snopes* trilogy challenges orthodox understandings of American politics. The trilogy is the chronicle of Faulkner's thirty-four years as an apocryphal writer. In it, Yoknapatawpha emerges as no myth or saga, but as an apocryphal "casebook on mankind,"[46] to use Faulkner's terminology, with no claims to any greater authority beyond that of its own words.

1. *Selected Letters,* pp. 62, 70, 72, 73, 74, 78.
2. *Ibid.,* p. 107.
3. *Ibid.,* p. 113.
4. *Ibid.,* pp. 115, 116.
5. Cleanth Brooks, *William Faulkner: The Yoknapatawpha Country* (New Haven, CT: Yale University Press, 1963), p. 179.
6. Watson, *Letters and Fictions,* p. 44.
7. Sally R. Page, *Faulkner's Women: Characterization and Meaning* (DeLand, FL: Everett/Edwards, 1972), p. 154; see also pp. 155 and 158.
8. Stonum, *Faulkner's Career,* p. 174.
9. *Faulkner in the University,* p. 31.
10. Kinney, *Faulkner's Narrative Poetics,* p. 73.
11. Critics generally distinguish Mink and Flem from one another without recognizing them both as two responses to the same system of class oppression. See, for example, Watson, *Letters and Fictions,* p. 58: "Flem's heedless disregard for his kinsman is illustrative of an inhumanity that is the more profound for being premeditated. It constitutes a denial and negation, not only of blood ties and human community, but of those individual rights and that dignity which Mink strove to assert and achieve by murdering Houston."
12. Waggoner, *From Jefferson to the World,* p. 185, sees Flem Snopes as "a Horatio Alger hero" who "parodies the American dream" and "caricatures the American success myth."
13. *Essays, Speeches and Public Letters* is the handiest, although not a complete collection of Faulkner's public writings and addresses.
14. *Selected Letters,* pp. 381, 387.
15. See Eileen Gregory, "Faulkner's Typescripts of *The Town*" and "Faulkner Material on the Versos of Typescripts of *The Town* and *The Mansion*" in James B. Meriwether, ed., *A Faulkner Miscellany* (Jackson: University Press of Mississippi, 1974), pp. 113–38.
16. *Selected Letters,* p. 390.
17. *Ibid.,* p. 391.
18. *Ibid.,* pp. 399–400.
19. *Faulkner: A Biography,* p. 1605.
20. *Selected Letters,* telegram to Saxe Commins, August 25, 1956, p. 403.
21. *Selected Letters,* p. 402.
22. Gold, *William Faulkner: A Study in Humanism,* p. 157, sees two principal techniques at work in *The Town:* "One is anecdotal. The other is discursive. This, I believe, clearly indicates that on the one hand Faulkner wishes to return to the imaginative power of his early fiction . . . and on the other hand Faulkner cannot escape an awareness of the limelight in which he now stands. He knows that now his novels are eagerly awaited, and he feels compelled to make his 'message' unmistakable."
23. Brooks, *William Faulkner: The Yoknapatawpha Country,* p. 216.
24. See, for example, Watson, *The Snopes Dilemma,* p. 142: "Throughout *The Town* the theme of the moral idealist's inability to act positively in the real world provides the vehicle by which Flem's amorality is revealed."
25. See, for example, Gold, *William Faulkner: A Study in Humanism,* pp. 154 and 155: "Eula becomes a kind of sacrificial figure in the power struggle for money and respectability," and "Eula is capable of love, of giving and accepting real love (characterized by selflessness), but in her world she can find none."

26. Beck, *Man in Motion,* p. 129. sees Gavin as a man with "probity . . . and aspiration, benevolence, and fidelity" who is, in fact, "a rare modern instance, a rounded man. He seems heir of several streams out of these last three centuries . . . he is rational, and intuitive, and engaged, one who, therefore, is because he thinks, feels, and acts"; Noel Polk, "Faulkner and Respectability," in *Fifty Years of Yoknapatawpha: Faulkner and Yoknapatawpha 1979* (Jackson: University Press of Mississippi, 1980), p. 123, suggests that Gavin imagines Flem Snopes as his very own "opposite number, the Compleat Villain," in order to accentuate his role "as morally superior person"; Watson, *The Snopes Dilemma,* p. 107, agrees with Beck, characterizing Stevens as clinging "to his belief in the innate righteousness of principled existence, and his opposition to the amoral forces that he perceives to be at work in Jefferson."

27. On the peasant realism of the book, see John Pikoulis, *The Art of William Faulkner* (Totowa, NJ: Barnes and Noble Books, 1982), pp. 147–48.

28. Waggoner, "Past as Present: Absalom, Absalom!" in Warren, ed., *Faulkner: A Collection of Critical Essays,* p. 185.

29. See William Faulkner, "On Marriage," *New Orleans Item-Tribune,* April 4, 1925, p. 1, prize-winning response to the question "What is the Matter with Marriage?" in 250 words or less. "The first frenzy of passion, of intimacy of mind and body, is never love. That is only the surf through which one must go to reach the calm sea of real love and peace and contentedness."

30. Noel Polk, "Faulkner and Respectability," in Fowler and Abadie, eds., *Fifty Years of Yoknapatawpha,* p. 123.

31. *Selected Letters,* p. 407.

32. *Ibid.,* pp. 412, 413.

33. *Ibid.,* pp. 416, 419.

34. *Ibid.,* pp. 420, 424, 425.

35. *Faulkner: A Biography,* pp. 1712–13.

36. *Ibid.,* p. 1734.

37. *Selected Letters,* p. 430.

38. *Ibid.,* pp. 425–26.

39. *Ibid.,* p. 422.

40. Francois Rabelais, *The Histories of Gargantua and Pantagruel,* translated and with an introduction by J. M. Cohen (New York: Penguin, 1955), p. 243.

41. Noel Polk, "Idealism in *The Mansion,*" in Gresset and Samway, S. J., eds., *Faulkner and Idealism,* p. 121; but compare Brooks, *William Faulkner: The Yoknapatawpha Country,* p. 221, where Mink is called "the only Snopes with a sense of honor."

42. Rankin, "Chasing Spotted Horses," in Carey, ed., *Faulkner: The Unappeased Imagination,* p. 142; see also Lynn G. Levins, *Faulkner's Heroic Design: The Yoknapatawpha Novels* (Athens: University of Georgia Press, 1976), p. 169, who sees in Mink, Faulkner's reduction of a character "as far as it would go and still deserve to be called man" and then standing "back to see if there were anything in what remained that would still stand forth and declare its humanity."

43. Watson, *The Snopes Dilemma,* p. 148.

44. Stroble, "Flem Snopes," in Carey, ed., *Faulkner: The Unappeased Imagination,* p. 207.

45. Gold, *William Faulkner: A Study in Humanism,* p. 169.

46. In 1947, Faulkner described the works of Shakespeare as a "casebook on mankind" which could be used "as a yardstick" to measure and assess human behavior. See *William Faulkner of Oxford,* p. 132.

Epilogue   The Nobel Prize Address
and the Will to Apocrypha

Faulkner made an important and vital distinction in the first line of his Nobel Prize Address between "me as a man" and "my work."[1] The award he received in Stockholm was made to the work, to the apocrypha, and not to the man, he claimed, who held it "only . . . in trust." While the work must speak for itself, the man would use the moment "as a pinnacle from which I might be listened to by the young men and women" who are writing. At this juncture, Faulkner steps outside his vocation as "author" and into the "visible" world. "We really live in the world of our mind, we only move about in the visible one," Faulkner told a friend after giving his speech. "What I said [in Stockholm] I would have *liked* to be true."[2] What Faulkner delivered in the Nobel Prize Address was a statement in defense of his apocryphal vision, a declaration of apocryphal principle in the guise of advice to young writers.

The only things "worth writing about," Faulkner claimed, are "the problems of the human heart in conflict with itself." These "problems" are the difficulties the writer ought to recognize, difficulties the "heart" has in accepting its time and its place in the physical world, that is, in "reality." This presumably includes preconceptions and values—ideologies—that are inherited and become burdens to independent, genuine reactions to circumstances. This would also include the "problems" faced by the human heart as it attempts to communicate amid the cacophony of voices in the community, all "trying to say." The "heart in conflict with itself" is in conflict, or dialogue, with what it knows and what it has been told, between what it creates and what it is given. A product of a certain set of historic circumstances and definitions with which it must struggle to form its own individuality and voice, the heart (Faulkner's code word for authenticity) faces overwhelming external forces that threaten to overpower and consume it with meanings and official explanations. Against these forces stands the apocryphal "writer"; against these forces also stand this "man" and his "work." In principle, the will to apocrypha is the will to say no (or nope) to the forces that would still or silence the heart.

The predicament is a familiar one in the Faulkner canon, where the individual faces an onslaught of encoded messages and social configurations into which the self, in all its personal, psychological confusion and multiplicity, must be inserted. Like Horace Benbow, Faulkner's characters are in search of "a hill to lie on," a place of rest in the social cosmos, a place to call home. Recall Quentin Compson in Rosa Coldfield's "office" receiving the local History, or Joe Christmas learning about sexuality from Joanna Burden, or Darl Bundren's confrontation with the absurd and futile actions of his clan. Again and again (or, as Faulkner would prefer, tomorrow and tomorrow), someone is telling or showing someone else something with which that person must deal according to personal capabilities. In *Pylon*, the process is likened to getting drunk: one may accept the intoxicant with its destabilizing effects, or one may vomit. The Reporter repeatedly does the latter until late in the novel when he finally holds down his liquor, and the narrative concludes with its apocryphal declarations. In most of the fiction before *The Portable Faulkner*, however, Faulkner's receivers of knowledge usually vomit. Quentin may say no to Rosa's depiction of Sutpen, but he still cannot by the end of *Absalom, Absalom!* "hold down" the South in his gut. Joe Christmas flees from knowledge of Joanna and into oblivion, refusing to hold down any definition of himself. And Darl's psychotic "yes yes yes yes yes" is the flipside of the coin he obsesses over at the end of *As I Lay Dying*, the other side being a repetitive, purposeless negation. Again and again, until his encounter with Malcolm Cowley, Faulkner portrayed the devastating, stifling effects of unassimilable knowledge and the self-defeat that inevitably follows saying no, but doing and saying nothing more. The few exceptions, such as Vardaman Bundren, often seem muted behind the chorus of defeated characters. In Faulkner's fiction, revelation is a prelude to declaration or action, or else it remains a valueless intoxicant, a kind of poison.

Action—human action in society—of course, is precisely what Faulkner's political apocrypha addresses. Long before his encounter with Malcolm Cowley and long before the Nobel Prize Address, Faulkner had portrayed the consequences of political inertia and of the failure to act. From Quentin Compson's narcissistic suicide through Isaac McCaslin's perverse and archaic love affair with the wilderness, Faulkner had given full view to the destructiveness and missed opportunity inherent in human apathy. When Cowley was preparing *The Portable Faulkner,* he had *Go Down, Moses* in hand as Faulkner's most recent accomplishment, a novel that has undergone various stages of misunderstanding, including the one emblemized by the persistently anthologized section "The Bear." (If anything, the entire novel works to undermine the supreme delusion which "The Bear" represents.) The fact that Cowley had *Go Down, Moses* fresh in his mind while producing *The Portable Faulkner* is further testimony to the distance between the two men's understanding of Faulkner's literary practices. ("The Bear" appears in *The Portable Faulkner* as representative of "1883" under Cowley's heading of "The Last Wilderness.")

Go Down, Moses is Faulkner's grand statement against the passivity to which intellectual clarity can lead and against the righteousness of condemning one's world without acting to change it. The fact that Isaac has been so often viewed as saintly[3] displays the level of misunderstanding that has dogged Faulkner's writing. Isaac is a personification of orthodox political failure and of the exhaustion of "individualism" in the American sense of the word. He may be a nice old man and may even be ethically "correct," but he is still a pathetic example to his community. Faulkner clearly intended Isaac McCaslin as such. He told Cynthia Grenier in 1955 that "a man ought to do more than just repudiate" in answer to her question about Isaac. "He should have been more affirmative instead of shunning people."[4] It may have been the world's political climate which led Faulkner to take a stand against political dispassion in the early 1940s. At the same time, he insisted that his material was not literally limited to the South. The principle of what he told Malcolm Cowley in 1944—

"that my material, the South, is not very important to me. I just happen to know it . . . life is a phenomenon but not a novelty,"[5]—he presaged in *Go Down, Moses*. During the important dialogue between Isaac and McCaslin Edmonds in "The Bear," McCaslin quotes a passage from a poem to make his point about constancy. Ike protests that the poem is irrelevant because the poet is "talking about a girl." McCaslin quickly corrects him. "He had to talk about something," he says (297). In *Go Down, Moses*, Faulkner is "talking about" hunting, race relations, and masculine initiations, but what he means is the establishment of a groundwork for the rebellion against the injustices of the father, the display of one man's obvious failure to displace the father when the time had come, and the inherent absurdity of such obsolete "systems of thought" as racial division. If there is a dirty word in *Go Down, Moses*, that word is heritage.

The inheritance of meaning, a motif that runs through *Go Down, Moses*, is suggested from the opening pages of the novel. Although this is a book about Isaac McCaslin's consciousness, four of its seven stories do not concern him directly, and the first of these, "Was," takes place before he was born. "Was" is included not because it is "something he had participated in or even remembered" but because Ike knows of its content through "the hearing, the listening." Because Ike's father was "near seventy when Isaac, an only child, was born," his cousin McCaslin became more like his "brother than cousin and rather his father than either" (4). Thus, in the prefatory fragment that opens the novel, "father" is suggested to mean not simply a biological function but an entire epistemological system. From the "father" Isaac's consciousness is formed from the listening to and the hearing of the stories and traditions growing "out of the old time, the old days." Since Isaac's real father is too old to serve this purpose, the community provides a surrogate. In any event, the child is socialized and the community's structure is preserved. It is his own eventual role as "father" which Isaac rejects, as Faulkner states in the opening line "a widower now and uncle to half a county and father to no one." What Ike fails to see, however, is that he need not father a son in order to be a "father" in the community. His very passivity, even in repudiation, enforces the perpetuation of social forms.

What Isaac would like to find in life is a sanctuary from the world he has inherited. He is heir to a long line of Faulknerian escapists, including but not limited to Quentin Compson, Horace Benbow, Joe Christmas—all in search of that "hill to lie on." Frederic Jameson has written against the myth of depoliticized human existence in any form, whether religious, psychological, or literary. Escape from "politics" is impossible, Jameson argues, and the only kind of "effective liberation from such constraints begins with the recognition that there is nothing that is not social and historical—indeed, that everything is 'in the last analysis' political."[6] Even where Faulkner's content is not politically charged, his "literary procedure," as Hannah Arendt points out, "is highly 'political.'"[7] In *Go Down, Moses,* Faulkner's narrative strategy amounts to a demonstration of Jameson's statement of the inescapable reality of the political content of twentieth-century life.[8] When Isaac turns "apostate to his name and lineage by weakly relinquishing the land which was rightfully his to live in town on the charity of his grand-nephew" (39–40), he not only foresakes his principles but acquiesces in a system of injustice.

The man who is most responsible for Isaac's perversion is Sam Fathers, another surrogate father to Ike, who unwittingly struggles with McCaslin Edmonds for the boy's soul in "The Old People" and in "The Bear." When Ike claims that "Sam Fathers set me free" (301), he means that the old Indian–Negro gave him an escape route wherein he could find an idealistic justification for repudiation. In the woods, at the end of "The Bear," it is to the snake, the "ancient and accursed," the representative of "old weariness and of pariah-hood and of death" that Isaac salutes: "Chief . . . Grandfather" (329–30). Here Ike has chosen paradise over politics and has escaped into the realm of the serpent. Yet "even in the act of escaping," Faulkner explains, "(and maybe this was the reality and the truth of his need to escape) was heresy" (294), a heresy Ike tried to cover with a profane attempt to imitate Christ. By his own orthodoxy, Ike is apostate, heretic. By acting alone and as an "individual," he is worse; he saves nothing but his own pathetic martyrdom. As Joseph Gold has aptly stated, "Christ gave up his woodworking tools to undertake the work of men, while Ike gives up men in order to become a carpenter."[9] When Faulkner explains that Isaac chose carpentry in order to emulate Christ, he characterizes Isaac's motivation as being "simple enough" but asserts his ends as being "always incomprehensible to him" (309–10). What Sam Fathers taught Isaac McCaslin was the powerlessness and the fatalism of the dispossessed. Hence, like Fathers (and like the serpent), Ike's definition of freedom is death, and the way he frees his son is never to father one. His wife's derisive laughter is aimed at a helpless and self-loathing man, who despite the devotion of a woman who loves him (352) still considers the wilderness as "his mistress and his wife" (326). And like the wilderness, Isaac is an anachronism, "the two spans running out together, not toward oblivion, nothingness, but into a dimension free of both time and space" (354), or in a word, death.

McCaslin Edmonds counters Sam Fathers' anachronism by insisting that Isaac not flee from contradiction but accept it as motivational. He tells Isaac, "You cant live forever, and you always wear out life long before you have exhausted the possibilities of living." If Isaac is looking for natural metaphors, McCaslin tells him that the earth itself does not "just keep things, hoard them; it wants to use them again" (186). In either case, what McCaslin means is that Isaac cannot expunge contradiction, alteration, and re-creation from his life or from history. The wilderness, which symbolizes for Isaac a kind of classless, raceless, sexless utopia, does not coincide with the realities of the community, which is class oppressive, racist, and sexually antagonistic. Even if in "the timeless woods" (200) men are not racially distinct (and this is in Faulkner's rhetoric only; in his depiction of the hunt itself, racial hierarchy remains), in the community they are historically intertwined despite themselves. None of us is free, McCaslin says, "not now nor ever, we from them nor they from us" (299). History is not the record of individuals acting with singularity of purpose, in McCaslin's view, but of individual *articulations* representative of class and community interests. And so Isaac's repudiation has profoundly political implications. Isaac believes he has taken a stand against injustice; in actuality, he has made himself irrelevant (as irrelevant as his primitive hunting skills) to modern political existence.

Ike sees the wilderness as his mistress and his wife, and we see the wilderness disappearing before the workings of a masculine culture. In "Delta Autumn," the men must drive "farther and farther" every year to find the wilderness, "the territory in which game still existed drawing yearly inward" just as Isaac's "life was drawing inward" (335). Indeed, Isaac realizes at the end of his life that his repudiation was wholly selfish and historically reactionary. There will be "just exactly enough" (354) wilderness to last until he dies, when both he and it will have given way to the forces each of them passively witnesses destroy the other. Now the men even kill does, symbolizing the effective killing off of the feminine and the triumph of a kind of lockstep masculine tradition.[10] When the conversation turns to Hitler (338), Faulkner's understanding of the implications of intellectual and creative submission to authority are made clear. And when the woman shows up at the end of "Delta Autumn" with Roth's child, Isaac is confronted with the fruit of his acquiescence. The existence of the child—the product of the blind duplication of the great-grandfather's original sin by the grandson—demonstrates the political implications of repudiation, even "in principle" (351). When the woman questions Isaac as to whether he has "lived so long and forgotten so much that you dont remember anything you ever knew or felt or heard about love" (363) she is condemning not only him but also the entire principle of the masculine "hunt," the flight from community, and the pastoral fantasy represented by Ike's wilderness romance.

In the world of *Go Down, Moses* there are too many fathers and too few mothers, too much naming and not enough nurturing, too much force and violence and too little understanding and change. In a short story written ten years earlier, the German prisoner in Faulkner's "Ad Astra" claims that "the word *father* iss that barbarism which will be first swept away" in the coming of a more humane world; "it iss the symbol of that hierarchy which has stained the history of man with injustice or arbitrary instead of moral; force instead of love."[11] Heritage and blind adherence to traditional social forms perpetuate racial injustice in *Go Down, Moses*. The clearest example of this is in Roth Edmonds' fraternal relationship to Henry Beauchamp, the son of the black woman who suckled and raised both boys. Roth and Henry are inseparable as boys until Roth is initiated into his heritage. "Then one day the old curse of his fathers, the old haughty ancestral pride based not on any value but on an accident of geography, stemmed not from courage and honor but from wrong and shame, descended to him" (111), and Roth refuses to fraternize any longer with Henry. "So he entered his heritage," Faulkner smugly concludes. "He ate its bitter fruit" (114). Significantly, Roth's mother died at childbirth, and he was mothered by the black woman, Molly Beauchamp. Yet the mother is denied, and "out of the tragic complexity of his motherless childhood" emerges the man who will carry on the injustices of the fathers, blind to the compassion of his invisible mother.

From the time Eunice "drownd herself" in 1833 through Lucas and Zack's standoff over Mollie and through the appearance of the woman in "Delta Autumn," the world of *Go Down, Moses* has been marked by a perversion of human love and human sexuality. It is a world where Eden is understood as without women and children and where its chief representative consciousness, Isaac McCaslin, defines his son's freedom by his never being born. This perversion of sexuality is at the root of the racism that permeates social power structures and marks a peculiar human failure to understand its own nature and to live in peace with its own compulsions. More important than this identification of the source of human injustice is the condemnation in *Go Down, Moses* of those who see but do not act, or who understand but choose to live in the comfort of self-righteous humility. As Faulkner's novel illustrates, even repudiation is a political stand, one which acquiesces in the very injustices that it intellectually disavows.

Go Down, Moses is a demand that the living take responsibility for the world as they find it. Despite its rhetorical homage to the "old time," *Go Down, Moses* is not a nostalgic book nor does it romanticize the past. Rather, it affirms the power and the right of the living generation to assert its will on the world, a will for which it is wholly responsible even if it does not execute it. In *Go Down, Moses,* Faulkner suggests that even though "meaning" is our most burdensome inheritance—the definitions, the structures, the injustices, all here before our birth—it need not be wholly deterministic of our fates. When those men finally kill the old bear (and it seems about time that critics recognize that Old Ben is dead, and deservedly so), they acknowledge the passing of one era and the beginning of another. Only Isaac wants to stay in the woods. The worst we can do in the face of "the old haughty ancestral pride," the curse of the fathers, is to seek refuge or sanctuary in "the wilderness" of intellectual renouncement or withdrawal. The best we can do is to overturn the heritage, as in the case of Lucas Beauchamp,[12] *"who fathered himself"* (118) and defined for himself the limits of what he would stand. "It was as though he were not only impervious to that blood" which symbolized his heritage, "he was indifferent to it." Faulkner continues: "He didn't even need to strive with it. . . . He resisted it simply be being the composite of the two races which made him, simply by possessing it," or accepting the contradiction which defined him. Instead of seing himself in an Isaac (or Quentin, or Joe Christmas) manner, as a kind of "battleground and victim" of his heritage, Lucas "was a vessel, durable, ancestryless, nonconductive, in which the toxin and its anti stalemated one another, seethless, unrumored in the outside air" (104). Although Beauchamp is politically dispossessed, he stands in contradistinction to Isaac as a man neither crushed nor conquered by his myriad and many fathers, but triumphant over them.

Intellectual and political complacency, or more accurately, intellectual complacency as a form of political apathy is what Faulkner is talking about in *Go Down, Moses,* not the woods or the hunt or, least of all, a bear as symbol of either. He is "still talking" about these matters in the Nobel Prize Address. Maturing in the 1930s, Faulkner well knew the problematic place of the writer in ideological debate, struggle, and change. A few years later, for example, Faulkner would see "The Bear" excised (or perhaps resurrected) from its context in *Go Down, Moses* and reprinted in Cowley's *The Portable Faulkner,* presented as a symbol of what Faulkner stood *for,* not *against,* in the novel. He would be celebrated by Malcolm Cowley and others for mythologizing the very orthodoxy he condemned in *Go Down, Moses* and throughout his apocrypha. After Cowley, Faulkner would try again and again to say what he meant, or as the Reporter says in *Pylon,* "to explain." At Stockholm in 1950, Faulkner would explain his apocrypha as a political stance.

The specific "reality" that threatens the young writer, according to the Nobel Prize Address, is the terror and fear characteristic of the atomic, or the nuclear age. "Our tragedy today is a general and universal physical fear so long sustained by now that we can even bear it." The resignation to apocalyptic terror, a characteristic more "universal" today than it was in 1950, has become so much a part of the environment that we have, like Temple Drake of *Sanctuary,* gotten "used to being" afraid of physical annihilation. "There are no longer problems of the spirit. There is only the question: When will I be blown up?" The writer, Faulkner admonishes, must reject fear as "the basest of all things" and return to "the old verities and truths of the heart." These truths are the familiar Faulknerian formula of "love and honor and pity and compassion and sacrifice." Behind the rhetoric, however, lies a coherent statement of the meaning of Faulkner's apocryphal vision not just to the "work" but to the man.

If the young writer does not say no to the official, pre-established world or to the writer's "time and place," Faulkner claims, then he "labors under a curse." As a result, the writers words are meaningless and ephemeral. To the apocalyptic terror of the present age and to apathetic resignation as well as to the optimists who believe that humanity will merely survive ("in the last red and dying evening . . . still talking"), Faulkner says no: "I refuse to accept this." It is the "duty" of the poet and the writer to address the human capacity not merely to survive but to say no and to construct alternatives, not merely to exploit human fears or to satisfy the glands but to provide direction and courage by the example of creating something which, before the words were written, did not exist. "It is his privilege to help man endure by lifting his heart, by reminding him of . . . the glory of his past" and by giving him the basis on which to "refuse to accept" reality as he finds it. In the Nobel Prize Address, Faulkner simultaneously admonishes and expresses faith. He "declines to accept" the fallen present and encourages a belief in the human potential for rebellion and change, for foundation. The tension between rejection and faith amounts to an assault on the terror of the age, an attack which is fundamentally rebellious. "The poet's voice," Faulkner concludes, shifting his emphasis away from "me as a man" and back to his works, "need not merely be the record of man, it can be one of the props, the pillars to help him endure and prevail." Man's record—the rapacity, the greed, the failures, and the injustice—is far from inspirational unless the poet can transform that record into something more than mindless chronology.

In the Nobel Prize Address, Faulkner argues that the transformation of the human record—the apocryphal vision—must be preceded by an act of intrinsic rebellion against orthodox reality and followed, or accompanied by an act of undeviable faith in the human spirit and in the human capacity for self-direction and the creation of alternative fields of action. Faulkner's great legacy, largely muted by the suppression of its apocryphal essence, is the insistence upon human rebellion as the very stuff of human spirituality. While the writer moves about in the "visible" world of inheritance, heritage, and history, he never loses sight of the world he would "*like*" to be true." When Faulkner labors to create his apocrypha, he acts against the visible world in the name of *its* impermanence and in the name of its being the product of someone else's imagination. The making of an apocrypha is compelled by the impulse to say no and by the will to put the possible in place of the merely real.

1. *Essays, Speeches, and Public Letters,* pp. 119–21.
2. Longstreet, *William Faulkner in California,* p. 33.
3. For example, see R. W. B. Lewis, "William Faulkner: The Hero in the New World," in Warren, ed., *Faulkner: A Collection of Critical Essays,* p. 208: "In 'The Bear' we meet Faulkner's first full-fledged hero in the old heroic meaning of the word"; Arnold Goldman, "Faulkner and the Revision of Yoknapatawpha History," in *The American Novel and the 1920s* (London: Edward Arnold Ltd., 1971), p. 190:

"Through Ike McCaslin Faulkner has traced just how far you have to go to redeem history and what the process can do to you, in hope and in glory, and in shame and defeat"; and Waggoner, *William Faulkner: From Jefferson to the World,* p. 207: "Isaac will do what he can to break the pattern of inherited injustice: he will at least refuse to profit by it."

4. *Lion in the Garden,* p. 225. Many critics have seen Ike similarly. Gold, *William Faulkner: A Study in Humanism,* p. 63: "Ike is more like Pontius Pilate than like Christ. His ineffectuality is pathetic, not tragic, and the persistent reference to his lack of posterity is to symbolize his isolation"; Hunt, *William Faulkner: Art in Theological Tension,* p. 167: "Isaac assumes he can slough off the sin and act in the heart's truth. That he is unable finally to do so testifies to the accuracy of his diagnosis and to the fallacy of his solution. And at the same time it points up the tragic inadequacy of even the heart's truth, for his heart gives him the desire but not the capacity to fulfill it"; and Myra Jehlen, *Class and Character in Faulkner's South* (New York: Columbia University Press, 1976), pp. 2 and 9, characterizes Isaac as "a frustrated Natty Bumppo" who "becomes class conscious: instead of ideals, he discovers ideology."

5. *The Faulkner-Cowley File,* pp. 14–15.

6. Fredric Jameson, *The Political Unconscious: Narrative as Socially Symbolic Act* (Ithaca, NY: Cornell University Press, 1981), p. 20.

7. Hannah Arendt, *On Revolution* (New York: Viking Press, 1963; rev. ed. 1965), p. 320n. In context: "How such guideposts for future reference and re-membrance arise out of this incessant talk, not, to be sure, in the form of concepts but as single brief sentences and condensed aphorisms, may best be seen in the novels of William Faulkner. Faulkner's literary procedure, rather than the content of his work, is highly 'political,' and, in spite of many imitations, he has remained, as far as I can see, the only author to use it."

8. See, for example, Weldon Thornton, "Structure and Theme in Faulkner's *Go Down, Moses,*" in Cox, ed., *William Faulkner: Critical Collection,* p. 333: "In Faulkner's presentation, freedom for any creature, including man, is self-realization, and since man is, in Faulkner's view, an essentially social being, this self-realization can come only through accepting one's fellow men and one's social responsibilities. For Faulkner, then, freedom and responsibility are complementary facets of the same thing, two sides of the same coin."

9. Gold, *William Faulkner: A Study in Humanism,* p. 66.

10. See, for example, Ursula Brumm, "Wilderness and Civilization: A Note on William Faulkner," in Hoffman and Vickery, eds., *William Faulkner: Three Decades of Criticism,* pp. 130 and 133: "His sorrow about the vanishing of the wilderness is so acute and more articulate than Cooper's, and he comes to a conclusion which to my knowledge no European has ever drawn with such severity: at the root and beginning of civilization and all its achievements is rapacity, and civilized man has to bear the burden of the guilt always and everywhere." Brumm continues, finding that in Faulkner, "tradition itself is a part of the curse, it is its continuance through time."

11. William Faulkner, *Collected Stories* (New York: Random House, 1950), p. 417. "Ad Astra" was first published in 1931.

12. David M. Wyatt, "Faulkner and the Burdens of the Past," in Brodhead, ed., *Faulkner: New Perspectives,* p. 116, identifies Lucas as "a new kind of hero" in Faulkner.

Index

Aiken, Charles, 26
Anderson, Sherwood, 10–11, 47, 145, 159
Apocrypha (Biblical), 15–19, 27, 31, 56, 103–5, 134
Apocrypha (Faulknerian), 3–4, 12, 13–22, 23–24, 26–27, 31, 34, 35–36, 38, 42, 47–49, 53–54, 61, 67–70, 75–76, 80–83, 85–86, 88–89, 95, 97, 103–5, 133–37, 140, 148–49, 160, 163, 168–69, 182, 189, 193–94, 196–97, 209–10, 212–14, 220–21. *See also* Yoknapatawpha County
Arendt, Hannah, 216
Arpad, Joseph, 151

Bacher, William, 95
Barnstone, Willis: *The Other Bible,* 15–17, 27
Beck, Warren, 25, 147
Bedell, George, 74
Beskow, Per, 103–5
Bezzerides, A. I., 52
Bloom, Harold, 61
Blotner, Joseph, 11, 47–48, 49, 51, 100, 150, 183, 195
Brooks, Cleanth, 170, 184

Broughton, Panthea Reid, 30
Butterworth, Keen, 108

Camus, Albert, 113, 114
Cochran, Louis, 49
Coindreau, Maurice, 52, 54
Collins, Carvel, 37–38
Commins, Dorothy, 52
Commins, Saxe, 52, 100–3
Coughlin, Robert, 52, 54, 127
Cowley, Malcolm, 5–14, 18–19, 24, 37–39, 41–42, 97–98, 100, 101, 156, 159, 168, 214, 220; *The Faulkner-Cowley File,* 6; *The Portable Faulkner,* 6–9, 12–14, 19, 38, 39, 97–98, 126, 161, 213, 214, 220.

Dardis, Tom, 95

Faulkner, Estelle, 11, 48
Faulkner, Jill, 126, 181
Faulkner, William: biography, 48–58, 143–44, 149–51, 155–62; civil rights, 139–44, 182; conflict, 36, 59–61, 96, 101–2; Malcolm Cowley, 5–

223

10, 12–14, 37–39, 41–42, 97–98, 213–14; depression, 12; Albert Erskine, 194–96; fame, 5, 10–11, 18, 150–51, 183–84; history, 35, 81, 83, 221; Hollywood, 12, 41, 51, 95–97; incompletion, 127–31, 144; individualism, 37, 141–43, 179, 198, 204–5, 207–9, 213; intoxication, 3, 53–58, 69, 81, 150, 213; lying, 22–23; the Nobel Prize, 4–5, 11, 50, 102, 137, 160; racism, 84, 88–89, 138–39, 141, 143, 187–88, 202, 219–20; short story writing, 31; stealing, 27–28, 29, 36, 47–48, 67–69; works: *A Fable*, 4, 5, 17, 22, 38, 42, 58, 68, 82, 85, 95–122, 126, 127, 129, 135, 138, 139, 142, 148, 153, 169, 181, 182, 197, 207; *Absalom, Absalom!*, 5, 13, 29, 35, 56–57, 59, 69, 81–82, 83, 96, 100, 145, 147, 148, 169, 185, 191, 213; "Ad Astra," 59, 218; "Appendix: Compson," 13, 38–42, 174, 207; *As I Lay Dying*, 51, 58–69, 72, 76, 80, 148, 213; *Big Woods*, 181; *The Collected Stories of William Faulkner*, 98; "The De Gaulle Story," 20–22; *Dr. Martino and Other Stories*, 145; *Go Down, Moses*, 7, 12, 31, 47, 57, 84, 100, 148, 187, 214–20; *The Hamlet*, 145, 146, 148, 149, 152–55, 168, 169–81, 184, 185, 186, 192, 197, 198, 203, 207, 208, 209; *Intruder in the Dust*, 11, 58, 83–89, 98, 106, 139, 143, 182; *Knight's Gambit*, 59, 98; *Light in August*, 5, 29, 83, 84, 143, 170; *The Mansion*, 148, 149, 152, 160–63, 169, 184, 186, 193, 194–210; *Mosquitos*, 94, 99; "Nobel Prize Address," 61, 129, 212–13, 220–21; "Notes on a Horsethief," 98, 114; "On Privacy" (essay), 141; "Pine Manor Junior College Address," 126–27, 128–29, 137–39; *Pylon*, 56–57, 58, 69–82, 96, 99, 213; *The Reivers*, 27–33, 36, 48, 84, 85, 88, 162; *Requiem for a Nun*, 38, 57, 98, 116, 121, 128, 129–37, 151, 169; *Sanctuary*, 5, 7, 8, 11, 29, 31, 57, 83, 84, 100, 132, 151, 173, 174, 220; *Sartoris*, 19, 145; *Snopes* trilogy, 4, 42, 58, 68, 82, 85, 126, 144, 145–49, 162–63, 168–210; *Soldier's Pay*, 27, 99; *The Sound and the Fury*, 5, 7, 13, 29, 38–42, 57, 59, 61, 70, 127, 145, 148; "Spotted Horses," 147; *The Town*, 138, 148,

155–60, 163, 168, 169, 172, 174, 177, 182–94, 197, 198, 200, 201, 206, 208, 209; *The Unvanquished*, 30, 83, 146, 152; *The Wild Palms*, 83, 99, 146, 148, 151, 170. See also Apocrypha (Faulknerian)

Gargantua and Pantagruel (Rabelais), 199
Gilmore, Thomas P., 55
Gnosticism, 15, 17–18, 54, 104
Gold, Joseph, 25, 30, 86, 183, 184, 207, 216

Hawks, Howard, 51–52, 181
Hemingway, Ernest, 7, 8, 13
Howe, Irving, 9

Irwin, John T., 25

James, William: *Pragmatism*, 35
Jameson, Frederic, 215–16
Jehlen, Myra, 33

Kermode, Frank, 14, 34
Kerr, Elizabeth, 147
Kinney, Arthur, 24, 179

Lester, Cheryl, 7
Lewis, R. W. B., 23
Linscott, Robert, 54, 55
Longstreet, Stephen, 50, 103

McAlexander, Hubert, Jr., 23
McLuhan, Marshall, 70
Magny, Claude-Edmonde, 23, 25
Mazzeo, Joseph, 35
Millgate, Michael, 24, 71–72
Minter, David, 10, 51

Oates, Stephen, 52–53
Oesterly, W. O. E., 31
Oxford, Mississippi, 26–27

Page, Sally, 170
Pagels, Elaine, 17, 54
Parker, Robert Dale, 62
Perry, Thomas, 72
Pitavy, Francois, 71
Pouillon, Jean-Jacques, 23
Polk, Noel, 161, 192
Prohibition, 57–58

Rankin, Elizabeth, 147–48
Rhyle, Gilbert, 49